Inside the Russian Revolution

Inside the Russian Revolution

Rheta Childe Dorr

Edited and Introduction by
Victoria I. Zhuravleva

ANTHEM PRESS

Anthem Press
An imprint of Wimbledon Publishing Company
www.anthempress.com

This edition first published in UK and USA 2026
by ANTHEM PRESS
75–76 Blackfriars Road, London SE1 8HA, UK
or PO Box 9779, London SW19 7ZG, UK
and
244 Madison Ave #116, New York, NY 10016, USA

Copyright © Victoria Zhuravleva 2026 editorial matter and selection;
individual chapters © individual contributors

The moral right of the authors has been asserted.

All rights reserved. Without limiting the rights under copyright reserved above,
no part of this publication may be reproduced, stored or introduced into
a retrieval system, or transmitted, in any form or by any means
(electronic, mechanical, photocopying, recording or otherwise),
without the prior written permission of both the copyright
owner and the above publisher of this book.

British Library Cataloguing-in-Publication Data
A catalogue record for this book is available from the British Library.

Library of Congress Control Number: 2025947754
A catalog record for this book has been requested.

ISBN-13: 978-1-83999-525-5 (Hbk) / 978-1-83999-526-2 (Pbk)
ISBN-10: 1-83999-525-4 (Hbk) / 1-83999-526-2 (Pbk)

Cover Credit: Harris & Ewing photograph collection, Library of Congress
Prints and Photographs Division Washington, USA.

This title is also available as an eBook.

Figure 0.1 Ekaterina Breshkovskaya, the "Little Grandmother of the Russian Revolution." Courtesy of the Russian State Documentary Film and Photo Archive.

CONTENTS

Figures ix

Acknowledgments xi

Editor's Introduction xiii

Chapter 1. Topsy-Turvy Land 1
Chapter 2. "All the Power to the Soviet" 7
Chapter 3. The July Revolution 15
Chapter 4. An Hour of Hope 23
Chapter 5. The Committee Mania 29
Chapter 6. The Woman with the Gun 35
Chapter 7. To the Front with Bochkareva 41
Chapter 8. In Camp and Battlefield 45
Chapter 9. Amazons in Training 51
Chapter 10. The Homing Exiles—Two Kinds 57
Chapter 11. How Rasputin Died 67
Chapter 12. Anna Vyrubova Speaks 75
Chapter 13. More Leaves in the Current 83
Chapter 14. The Passing of the Romanovs 89
Chapter 15. The House of Mary and Martha 97
Chapter 16. The *Tavarishi* Face Famine 105
Chapter 17. General January, The Conqueror 111
Chapter 18. When the Workers Own Their Tools 117

Chapter 19. Why Cotton Cloth Is Scarce	123
Chapter 20. Mrs. Pankhurst in Russia	129
Chapter 21. Kerensky, the Mystery Man	137
Chapter 22. The Rights of Small Nations	145
Chapter 23. Will the Germans Take Petrograd?	151
Chapter 24. Russia's Greatest Needs	159
Chapter 25. What Next?	165
Index	173

FIGURES

0.1	Ekaterina Breshkovskaya, the "Little Grandmother of the Russian Revolution"	v
3.1	Typical crowd on the Nevsky Prospect during the Bolshevik or Maximalist risings	18
5.1	Kerensky watching the funeral of victims of the July Bolshevik risings	31
6.1	Maria Bochkareva, Mrs. Emmeline Pankhurst and the Women's Battalion of Death	37
11.1	Prince Felix Ysupov, at whose palace on the Moika Canal Rasputin was killed, and his wife, the Grand Duchess Irina Alexandrovna, niece of the late tsar	69
12.1	Grigori Rasputin and some of his female devotees	78
15.1	The Grand Duchess Elizabeth Feodorovna, sister of the late Tsarina, and widow of the Grand Duke Sergei, who was assassinated during the Revolution of 1905, is now abbess of the House of Mary and Martha in Moscow	100
21.1	Alexander Fyodorovich Kerensky	139

ACKNOWLEDGMENTS

I've been working on this book for several years, yet this work would not have been started or completed had it not been for the enthusiasm and generous support of William Benton Whisenhunt. In cooperation with Norman E. Saul, he launched the "Americans in Revolutionary Russia" series at Slavica Publishers and managed to have it renewed at Anthem Press. I am also grateful to William and Norman for suggesting that I annotate Rheta Dorr's travelogue. As a scholar, I found studying the life, work and writings of the U.S. journalist, feminist and political activist to be a true academic pleasure. I would also like to thank my colleague and friend David S. Foglesong, who helped me with materials from the U.S. press. Special thanks to my former doctoral students Igor Tarbeev and Victoria Avanskaya for their assistance at the final stage of the book project. Finally, I extend my sincere gratitude to the Anthem Press team who helped transform my manuscript into a book about Rheta Childe Dorr's journey into the Russian Revolution.

EDITOR'S INTRODUCTION
Victoria I. Zhuravleva

Rheta Childe Dorr: Inspired and Sobered by the Russian Revolution

> I went to Russia a socialist by conviction, an ardent sympathizer with revolution, having known personally some of the brave men and women who suffered imprisonment and exile after the failure of the uprising in 1905–6. I returned from Russia with the very clear conviction that the world will have to wait awhile before it can establish any cooperative millenniums, or before it can safely hand over the work of government to the man in the street.[1]

These are the words of Rheta Childe Dorr, an American journalist, feminist and political activist, summing up her firsthand observations and eyewitness testimony of the 1917 Russian Revolution as it developed between February and October.

Dorr's book *Inside the Russian Revolution* was published in the United States in late 1917 and was never reprinted. Unlike other American observers of the Russian Revolution, Rheta Childe Dorr did not merit any major studies save for some encyclopedia entries and short sections in general works on women journalists, muckrakers, suffragettes and feminists; no collection of her personal papers survives in any archive.[2] And yet, her work and writings embodied the pro-reform spirit of the public and political life of the Progressive Era in the United States that manifested in many phenomena from muckraking journalism and trade unionism to the suffrage movement and feminism.

Dorr also demonstrated the increased interest in the Russian Revolution that was typical for many Americans of various political views. Looking at the events in faraway Russia and making sense of Russia's revolutionary message, they fine-tuned their own ideological creeds and visions of their own reformism. Simultaneously, they were crafting a perspective on the Russian Revolution that subsequently affected Americans' perceptions of and discourse on Soviet Russia.[3]

Additionally, like many other American women observers of revolutionary Russia, Dorr rejected abstract political philosophizing and theorizing and sought to record the specific ways in which different people experienced war, revolution and economic upheavals. This "technique of vivid impressionism" framed the discourses that American women generated on the subject of the Russian Revolution of 1917 in correlation with their own identity as women.[4] Dorr stood out among many U.S. journalists in her unprecedented ability to see different sides of the revolutionary process and to create a nuanced and balanced travelogue about the prospects of democratic reform in Russia, Bolshevik authoritarianism and naivete of the Russian people. It was precisely this vision that helped her book survive the test of time.

From Woman's Page Editor to Foreign Correspondent

Rheta Louise Childe[5] was born in Omaha, Nebraska, on November 2, 1866. She was the second child among four daughters and two sons of Lucie Child (née Mitchell) and Edward Payson Child, a druggist from New York. Her parents soon moved the family to Lincoln. At the age of 12, defying her father's prohibition, she attended a lecture on women's rights delivered by Elizabeth Cady Stanton and Susan B. Anthony, two charismatic leaders of the women's equality movement in the United States. The lecture inspired the young girl to fight for women's equality. She donated a silver dollar to the good cause and joined the National Suffrage Association. Her father punishing her for disobedience only entrenched Dorr in her rebellious spirit and convinced her of the need to defend her right to independent opinion.[6]

Dorr started working at 15 to buy her own clothes and generally support her large family financially. Once she graduated from school, she went on to study at the University of Nebraska. In 1890, after a two-year stint at a post office, she decided to go to New York to see the world. In this American metropolis, Dorr both understood that her vocation lay in writing and met her future husband, the businessman John Pixley Dorr. They married in 1892, when Rheta was 26 and John was 40. She later admitted she had been led into the marriage by a mixture of young love and vaulting ambition. The Dorrs went back to Nebraska for a few months and then moved to Seattle where John and his brother were in business. Rheta's only son Julian was born there in 1896. The loving couple was apparently remarkably happy for the first four years of their marriage, yet they ultimately divorced in 1898 since Dorr's husband, a man of conservative views, did not agree with her ideas of women's equality and her passion for journalism.[7]

Rheta "wanted all the freedom, all the opportunity, all the equality there was in the world,"[8] and she went back to New York with her young son to make a new start in life. For three years, Dorr pounded the pavement going from newspaper to newspaper in attempts to break into the male-dominated world of American journalism. City editors reminded her that men had to work all their lives while she was clearly just biding her time until she married again. A window of opportunity for Dorr opened in 1900 after she got Theodore Roosevelt to pose for a photo as he was officially notified that he had been chosen as the running mate of the Republican nominee for president, William McKinley. Dorr was paid an unusually high fee of $25 since Colonel Roosevelt had blankly refused to be photographed, yet Dorr was able to convince him to change his mind and promised to keep the photographers in line. This success brought her an offer to join the staff of the *New York Evening Post*, where she remained from 1902 until 1906 writing on the women's activities. Later, Dorr would say that during her time with the *Post*, she "was taught to write good, clear English and forced into habits of straight thinking and accurate statement" that was very useful for her professional career as a writer.[9]

The main thing, however, was that she became part of the world of working women and their struggle to improve their conditions, which helped transform her from a newspaper reporter into an investigative journalist (muckraker). Dorr witnessed female workers being forced to move from job to job and decided to speak about their needs and goals. She had become a feminist to fight against the restrictions of women's freedoms affecting educated middle-class ladies and factory girls alike.[10]

To better understand the needs of working women, Dorr even moved to New York's East Side, studying her neighbors' lives and talking to them. She taught at the University Settlement in Rivington Street and in exchange was boarded with the settlement's residents. While working at the *New York Evening Post*, Dorr wrote about the plight of factory girls, about women's clubs and charitable activities; she met prominent reformers and suffragists and became very active in the General Federation of Women's Clubs' investigation of the conditions of women and children working at various factories. Dorr supported all women's equality initiatives of her time as women agitated for suffrage, worked to develop their trade unions, fought to be admitted to higher education, to gain professional recognition and to secure equal pay for equal work. Since then, her circle of acquaintances included members of the settlement house movement who founded the famous social centers for residents of New York's poor districts populated by immigrants; radicals from among Russian Jewish emigrants; famous American female activists; leaders of various reform movements of the Progressive Era.[11]

Later, Dorr continued her muckraking journalism at *Everybody's* magazine. But before that, in 1906, she traveled to Europe to cover the coronation of King Haakon of Norway. He was the first elected ruler of independent Norway after its secession from Sweden. Dorr's trip to Scandinavia was funded by the *New York Evening Post*, the *Boston Transcript* and *Harper's Weekly*, which then published her articles.[12]

In the meantime, a revolution was brewing in Russia, a revolution of which Dorr had heard much from the Russian Jewish emigrants on the Lower East Side. She had made the acquaintance of the "grandmother of the Russian Revolution," Ekaterina Breshko-Breshkovskaya,[13] who arrived in the United States in December 1904 with a lecture tour to collect money for the revolutionary movement and to explain its true goals to Americans.[14] It was not surprising that Dorr decided to take a self-funded short trip to Russia where she met many revolutionaries, including terrorists, and became, once and for all, enamored of Russia's fight for freedom. From St. Petersburg, she went to Copenhagen to a meeting of the International Woman Suffrage Alliance, where she met Emmeline Pankhurst,[15] one of the leaders of radical suffragettes in Great Britain, who would go on to become Dorr's close friend.[16] Under the influence of the British movement and using techniques of the political left, the American women's suffrage movement blossomed after 1907. Dorr was among those suffragists who witnessed or joined the English suffrage campaigns from 1906 to 1911.[17]

In November 1906, she returned to New York and quit the *Post* that offered her no career prospects. Dorr convinced John O'Hara Cosgrave, the editor-in-chief of *Everybody's*, to pay her $35 a week for a series of articles "The Woman's Invasion." She planned to investigate and describe to the American reading public women's exodus from homemaking into factories and their grueling working conditions. Dorr became the first journalist to dare immerse herself in that world and depict it from the inside. For over a year, she worked in various places, toiling from morning till night as a seamstress, a washerwoman, a sales assistant and an assembly-line worker. Every week, she sent her notes to the magazine's editor. But he wanted ready-to-print articles. Ultimately, Dorr had to agree to collaborate with the talented journalist William Hard who promptly transformed the material she collected into magazine pieces. Dorr was shocked, however, when *Everybody's* advertised a series of articles she had conceived, based on materials she had collected, yet credited Hard alone. She sued and won, forcing the magazine to publish the articles with a joint byline. Still, "The Woman's Invasion" as told by Hard did not sit right with her. Hard emphasized American women breaking the bonds of homemaking slavery and triumphantly expanding their range of occupations, thereby gaining an opportunity to earn money for clothes and entertainment. Dorr had wanted to tell a story of former housewives becoming working women, undergoing their own personal transformations and affecting the labor market. She was certain that American women faced a tough struggle for their right to work and for equal pay with men.[18]

These ideas were reflected in Dorr's first book *What Eight Million Women Want* (1910) that summarized her journalistic investigations and was chiefly based on her articles published in *Hampton's Magazine*. Since 1910, she has been on staff of this periodical, and her stories about women's clubs and hard conditions of women's work, about their fight for suffrage, and against double standards helped solidify the magazine's standing as a muckraking outlet and placed Dorr herself at the forefront of the crusade for women's equality.[19]

In 1912, *Good Housekeeping* magazine sent Dorr to Paris to interview Emmeline Pankhurst whom Dorr had met in 1906. Their close acquaintance and Dorr's knowledge of the activities of radical British suffragettes served to complete the American journalist's transformation into a social activist whose main goal in life was fighting for equal rights for women. Dorr accompanied Pankhurst on her lecture tour of the United States and later, during the winter of 1913–1914 in Paris, helped her write her autobiography, *My Own Story*. Pankhurst included a special Acknowledgment section in her book expressing her deep obligation to Dorr for her invaluable assistance in the preparation of this book.[20]

After Paris, Dorr decided to visit Finland, then a Grand Duchy of the Russian Empire. That trip helped her realize why American women made such a slow progress toward suffrage. She believed them to lack the art of passive resistance that Finns had mastered living under the Tsarist regime and that Finnish women were better at than men as they had been honing this art for centuries.[21] Back home from her second visit to Russia, Dorr became the first editor of *The Suffragist*, a weekly launched in November 1913 by the Congressional Union for Suffrage. This periodical was closed down in August 1920 after the United States Congress passed the 19th Amendment to the Constitution granting women equal suffrage with men.

Early in the 1910s, like many muckrakers, such as Sinclair Lewis or "gentlemen socialists" Ernest Poole, Arthur Bullard and English Walling, who had graduated from prestigious universities and participated in the settlement house movement, Dorr became a member of the Greenwich Village branch of the Socialist Party. It was nicknamed the Highbrow branch since it counted many well-known writers, artists and social workers among its members. They had their social program and professed their belief "in the helplessness of the old political parties, both in the octopus grip of the money barons."[22] Dorr knew nothing of socialism at the time but was inspired by the activity of the English Fabian Society and believed that socialism was a cure-all for the social ills of the time.[23]

Dorr's passion for women's issues never flagged. From 1912 to 1917, she was part of the feminist circle called Heterodoxy, a group that took pride in their unorthodox opinions. Beginning with 25 women in 1912, Heterodoxy epitomized the feminism of the time. They discussed cultural, political and scientific innovations, the progress of the Socialist Party, psychoanalysis, women's special affinity for peace and their own personal experiences as women.[24] "We thought we discussed the whole world," Dorr reflected on those years, "but we really discussed ourselves."[25]

World War I was the turning point in her life and thinking. In the spring of 1915, she resigned from the editorship of *The Suffragist* and turned a new page in her career by joining the staff of the *New York Evening Mail*. Dorr wrote 1,000-word daily articles and editorials and closely followed politics and the progress of the suffrage movement. By 1917, she found herself among American socialist-leaning reformers advocating support for Western democracies in their fight against the German Empire and the participation of the United States in the war on the side of the Triple Entente. In her *Evening Post* column, Dorr condemned internationalists and pacifists (her own former associates) as traitors and German propagandists, accused the Kaiser of trying to destroy Christian civilization and enslave mankind, and called World War I the most righteous war in the history of the world.[26]

Once the United States joined the war in April 1917, Dorr wanted one thing only: to become a war correspondent, which was a real breakthrough for American female journalists at that time. Her dream came true after her return from revolutionary Russia, where she spent five months, from May to September of 1917, as a correspondent for the *New York Evening Mail* (this part of her biography will be discussed later).

Having completed her "Russian revolutionary epic story" with dozens of articles and a book titled *Inside the Russian Revolution*, Dorr convinced the editor-in-chief to send her to France where her son was fighting. She sailed to Europe on December 1, 1917. The *New York Evening Mail* promised its readers her articles on the war-torn continent stressing that "Mrs. Dorr is one of the most remarkable figures in American journalism. She is essentially feminine in her appearance, and yet can brush aside more obstacles and solve more difficulties than most of her competing correspondents."[27] Obstacles and difficulties were not long in coming: the French authorities refused to recognize Dorr's credentials as a war correspondent insisting that the newspaper send over a man instead. As always, she persevered and came up with a solution. Dorr struck a deal with the leaders of the Young Men's Christian Association offering them a series of lectures on the events in revolutionary Russia in exchange for traveling around France. She remained in the war-torn country until May 1918, sending articles to her newspaper and collecting materials for her next book *A Soldier's Mother in France* (1918).[28]

In November 1918, Dorr resigned from the newspaper whose owner was accused of taking money from the German government. Now unemployed, she cared for her twice wounded son at a New York army hospital and simultaneously wrote columns for various newspapers. *The Pictorial Review* magazine commissioned her to write a series of articles on women's involvement in the 1920 elections and she decided to start by talking to Congressmen in Washington, DC. Soon after her arrival in November 1919, as Dorr was crossing a street to enter her hotel, she was run down by a motorcycle and severely injured. Dorr was taken to an emergency hospital where she was diagnosed with three broken ribs and a broken collarbone.[29]

The consequences of this accident would continue to plague her throughout her life. After being discharged from the hospital, despite her poor physical and mental health, she did write a series of articles on the 1920 electoral campaign. However, once this work was completed, Dorr realized she needed to take care of herself and went to Czechoslovakia to regain her health. On the way there, holding up on sheer willpower, she traveled through war-ravaged France to collect materials for her new articles. During this French trip, Dorr was hospitalized again, had surgery and was then transferred to an American hospital in Paris. Consequently, she started working in Prague only five months after her departure from New York.[30]

Dorr wrote for the *New York Tribune* on the political life in republican Czechoslovakia led by President Tomáš Masaryk; she visited Romania and Italy where she witnessed fascists led by Benito Mussolini appearing on the political stage. Soon she learned that Anna Vyrubova, Empress Alexandra Feodorovna's lady-in-waiting and confidante, whom Dorr met in the revolutionary Petrograd in 1917, was in Europe. She decided to meet with Vyrubova and to persuade her to write her memoirs. Their meeting took place in April 1922 in southern Germany. They worked on the book together for two months amid old letters, photographs and endless talks about the royal family and life at court. In 1923, *Memoirs of the Russian Court* was published.[31]

After three years in Europe, Dorr went back to the United States, in good health again and brimming with new ideas. The path of her thought paralleled the mainstream of her time—from liberal socialism of the prewar era, to wartime superpatriotism, to postwar retreat from radical reform. Summarizing her experience in postwar Europe, Dorr wrote in 1927 that her faith in socialism "began to evaporate in France where for some months I watched hard-boiled facts roll back the catastrophic German theory. But it needed three years of continuous residence in post-war Europe completely to convert me from socialism."[32]

In the 1920s, she continued working with the National Woman's Party toward what she saw as its constructive feminist goals. In 1924, Dorr published her autobiography *A Woman of Fifty* telling the story of her life and career against the backdrop of the history of American women's struggle for their rights and for their place in the labor market. She concluded her book saying, "I think the greatest thing my generation of women accomplished was the freeing of younger women to go farther than ourselves."[33]

After 1925, Dorr virtually abandoned journalism but continued to give lectures and write books. In 1928, she produced one of the earliest secondary studies of Susan B. Anthony, paying homage to the woman who had helped her find the cause of her life: fighting for women's equality in the United States. Dorr emphasized Anthony's influence on the success of thwenties-century Suffragists and dedicated this book to her granddaughter Lora so that she would know of the struggle of those women whose legacy she enjoyed.[34] Dorr's final book was published in 1929.[35]

She was crushed by the death of her beloved son in Mexico City. Julian Childe Dorr was very badly wounded during World War I, but despite these injuries, he graduated from Georgetown University School of Foreign Service. He married Jessie Theo Mannheim on his assignment to his first post in Czechoslovakia. Julian was subsequently transferred from Prague to Genoa, then to Barbados and then to Mexico, where he served as a United States consul under the Hoover Administration. He died on September 2, 1936, and outlived his wife by a mere six months.[36] These losses finally undermined Rheta Dorr's health. At the end of the 1930s, she was transferred from a hospital in New York to a sanatorium in Bucks County, Pennsylvania, and thereafter to the home of her doctor and friend Dr. Von Lohr, where she died of a cerebral hemorrhage on August 8, 1948.[37]

Revolutionary Russia in Dorr's Representations

Revolutionary Russia had a special place in Rheta Childe Dorr's life. She herself admitted that while observing the events of the Russian Revolution of 1905–1907, she "got a spiritual vision" comparable to "a religion rebirth."[38] Arriving in St. Petersburg in 1906 and staying in an apartment with Russian revolutionaries who reminded her alternatively of Girondists and of Sans-Culottes of the eighteenth-century French Revolution, Dorr was plunged headlong into the new world of revolutionary struggle for freedom in Russia.

Dorr gleaned information from an extremely wide range of sources: she attended State Duma meetings, on the one hand, and listened to stories of clandestine revolutionary propaganda amid workers and peasants, on the other. She met terrorists who were willing to sacrifice their lives at the altar of freedom and who kept telling her that were she Russian, and not a free American, she would have done the same. Dorr's connections in the Russian revolutionary milieu allowed her to attend underground gatherings that, as she later reported, fascinated her more than the Duma meetings. However, Dorr deemed both Duma deputies and Socialist Revolutionaries to be dreamers. She thought that Constitutional Democrats (*Kadets*),[39] the majority faction in the first Duma, "represented the best republican minds in Russia," but "had a program which lacked nothing but practical common sense." They wanted to westernize a gigantic empire overnight, disregarding the fact that Russia was only beginning to wake up from "a thousand years of oriental lethargy"; they wanted to introduce universal suffrage in a country where the majority of its population was comprised of illiterate peasants; they wanted to give land to peasants without having a clear plan of how to do it without undermining the Russian economic system. From Dorr's point of view, while Constitutional Democrats sought to cure Russia's ills by implementing universal revival theories without accounting for the true state of affairs, Socialist Revolutionaries,[40] in their turn, relied on revolutionary terror. She saw these visions of both liberals and radicals of the first Russian Revolution as threatening Russia's collapse.[41] However, Dorr arrived at this conclusion in her 1924 autobiography after her dramatic experience of the 1917 Russian Revolution, between the Tsar's overthrow and Bolsheviks coming to power.

Dorr was one of the three American women journalists reporting from revolutionary Russia in 1917. The other two were Bessie Beatty[42] of the *San Francisco Bulletin* and Louise Bryant[43] of the *Bell Syndicate*. However, these American women had different "Russian experiences." Beatty was a neutral observer, Bryant a supporter of Communism and Dorr a consistent critic of the Bolsheviks and of giving power to the uneducated population. Beatty and Dorr stayed at the same hotel where they took shelter from stray bullets during the July uprising. But Dorr was the first to provide a detailed description of it for the American press and then in her book *Inside the Russian Revolution*. Both Beatty and Dorr crept through the streets of chaos-torn Petrograd and admired the bravery of the Women's Battalion of Death. But Dorr was the first to present the story of its commander Maria Bochkareva[44] to the American public. Dorr was also the first among the women correspondents to transform her observations into a systemic series of articles and into a book. She left revolutionary Russia in September, while Beatty stayed there until late January 1918, witnessing the Bolsheviks coming to power. In their turn, Bryant and her husband John Reed[45] found themselves inside the October Revolution, drawing inspiration from its culmination and finale. So, Dorr's *Inside the Russian Revolution* was published in 1917, Beatty's *The Red Heart of Russia* in 1918, and Bryant's *Six Red Months in Russia* in 1919.[46]

It was the first time in the history of American journalism when three women foreign correspondents competed not only with men but also between themselves.⁴⁷ They sought to show American readers the "first-hand" truth of the Russian Revolution, the truth as they saw it since both their political views and their manner of presenting information differed.⁴⁸

Dorr heard of the 1917 February Revolution at the office of the *New York Evening Mail* and demanded that the paper send her to Russia since she had for ten years been following the Russian revolutionary movement and visited the Russian Empire twice. No one in the office objected since they had recognized Dorr's status as a professional journalist who could hold her own against male correspondents. Before departure, the editor asked her not to wax philosophical, not to write about the Russian soul and to diligently do her journalistic duty: observe and then describe her observations. She adopted this "method of vivid impressionism" when she arrived in Petrograd in May 1917 and found herself inside the Russian Revolution.⁴⁹

Dorr knew the history of the French Revolution very well as she had studied it for many years, and she was certain that there was nothing more exciting than writing about a country in revolt. Dorr dreamed of becoming a second Arthur Young, the British journalist celebrated for his book on traveling through revolutionary France. Consequently, her observations were full of analogies between the Russian and the French Revolutions: her pen transformed members of the Provisional Government into Russian Girondists, while Bolsheviks were turned into Sans-Culottes; Empress Alexandra Feodorovna was the Marie Antoinette of the Russian Revolution and Anna Vyrubova was her Princesse Lamballe; Nicholas II being expelled from the Alexander Palace in Tsarskoe Selo was similar to Louis XVI being expelled from the Tuileries Palace; and Maria Spiridonova⁵⁰ reminded Dorr of Charlotte Corday.⁵¹ The American journalist felt as if she suddenly found herself in Paris in 1792 among Lafayettes and Mirabeaus, enlightened lawmakers, thinkers, adherents of ideals and reason on the one hand, and revolutionary fanatics, Dantons, Marats and Robespierres, on the other. The more Dorr observed, the more she was terrified by the similarities with the French radicalism, uncontrolled mutiny of the people and political violence and terror, emphasizing that the stunning likeness of the two revolutions lay "in the facility with which both were snatched away from the sane and intelligent men who began them and placed in the hands of fanatics, who turned them into mad orgies of blood and terror."⁵²

However, Dorr's five months spent observing revolutionary Russia ultimately made her abandon analogies between the two revolutions at all. She concluded that Alexander Kerensky⁵³ and other leaders of the Russian Revolution were entirely unlike the leaders of the French one; that is, the Russians did not produce their own Dantons, Mirabeaus and Robespierres.⁵⁴ The French Revolution was preceded by an ancient civilization, thereby allowing France to resume its progress toward freedom after the rule of terror. The Russian Revolution, on the other hand, hailed from "a long night of barbarism," which brought German agents, Bolsheviks, to power, and they subjugated the uneducated people.[55]

With the help of an interpreter (a Russian student), she talked to Petrograd residents in streetcars, on park benches and in lines of people waiting to buy food. She met representatives of various social groups and political parties ranging from members of the Provisional Government and Bolsheviks to aristocrats and former courtiers. She sought to give voice to different people inside the Russian Revolution. Dorr was the first to tell the American public the true story of Grigori Rasputin's murder[56] based on her interviews with one of the conspirators, Prince Felix Yusupov,[57] and with Anna Vyrubova, the closest friend of Empress Alexandra Feodorovna.[58] Ultimately, Dorr herself concluded that "Rasputin had to be killed, and he was."[59] In the TV interview Yusupov and his wife Princess Irina Alexandrovna gave in Paris in 1967, they confirmed all the facts the American journalist listed in 1917.[60]

With her own eyes, Dorr watched the Constitutional Democrats and the Provisional Government's impotence, on the one hand, and the growing power of the Soviets (councils) and the Bolsheviks, on the other. She gave Alexander Kerensky his due, stressing that no one else would have been able to demonstrate to the freedom-crazed Russian people engulfed in anarchy that a working government is a must if the state is to continue to exist.[61] However, she criticized Kerensky for fearing to take radical steps proposed by General Lavr Kornilov.[62] Dorr believed that he could have saved Russia and the Russian army from Bolsheviks because Kornilov was "a true patriot" and was ready and willing "to pay the awful price" for it.[63] However, the diarchy that emerged in Russia and the impotence of the Provisional Government allowed Bolsheviks (whom she collectively called *Tavarishi* [comrades], and believed to be agents of Germany[64]) to unleash a wave of terrorism, thereby pushing the country on the brink of famine and ruin to conclude a separate peace treaty with Germany.[65]

Dorr accused the staff of the U.S. Embassy and Consulate, members of the Elihu Root mission[66] sent by President Woodrow Wilson and the majority of American correspondents of lacking a realist view of the situation. They refused to see the obvious and to understand that Russia was sinking into chaos, choking on the blood of murders and massacres, engulfed in banditry in the streets of Moscow and Petrograd; they refused to see that Russia's army was demoralized and disintegrating, and the country in search of freedom was, in fact, on its way to a Bolshevik dictatorship.[67] In this respect, Dorr was more insightful than many American observers. She admired Constitutional Democrats and their leader Pavel Miliukov,[68] but was disappointed they could not keep their hold on power in Russia. Dorr criticized Kerensky and justified Kornilov's plans since she believed that a temporary dictatorship would help Russia that was drunk on freedom.[69] Dorr demonized the Bolsheviks whose actions let the genie of anarchy out of the bottle, and the absolute power of those who were not ready to wield power. Therefore, the Soviets ruled Russia, soldiers did not want to fight and slaughtered their officers, workers allowed themselves not to work and curtailed the workday and workers' committees took control of factories and plants violating their owners' rights.[70]

As a feminist who had no doubts that women were not merely equal to men, but even better than men when it came to loyalty to ideas and to the sense of duty, Dorr particularly focused on Russian women in revolutionary Russia. Her articles and books gave voice to all of them, from the revolutionaries Vera Figner,[71] Maria Spiridonova and Ekaterina Breshko-Breshkovskaya (Dorr's book began with her portrait), to Empress Alexandra Feodorovna and her closest friend Anna Vyrubova, to the Grand Duchess Elizabeth Feodorovna[72] (who took the veil), the wife of Grand Duke Sergei Alexandrovich.[73]

Dorr was inspired by the Provisional Government's policy that enfranchised Russian women and allowed them to fight alongside men. Women's battalions in general and Maria Bochkareva's Women's Battalion of Death, in particular, were of special interest to the American press.[74] All female correspondents from the United States covering the 1917 revolution in Russia wrote about it.[75] Dorr devoted several articles and a few chapters in her book to Bochkareva and her Battalion of Death. Rheta told the true story of Maria herself, recorded from her own words and portrayed several women warriors who came from all walks of life, from aristocrats to peasants. When Dorr failed to secure an official permit in time, she secretly traveled with Bochkareva's battalion to the Dvinsk front as a nurse and stayed for nine days in the barracks with the women until they were sent into battle. Then she visited them in the hospital in Petrograd. By that time, the Women's Battalion of Death had earned its glory, and the journalist listened with bated breath to the gravely wounded Bochkareva's and her comrades-in-arms' firsthand stories of their first battle. Ultimately, Dorr was the first to tell Americans the most complete and reliable story of these warrior women that constituted a stark contrast with the contradictory and distorted information printed elsewhere.[76] She believed the Russian women and the Cossacks to be the "two fighting elements which are ready to die to restore peace, order and bright honor to their distracted land." Dorr concluded that "a country that can produce such women cannot possibly be crushed forever. It may take time for it to recover its present debauch of anarchism but recover it surely will."[77]

The American journalist was captivated by the revolutionary drama unfolding before her very eyes in Russian history. Yet, with her front-row seat, as it were, Dorr could only observe without being able to write down what she saw. She watched and accumulated information. Returning to the United States in September 1917, Dorr realized that no one truly understood what was going on in revolutionary Russia, who Kerensky was and what goals the Soviets set for themselves. The editor gave her total freedom, and she immersed herself in reliving her Russian experience. For five weeks, from morning till night, Dorr was typing up her articles, living in the world of memories and surprised that she no longer saw Petrograd roofs and the Kremlin's belfries from her windows. On September 24, the *New York Evening Mail* advertised a series of her articles emphasizing that "Mrs. Dorr, speaking from the viewpoint of a patriotic woman, who passionately desires allied success over German militarism, will tell the solemn truth about the black chaos that holds Russia in its grip."[78] Between late September and early December, the *Mail*'s front pages regularly featured Dorr's extensive articles that were promptly syndicated in the *Washington Evening Star*, the *San Francisco Chronicle* and the *St. Louis Post-Dispatch*. Dorr was very selective in accepting lecture engagements, although she received a great many high-paying offers. The journalist was writing her articles and her book and did not respond to American radicals (including Louise Bryant) who attacked her for her perspective on the Russian Revolution.[79]

Dorr's *Inside the Russian Revolution* was the story of the Provisional Government fighting against Bolsheviks as Russia lay bleeding around them; it was a rumination on the possible ways of helping the country go back to stability, and on the absolute power of the man in the street who recognized no authority whatsoever. In Dorr's opinion, Russia's problem lay in understanding freedom as anarchy and in total refusal to obey anyone except Soviets. She never thought that Russia needed lessons in democracy as it had democracy in spades. This huge country needed a stable government to restore order, a capable army to finish the war, political and economic leaders who were trusted by the Russian people that in turn needed to be educated and taught "how to establish a peaceful federation on republican lines." From her point of view, those were all the things that the United States could help Russians with in order to save democracy. Dorr believed that Americans "must loan money to Russia even though they lose the money, send her food and supplies even though they be received without much gratitude."[80] She continued to hope that the famine that was clearly looming ahead in Russia would result in the Bolsheviks' power collapsing.[81] It did not happen in 1917 or in 1921–1922 when the American Relief Administration (ARA) came to the aid of the starving Soviet Russia.

Observing the events in Russia, Dorr concluded that the Russian Revolution of 1917 was a warning for all those who believe socialism to be the best socioeconomic development model (and that included herself): "I believe that the world is for the many, not the few. But Russia has demonstrated that there is no advantage to be gained by taking all power out of the hands of one class and placing it in the hands of another [...]. The lesson of Russia to America is patient, intelligent, clear-sighted preparation for the next economic development. Beginning with the youngest children, we must contrive for all children a system of education which will create in the coming generation a thinking working class, one which will accept responsibility as well as demand power, and into whose hands we can safely confide authority and destiny."[82]

Thinking about her life, she admitted that whenever she met anarchists and radicals of various persuasions, she always came to be disappointed with the discussions of their specific programs, which invariably brought her back to feminism with its legally achievable goals, and buttressed her faith "in the American Constitution as a perfectly good means of securing as much justice as the human race in this era is capable of comprehending."[83] Dorr's sobering experience of the Russian Revolution was certainly conducive to her transitioning from socialism to moderate reformism with its program of achieving greater equality through gradual reforms. As she wrote in 1927, "I became a socialist by getting religion. I got converted away from it by the logic of fact [...]. My faith in socialism became held out after five months in revolutionary Russia with the socialist Kerensky demonstrating every day the futility of theories when opposed to facts [...]"[84]

However, that did not take away Dorr's faith in the future of Russia. In her opinion, this country was gravely ill with freedom in 1917, but would be reborn into a new life, even if at the cost of tremendous suffering. Although Dorr believed that in some aspects, Russians still lived in the sixteenth century, she emphasized that they were the fastest learners among all European nations.[85] Dorr did not expect the Russian "safely democratic civilization" to be shaped during her lifetime, yet she did not deny that Russia's fight for freedom was an inspiring experience and already did make and would go on to make its contribution to global democracy. And Russians should count on Americans' help in this struggle.

Summing up her years-long observations of the Russian Revolution, Dorr wrote: "Hapless Russia, twice have I seen you under your Tsar, once under your more ruthless tyrant, the mob. Perhaps I shall not live to see you free from the chains you have striven so long to break, but slave or free you will always hold part of my heart, for from your blood-stained, scarred and martyred soil I too picked up a torch."[86]

Such was the outcome of Rheta Childe Dorr's journey into the Russian Revolution. The way she perceived it was tied to her identity as a woman and to her vision of the ways of reforming American society itself. Dorr's ability to create a multifaceted picture of revolutionary politics made her writings about the Russian Revolution widely known at that time.[87] However, despite their importance, they were soon eclipsed by other books about the 1917 October Revolution.

Meanwhile, Dorr's narrative about the prospects of Russia's renewal fitted into several discourses of viewing Russia that existed in American society in the early twentieth century and were connected with the construction of its national identity: her book was liberal and messianic in nature because she believed in the future of the Russian people that had just entered the American "freedom school" and were in need of a long education as well as help from the United States. Her travelogue was also radical in what concerned the significance of the Russian revolutionary message (both inspiring and sobering) for all humanity. Along with the pessimistic conservative discourse that described the revolutionary Russian style as a circular movement from freedom via anarchy toward dictatorship, the first two discourses were incorporated into the works of American Slavists, into political writings, and into journalism. All these discourses remain relevant even now as they formed the foundations of what can be termed the American understanding of the Russian Revolution as a phenomenon.

Notes

1 Rheta Childe Dorr, *Inside the Russian Revolution* (New York: The Macmillan Company, 1917), 1.
2 Some of Rheta Childe Dorr's correspondence related to suffrage may be found in the National Woman's Party Papers, Library of Congress, Manuscript Division, Washington DC.
3 Victoria I. Zhuravleva, "The Study of the Russian Revolution in the US: Academic Discourse as an Identity Discourse," in *AMERICANA* XVI, edited by Alexander Kubyshkin and Ivan Kurilla (Saint-Petersburg–Volgograd: Herzen State Pedagogical University of Russia and Volgograd State University, 2020), 148–65; Victoria I. Zhuravleva, "Image of Russian Revolution in American Radical Discourse: The Russia's Social Mission vs the US Liberal Mission," *ISTORIYA* 11, no. 12 (98), Part I (2020), https://history.jes.su/s207987840012984-1-1/.
4 Choi Chatterjee, "'Odds and Ends of the Russian Revolution,' 1917–1920: Gender and American Travel Narratives," *Journal of Women's History* 20, no. 4 (Winter 2008): 10–33; Julia L. Mickenberg, "Suffragettes and Soviets: American Feminists and the Specter of Revolutionary Russia," *Journal of American History* 100, no. 4 (March 2014): 1021–1051.
5 The original spelling of the family name did not have the final "e." Rheta added the letter later in life as a stylistic embellishment.
6 Rheta Childe Dorr, *A Woman of Fifty* (New York: Frank & Wagnalls Company, 1924), 10–12.

7 Dorr, *A Woman of Fifty*, 18–39, 47–48, 50–54; Robert Edgar Riegel, *American Feminists* (Lawrence: University of Kansas Press, 1966), 173–75; John Jakes, *Great Women Reporters* (New York: G.P. Putnam's Sons, 1969), 108–9; Susan G. Motes, "Rheta Dorr," in *American Newspaper Journalists, 1901–1925*, edited by Perry J. Ashley (Detroit: Gale Research Co., 1984), 78–80.
8 Dorr, *A Woman of Fifty*, 101.
9 Dorr, *A Woman of Fifty*, 103.
10 June Sochen, *Movers and Shakers: American Women Thinkers and Activists, 1900–1970* (New York: Quadrangle, 1973), 12, 28, 31, 33.
11 Dorr, *A Woman of Fifty*, 87–94, 107–25; Louis Filler, *Crusaders for American Liberalism* (New York: Harcourt, Brace and Company, 1939), 348; Eshbel Ross, *Ladies of the Press. The Story of Women in Journalism by an Insider* (New York and London: Harper & Brothers, 1936), 3–13, 112–13.
12 See, for example, Rheta Childe Dorr, "Crowning a King in Norway," *Harper's Weekly* 50 (July 28, 1906): 1054–57.
13 Ekaterina Konstantinovna Breshko-Breshkovskaya (née Verigo, 1844–1934), also known in English sources as Catherine Breshkovsky, was a major figure in the Russian socialist movement, a *Narodnik* and later one of the founders of the Socialist Revolutionary Party. She spent decades in a tsarist prison and exile for her political views. Also popularly known as "*babushka*" (grandmother), Breshkovskaya was the grandmother of the Russian Revolution. After the October Revolution, she became a vocal opponent of the Bolshevik government.
14 Victoria I. Zhuravleva, *Understanding Russia in the United States: Images and Myths* (Moscow: Russian State University for the Humanities, 2012), 637–43.
15 Emmeline Pankhurst (1858–1928) was a British political activist who organized the British suffragette movement. Her 40-year campaign achieved complete success in the year of her death, when British women were finally fully enfranchised.
16 Dorr, *A Woman of Fifty*, 155–59; Motes, "Rheta Dorr," 81; Jakes, *Great Women Reporters*, 111–13.
17 Nancy F. Cott, *The Grounding of Modern Feminism* (New Haven: Yale, 1987), 26–27.
18 Motes, "Rheta Dorr," 80–81; Dorr, *A Woman of Fifty*, 193–98.
19 Filler, *Crusaders for American Liberalism*, 272–73; See also Dorr's articles in *Hampton's Magazine*, 1910–11.
20 Emmeline Pankhurst, *My Own Story* (New York: Hearst's International Library Co., 1914).
21 Dorr, *A Woman of Fifty*, 236–67.
22 Rheta Childe Dorr, "A Convert from Socialism," *North American Review* 224 (November 1927): 500.
23 Dorr, *A Woman of Fifty*, 215.
24 Judith Schwarz, *The Radical Feminists of Heterodoxy* (Lebanon: New Victoria Publishers, 1982), 13, 23–27; Cott, *The Grounding of Modern Feminism*, 38–39.
25 Dorr, Woman of Fifty, 270–78.
26 Filler, *Crusaders for American Liberalism*, 348.
27 "Mrs. Dorr Now in Europe for Mail. Special Writer Will Tell of Both Battles and Politics," *New York Evening Mail*, December 13, 1917.
28 Dorr, *A Woman of Fifty*, 375–76, 380–89; Motes, "Rheta Dorr," 82–83.
29 "Mrs. R.C. Dorr Injured. In a Washington Hospital After Being Run Down by a Motorcycle," *New York Times*, November 20, 1919, 17.

EDITOR'S INTRODUCTION xxix

30 Dorr, *A Woman of Fifty*, 394–408.
31 Ross, *Ladies of the Press*, 115–16.
32 Dorr, "A Convert from Socialism," 502.
33 Dorr, *A Woman of Fifty*, 446.
34 Rheta Childe Dorr, *Susan B. Anthony. The Woman Who Changed the Mind of Nation* (New York: Frederick A. Stokes Company, 1928).
35 Rheta Childe Dorr, *Drink Coercion or Control?* (New York: Frederick A. Stokes, 1929).
36 "Wife of American Consul at Mexico Buried with Honors in Arlington Cemetery. Was Yeomanette in war. Received Victory Button for Her Work," *New York Times*, March 15, 1936, 13; "Rites for Julian C. Dorr. Ashes of Former Envoy to Mexico are Buried at Arlington," *New York Times*, October 7, 1936, 27.
37 "Rheta C. Dorr, 82, Author, Feminist, Reporter, War Correspondent, First Editor of Suffragist, Dies in New Britain, Pa.," *New York Times*, August 9, 1948, 19.
38 Dorr, *A Woman of Fifty*, 136.
39 The Constitutional Democrats (*Kadets*) advocated a radical transformation of Russian governance into a constitutional monarchy. The party was founded in October 1905 by the Union of Liberation and other liberals from the zemstvos, local councils that often were centers of liberal opinion and agitation. The *Kadets* dominated the first Duma of 1906, but the tradition of despotic rule and the growth of revolutionary fervor and agitation during World War I caused other groups to claim the nation's attention. Four members of the Provisional Government's first cabinet were *Kadets*.
40 The Socialist Revolutionary party (SRs) was founded in January 1902 and became the largest political party in Russia in the crucial revolutionary year of 1917. Heirs to the earlier populist movement, the SRs were unabashed proponents of peasant rebellion and revolutionary terror. They undertook propaganda work in both rural areas and factories and emphasized the socialist transformation of rural Russia and a democratic system of government as their political goals.
41 Dorr, *A Woman of Fifty*, 138–44.
42 Elizabeth Mary "Bessie" Beatty (1886–1947) was an American journalist and editor who traveled to Russia to cover the Russian Revolution in a column at the *San Francisco Bulletin* titled "Around the World in Wartime." She visited the trenches where disillusioned Russians were fending off the German advances, spent a week with Bochkareva's Women's Battalion of Death and interviewed peasants, soldiers and sailors. In July, she returned to St. Petersburg where eruptions of violence and periods of uneasy peace were visible right on Nevsky Prospect. On November 7, 1917, the day the Winter Palace fell, Beatty obtained a pass from the Military Revolutionary Committee gaining access to any place in the city; she was one of the first civilians to enter the Winter Palace after the removal of Alexander Kerensky's provisional government. Beatty was present at the meetings of important revolutionaries that decided the future of Russia.
43 Louise Bryant (1885–1936) was an American feminist, political activist and journalist, best known for her marriage to the writer, reporter and activist John Reed. They married in 1916, and in 1917, traveled to Petrograd to report on the Russian Revolution.
44 Maria Leont'evna Bochkareva (1889–1920) was the third daughter in a peasant family. She petitioned the government to allow her to enlist in the Imperial Army in order to protect Mother Russia against Germany in World War I. She was accepted into the active field army only after appealing personally to the tsar and served from early

1915 until May–June 1917. Then she organized her Women's Battalion of Death, the first all-female combat unit formed after the February Revolution by the Provisional Government to inspire the mass of war-weary soldiers to continue fighting in World War I. Nearly 2,000 women of all backgrounds responded to Bochkareva's initial appeal to "women-citizens" made at a propaganda event at the Mariinsky Theater on May 21, 1917. Her speech was subsequently published in newspapers. Bochkareva became the first Russian woman to command a military unit. After the October Revolution, when 20 of her female soldiers were lynched by an angry male mob, the battalion had to be disbanded. She was twice detained by the Bolsheviks, but managed to escape. In July 1918, Bochkareva visited the United States where she met President Woodrow Wilson, and then Great Britain where she had an audience with King George V, to plead for an Allied intervention in Russia. With British assistance, she came back to Russia and did her best to persuade the White authorities to allow her to raise a women's battalion again. She failed in her efforts, was captured by the Red forces at Tomsk and executed.

45 John Silas Reed (1887–1920) was an American journalist, poet and communist activist. He first gained prominence as a war correspondent for *The Metropolitan* during the Mexican Revolution and for *The Masses* during World War I. He is best known for his coverage of the October Revolution in Russia, which he wrote about in his 1919 book *Ten Days That Shook the World*. He hoped for a similar communist revolution in the United States and co-founded the short-lived Communist Labor Party of America in 1919. He died of spotted typhus in 1920 in Soviet Russia and was buried at the Kremlin Wall.

46 Bessie Beatty, *The Red Heart of Russia* (The Century Co., 1919); Louise Bryant, *Six Red Months in Russia*, edited and introduced by Lee A. Farrow (Bloomington: Slavica Publishers, 2017); Lyubov Ginzburg, "The Triumph and Anguish of the Russian Revolution: Bessie Beatty's Forgotten Chronicle," *Journal of Russian American Studies* 4, no. 1 (2020): 48–69, https://journals.ku.edu/jras/article/view/13658/12711; Helen Rappaport, *Caught in the Revolution* (London: Windmill Books, 2016).

47 The Canadian Florence Harper was the fourth female journalist and war correspondent. In 1916, she covered events on the Western Front, and in February 1917, she arrived in Russia as a special war correspondent for the American magazine *Leslie's Illustrated Weekly Newspaper*. During her time in Russia, she was authorized to take photos for the *New York Times*, a leading U.S. newspaper, and for Paramount Pictures, a U.S. film company. She was also a staff war correspondent and official photographer of the Central News Photo Service. Harper's *Runway Russia* was published in 1918 by Century Press in New York. For more information about her see Rappaport, *Caught in the Revolution*.

48 Julia Edwards, *Women of the World. The Great Foreign Correspondents* (Boston: Houghton Mifflin Company, 1988), 32–40.

49 Dorr, *A Woman of Fifty*, 318–20, 332.

50 Maria Alexandrovna Spiridonova (1884–1941) was a *Narodnik*-inspired Russian revolutionary. In 1906, as a novice member of a local combat group of the Tambov Socialist Revolutionaries (SRs), she assassinated one of the officials who led the governmental reprisals, General Luzhenovsky, the governor's advisor. Her subsequent abuse by police made her enormously popular with opponents of Tsarism throughout the empire and abroad. She spent over eleven years in Siberian prisons, was freed after the February Revolution and returned to European Russia as a heroine of the destitute, and especially of the peasants.

51 Charlotte Corday (1768–1793) assassinated the French revolutionary Jean-Paul Marat, one of the leaders of the radical Montagnard faction during the French Revolution. She was guillotined just four days after his murder.
52 Dorr, *Inside the Russian Revolution*, 10.
53 Alexander Fyodorovich Kerensky (1881–1970) was a Russian lawyer and key political figure of the 1917 February Revolution. He joined the newly formed Russian Provisional Government, first as the justice minister, then as the war minister, and after July 1917 as the government's second minister-chairman. A leader of the moderate-socialist *Trudoviks* (Laborist) faction of the Socialist Revolutionary Party, he was also vice-chairman of the powerful Petrograd Soviet. On November 7, his government was overthrown by the Lenin-led *Bolsheviks* in the October Revolution.
54 Dorr, *Inside the Russian Revolution*, 205–6.
55 Dorr, *A Woman of Fifty*, 341–42.
56 Grigori Yefimovich Rasputin (1869–1916) was a Siberian peasant and mystic; his ability to stem hemorrhages Aleksey Nikolayevich, the hemophiliac heir to the Russian throne, suffered from made Rasputin an influential favorite at the court of Emperor Nicholas II and Empress Alexandra Feodorovna. Rasputin reached the pinnacle of his power at the Russian court after 1915 when Nicholas II went to the troops at the front, leaving Alexandra in charge of Russia's domestic affairs, while Rasputin served as her personal adviser. Several assassination attempts were made, but none were successful until 1916. Then a group of extreme conservatives, including Prince Felix Yusupov, Vladimir Mitrofanovich Purishkevich (a member of the Duma) and Grand Duke Dmitry Pavlovich (the tsar's cousin) formed a conspiracy to eliminate Rasputin and save the monarchy from further scandal. About Rasputin see, Douglas Smith, *Rasputin: Faith, Power, and the Twilight of the Romanovs* (New York: Farrar, Straus and Giroux, 2016).
57 Prince Felix Felixovich Yusupov (1887–1967) was a Russian aristocrat from the House of Yusupov, who is best known for participating in the assassination of Grigori Rasputin and for marrying Princess Irina Alexandrovna, a niece of Emperor Nicholas II, in 1914.
58 Rheta Childe Dorr, "Russian Prince Who Slew Rasputin Tells Own Story of Murder Night," *New York Evening Mail*, October 6, 1917; Rheta Childe Dorr, "Terrors of Russian Court Revealed by Czarina's Confident," *New York Evening Mail*, October 9, 1917.
59 Dorr, *Inside the Russian Revolution*, 102.
60 Interview by the French director Robert Hossein with Prince Felix Felixovich Yusupov and Princess Irina Alexandrovna Yusupova on the murder of Rasputin in 1916. Paris, 1967 // https://www.youtube.com/watch?v-zlEjwhy1UR8. This interview became part of Robert Hossein's film "I Killed Rasputin."
61 Rheta Childe Dorr, "Russia Seeking Liberty, Finds Chaos," *St. Louis Post-Dispatch*, September 27, 1917; Rheta Childe Dorr, "Premier Kerensky Tries to Put Back Russia's Genie of Unrest into Bottle," *San Francisco Chronicle*, October 28, 1917; Rheta Childe Dorr, "Kerensky Seeks Help of Army in Moscow Flight," *New York Evening Mail*, November 9, 1917.
62 Lavr Georgiyevich Kornilov (1870–1918) was an Imperial Russian general. On August 1 (July 18), 1917, Kerensky appointed him commander-in-chief, but conflicts developed between Kornilov and Kerensky owing to their opposing views on politics and on the role and nature of the army. At the end of August, Kornilov sent troops

toward Petrograd. Kerensky, interpreting this as an attempted military coup d'état, dismissed Kornilov and ordered him to come to Petrograd. Kornilov refused, and railroad workers prevented his troops from reaching their destination. He was captured and imprisoned, but later escaped. After the Bolsheviks seized power in October 1917, Kornilov assumed military command of the anti-Bolshevik volunteer army in the Don region. Several months later, he was killed in the battle for Ekaterinodar (today's Krasnodar) in the south of Russia.

63 Dorr, *Inside the Russian Revolution*, 38.
64 Criticism of a "German-Bolshevik conspiracy" theory see in: David S. Foglesong, "Foreign Intervention," in Edward Acton, Vladimir Cherniaev, and William Rosenberg, eds. *Critical Companion to the Russian Revolution, 1914–1921* (London: Arnold, 1997); David S. Foglesong, "Revolutionary Russia in American Eyes," *Vestnik Sankt-Peterburgskogo universiteta*, Vol. 25, No. 5 (2002), 104–118.
65 Rheta Childe Dorr, "Terrorists Battle to Tera Russia into Score of Republics," *New York Evening Mail*, October 19, 1917; Rheta Childe Dorr, "Baffled Kerensky Vainly Struggling Against Terrorists," *New York Evening Mail*, October 20, 1917; Rheta Childe Dorr, "Russia, Liberty-Crazed, Beset by Thieves and German Spies," *Washington Evening Star*, October 17, 1917; Rheta Childe Dorr, "Real Russian Facts Secret; Bolsheviki Control Censor," *New York Evening Mail*, November 9, 1917.
66 The Root mission was appointed by the U.S. President Woodrow Wilson in April 1917 to go to Russia, chiefly for the purpose to encourage the Provisional Government to stay in the war. The mission, headed by former secretary of state Elihu Root, arrived in Petrograd in June and concentrated on developing contacts with moderates such as Alexander Kerensky. The mission thus reached the erroneous conclusion that an American-funded propaganda campaign could keep Russia in the war. The Bolshevik Revolution of October 1917 exposed the flawed strategy behind the Root mission and caught the Wilson administration almost completely unprepared.
67 Rheta Childe Dorr, "Russia Finds Anarchy in Fight for Millennium," *New York Evening Mail*, September 26, 1917; Rheta Childe Dorr, "Bloody of Lenin Radicals Spread Death in Russia to Force Separate Peace," *New York Evening Mail*, September 28, 1917; Rheta Childe Dorr, "Blood and Terror Ruling in Russia," *Washington Evening Star*, December 3, 1917; Dorr, *A Woman of Fifty*, 336–37.
68 Pavel Nikolayevich Miliukov (1859–1943) was a Russian statesman and historian who played an important role in the events leading to the 1917 February Russian Revolution. He served as the Foreign Minister (March–May 1917) in Prince Lvov's Provisional Government. He remains one of the greatest of Russia's liberal historians.
69 Rheta Childe Dorr, "Kerensky Feared to Let Kornilloff Save Russian Army," *New York Evening Mail*, September 29, 1917; Rheta Childe Dorr, "Korniloff, Kerensky, Kaledines Main Hope of Saving Russia," *New York Evening Mail*, November 12, 1917; Rheta Childe Dorr, "Korniloff-Kerensky Victory," *New York Evening Mail*, November 14, 1917.
70 Rheta Childe Dorr, "Fanatics Snatched Freed Russia from Hands of Wise Man," *St. Louis Post-Dispatch*, September 28, 1917; Rheta Childe Dorr, "Workers' Control Cuts Down Factory Output in Russia," *New York Evening Mail*, October 15, 1917; Rheta Childe Dorr, "Workers Sleep and Loaf While Russia Suffers Dire Want," *New York Evening Mail*, October 16, 1917; Rheta Childe Dorr, "Liberty in Russia Blocked by Soldiers and Workmen," *Washington Evening Star*, October 18, 1917.

71 Vera Nikolaevna Figner (1852–1942) was a leader of the Russian Revolutionary Populist (*Narodnik*) movement. Following a major policy split within the *Zemlya i Volya* ("Land and Freedom") Party in 1879, she joined the terrorist branch which formed the new *Narodnaya Volya* ("People's Will") Party. As a member of the party's executive committee, she helped prepare plans for assassinations of key political figures, including Emperor Alexander II. She was captured by police in 1883 and condemned to death by a military tribunal. Her sentence was commuted, however, to life imprisonment, and for the next 20 years she remained a prisoner in the Shlisselburg Fortress. After being exiled to Arkhangelsk in 1904, she was allowed to go abroad in 1906. There she joined the Russian Socialist Revolutionary Party, the offspring of the Populist movement, but upon her return to Russia in 1915 she devoted herself to literary and social work.

72 Grand Duchess Elizabeth Feodorovna (1864–1918) was a granddaughter of Queen Victoria, an older sister of Alexandra Feodorovna, the last Russian Empress and the wife of Grand Duke Sergei Alexandrovich of Russia (1857–1905), the son of Alexander II of Russia. Elizabeth Feodorovna became famous in Russian society for her dignified beauty and charitable works. After the Socialist Revolutionary Party's Combat Organization assassinated her husband with a bomb in 1905, she left the Imperial Court and became a nun, founding the Marfo-Mariinsky (Martha and Mary) Convent. She was arrested and ultimately executed by the Bolsheviks.

73 Rheta Childe Dorr, "Czarina's Aide Reveals Secrets of Russian Court," *New York Evening Mail*, October 8, 1917; Rheta Childe Dorr, "Abbess Feodorovna, Last of Romanoffs, Prays for Kerensky," *New York Evening Mail*, October 11, 1917; Rheta Childe Dorr, "Visit to Only Free Member of Royal Family in New Russia," *Washington Evening Star*, November 4, 1917.

74 For information about Russian women's battalions see: Laurie S. Stoff, *They Fought for the Motherland: Russia's Women Soldiers in World War I and Revolution* (Lawrence: University Press of Kansas, 2006).

75 Rappaport, *Caught in the Revolution*, 193–201.

76 Rheta Childe Dorr, "Mrs. Pankhurst in Russia to Organize Women to Service," *New York Evening Mail*, October 17, 1917; Rheta Childe Dorr, "Women of Russia Enlisting to Form a Division of 20000," *New York Evening Mail*, October 23, 1917; Rheta Childe Dorr, "Russia Mail Troops Hide as Women Go Into Battle," *Washington Evening Star*, October 22, 1917; Rheta Childe Dorr, "Woman Soldiers of Russia May Rescue to Republic," *Washington Evening Star*, October 21, 1917; Jakes, *Great Women Reporters*, 94–95.

77 Dorr, *Inside the Russian Revolution*, 49, 51.

78 Rheta Childe Dorr, "The Amazing Truth About Russia," *New York Evening Mail*, September 24, 1917.

79 Dorr, *A Woman of Fifty*, 373–75; Ross, *Ladies of the Press*, 111.

80 Rheta Childe Dorr, "Russia Looks to America for Aid in Readjustment," *New York Evening Mail*, September 30, 1917; Dorr, *Inside the Russian Revolution*, 216, 226, 234.

81 Rheta Childe Dorr, "Hunger Soon to End Merciless Rule of Russian Terrorists," *New York Evening Mail*, October 12, 1917; Rheta Childe Dorr, "Empty Dinner Pail Russia's Hope for Save Government," *New York Evening Mail*, October 22, 1917; Rheta Childe Dorr, "Fate of Russians This Winter," *New York Evening Mail*, November 5, 1917.

82 Dorr, *Inside the Russian Revolution*, 243.

83 Dorr, *Woman of Fifty*, 218–19.

84 Dorr, "A Convert from Socialism," 498, 502.
85 Dorr, *Inside the Russian Revolution*, 9, 242.
86 Dorr, *Woman of Fifty*, 147.
87 See, for example, reviews on her book, "Russia in Revolution," *The Courier-Journal* (Louisville, KY), January 7, 1918, 6; *Pittsburgh Daily Post* (Pittsburgh, PA), January 12, 1918, 8.

Chapter 1

TOPSY-TURVY LAND

Early in May 1917, I went to Russia, eager to see again, in the hour of her deliverance, a country in whose struggle for freedom I had, for a dozen years, been deeply interested. I went to Russia a socialist by conviction, an ardent sympathizer with revolution, having known personally some of the brave men and women who suffered imprisonment and exile after the failure of the uprising in 1905–6.[1] I returned from Russia with the very clear conviction that the world will have to wait awhile before it can establish any cooperative millenniums, or before it can safely hand over the work of government to the man in the street.

All my life I have been an admiring student of the French Revolution, and I have fervently wished that I might have lived in the Paris of that time, to witness, even as a humble spectator, the downfall of autocracy and the birth of a people's liberty. Well—I lived for three months in the capital of revolutionary Russia. I saw a revolution that presents close parallels with the French Revolution both in men and events. I saw the downfall of autocracy and the birth of liberty much greater than the French ever aspired to. I saw the fondest dream of the socialists suddenly come true, and the dream turned out to be a nightmare such as I pray that this or any country may forever be spared.

I saw a people delivered from one class tyranny deliberately hasten to establish another, quite as brutal and as unmindful of the common good as the old one. I saw these people, led out of groaning bondage, use their first liberty to oust the wise and courageous statesmen who had delivered them. I saw a working class that had been oppressed under tsardom itself turn oppressor; an army that had been starved and betrayed use its freedom to starve and betray its own people. I saw elected delegates to the people's councils turn into sneak thieves and looters. I saw law and order and decency and all regard for human life or human rights set aside, and I saw responsible statesmen in power allow all this to go on, allow their country to rush toward an abyss of ruin and shame because they were afraid to lose popularity with the mob.

The government was so afraid of losing the support of the mob that it permitted the country to be overrun by German agents posing as socialists.

These agents spent fortunes on the separate peace propaganda alone. They demoralized the army, corrupted the workers in fields and factories, and put machine guns in the hands of fanatical dreamers, sending them out into the streets to murder their own friends and neighbors. Everyone knew who these men were, but the mob liked their "line of talk," and the government was afraid to touch them. After one of the last occasions when, at their behest, the Bolsheviki[2] went out and shot up Petrograd, Lenin,[3] the arch leader, and some of his principal gangsters deemed it the part of discretion to retire from Russia temporarily, and they got to Sweden[4] without the slightest difficulty, no attempt having been made to stop them. Some of the minor employees of the Kaiser[5] were arrested, among them a woman in whose name the bank account appeared to be. But she too, and probably all the others, were later released. A government like this could not bring peace and order into a distracted nation. It could not establish a democracy. It could not govern. The sooner the Allied countries realize this, the better it will be for Russia and for the world that wants peace. It is not because I am unfriendly to Russia that I write thus. It is because I am friendly, because I have faith in the future of the Russian people, because I believe that their experiment in popular government, if it succeeds, will be as inspiring to the rest of the world as our own was in the eighteenth century. I think the most unkind thing any friend of Russia can do is to minimize or conceal the facts about the terrible upheaval going on there at the present time. Russia looks to the American people for help in her troubled hour, and if the American people are to help, they will have to understand the situation. No discouragement to the allies, no assistance to the common enemy need result from a plain statement of the facts. The enemy knows all the facts already.

Everything I saw in Russia, in the cities and near the front, convinced me that what is going on there vitally concerns us. Every man, woman and child in the United States must get to work to give the help so sorely needed by the allies. Whatever has failed in Russia, whatever has broken down must never be missed. We must supply these deficiencies. Our business now is to understand, and to hurry, hurry, hurry with our task of getting trained and seasoned men into France. After what I saw in the neighborhood of Vilna,[6] Dvinsk[7] and Jacobstadt,[8] I know what haste on this side means to the world. There are several reasons why the whole truth has not before been written about the Russian Revolution. It could not be written or cabled from Russia. It could not be carried out in the form of notes or photographs. It could not even be discovered by the average person who goes to Russia, because the average visitor lives at the expensive Hotel d'Europe,[9] never goes out except in a droshky,[10] and meets only Russians of social position to whom he has letters of introduction, and who naturally try to give him the impression that the troubled state of affairs is merely temporary. The visitor usually knows no Russian and cannot read the newspapers. There are two good French newspapers published in Petrograd, but the average American traveler is as ignorant of French as of Russian. Even if he could read all the daily papers, however, he would not get very much information. The press censorship is as rigid and as tyrannical today as in the heyday of the autocracy, only a different kind of news is suppressed. One of the modest demands put forth by the *Tavarishi* (comrades) when I was in Petrograd was for a requisition of all the white print paper in the market, the paper to be distributed equally among all newspapers, large and small. The object, candidly stated, was to diminish the size and the circulation of the "bourgeois" papers.

A great deal of news, as we regard news, never gets into the papers at all, or is compressed into very small space. For example, there have been a number of terrible railroad accidents on the Russian roads. Most of these ones never heard of unless someone he knew happened to be killed or injured. Sometimes a bare announcement of a great fatality was permitted. Thus, an express train between Moscow and Petrograd[11] was wrecked, forty persons being killed and more than seventy injured. This wreck got a whole paragraph in the newspapers, with no list of the dead and injured and no explanation of the cause. The fact is that the railroads are in a condition of complete demoralization and the only wonder is that more wrecks do not occur.

An acquaintance of mine in Moscow, the wife of a colonel in the British army, was anxious to go to Petrograd to meet her husband who was expected there on his way from the front. My friend's father, who is the managing head of a large Moscow business concern, tried to prevail on her to wait for her husband to reach her there, but she was anxious to see him at the earliest moment and insisted on her tickets being purchased. The day after she was to have gone her father called on me and told me of his intense relief at receiving, an hour before train time, a telegram from the colonel saying that he would be in Moscow the next morning.

"And what do you think happened to that train my daughter was to have taken?" he asked. It was the regular night express to Petrograd, corresponding somewhat to the Congressional Limited between New York and Washington. A few miles out of Moscow a difference arose between the engineer and the stoker, and in order to settle it they stopped the train and had a fight. One of the men hit the other on the head with a monkey wrench, injuring him pretty badly. Authority of some kind stepped in and arrested the assailant. The engineer's cab was bloodstained, and some authority unhitched the engine and sent it back to Moscow as evidence. The train all this time, with its hundreds of passengers, stood on the tracks waiting for a new engine and crew, and if it was not run into and wrecked it was because it was lucky.

About the middle of August, an American correspondent traveled on that same express train from Petrograd to Moscow. The night was warm, and as the Russian occupants of his carriage had the usual constitutional objection to raised windows, he insisted on leaving the door of the compartment open. In the middle of the night a band of soldiers boarded the train and went into every one of the unlocked compartments, five in all, neatly and silently looting them of all bags and suitcases. The American correspondent lost everything he possessed—extra clothes, money, passport, papers. There was a Russian staff officer in that compartment, and he lost even the clothes he traveled in, and was obliged to descend in his pajamas. The conductor of the train admitted that he saw the robbery committed, that he raised no hand to prevent it, nor even pressed the signal which would have stopped the train. "They would have killed me," he pleaded in extenuation. "Besides, it happens almost every night on a small or large scale."

There is only one way of getting at the facts of the Russian situation, and that is by living as the Russians do, associating with Russians, hearing their stories day by day of the tragedy of what has been called the bloodless revolution. This I did, as nearly as it was possible, from the end of May until the 30th of August, in Petrograd, Moscow and behind one of the fighting fronts. In Petrograd I lived in the Hotel Military, formerly the Astoria,[12] the headquarters of Russian officers and of the numerous English, French and Romanian officers on missions in Russia. This was the hotel where the bitterest fighting took place during the revolutionary days of February 1917.[13] The outside of the building is literally riddled with bullets, every window had to be replaced and the work of renovating the interior was still going on when I left. Under the window in my bedroom was a pool of dried blood as big as a saucer, and the carpet was stained with drops leading from the window to the stationary washbowl in the alcove dressing room. Over the bed were two bullet holes.

Since the revolution the Hotel Military has been a garrison, soldiers sleeping in several rooms on the ground floor and two sentinels standing day and night at the door and at the gateway leading into the service court. I do not know why, when I asked for a room, the manager gave it to me. Two other women writers had rooms there, but one was in a party that included American officers, and the other was introduced by an English officer attached to the British embassy. However, I took the room and was grateful, because whatever happened in Petrograd was quickly known in the hotel. Also, it faced the square on which was located the Marie Palace,[14] where the Provisional Government held many of its meetings, and where several important congresses were held. Whenever the Bolsheviki broke loose, this square always saw some fighting. It was an excellent place for a correspondent to live.

I spent much of my time in the streets, listening, with the aid of an interpreter, a young university girl, to the speeches that were continually being made up and down the Nevsky Prospect, the Liteyny and other principal streets. I talked, through my interpreter, with people who sat beside me on park benches, in trams, railroad trains and other public places. I met all the Russians I could, people of every walk of life, of every political faith. I spent days in factories. I talked with workers and with employers. I even met and talked with adherents of the old regime. I talked for nearly an hour with the last Romanoff left in freedom, the Grand Duchess Sergei,[15] sister of the former empress, widow of the Emperor's uncle. I went, late at night, to a palace on the Grand Morskaya[16] where in strictest retirement, lives the woman who has been charged with being the closest friend and ally of Rasputin, the one who, at his orders, is alleged to have administered poison to the young Tsarevitch. I traveled in a troop train for two days and nights with a regiment of fighting women—the Botchkareva Battalion of Death—and I lived with them in their barrack behind the fighting lines for nine days. I stayed with them until they went into action, I saw them afterward in the hospitals and heard their own stories of the battle into which they led thousands of reluctant men. I talked with many soldiers and officers.

Russia is sick. She is gorged on something she has never known before—freedom: she is sick almost to die with excesses, and the leadership that would bring the panacea is violently thrown aside because suspicion of any authority has bred the worst kind of license. Russia is insane; she is not even morally responsible for what she is doing. Will she recover? Yes. But, God! What pain must she bear before she gets real freedom!

Notes

1 The uprising of 1905–6 refers to the Revolution of 1905–7 in the Russian Empire.
2 Bolsheviki (the Bolsheviks) were a far-left faction of the Russian Social Democratic Labor Party (RSDLP) that, along with the Mensheviks, split off from the RSDLP at the Second Party Congress in 1903. While Bolshevism was based on Marxist philosophy, it also absorbed elements of the ideology and practice of the socialist revolutionaries of the late nineteenth century and was influenced by Russian agrarian socialist movements like the *Narodniks*. The Bolshevik Party was officially established in 1912 and seized power in Russia in October 1917.
3 Lenin (Ulyanov), Vladimir Ilyich (1870–1924) was a Russian revolutionary, politician and political theorist. The founder and leader of the Bolsheviks, Lenin led the October Revolution and established the first socialist state in the world.
4 Dorr made a mistake. In the aftermath of Petrograd street riots (the July Days), the Provisional Government publicly alleged that the Bolsheviks were German agents. Many leading Bolsheviks were arrested (including Leon Trotsky), and the party was outlawed. Because of threats to his safety and life, Lenin was forced to go to ground in

the guise of a Finnish haymaker living in a hut made of tree branches on the banks of Lake Razliv in Sestroretsk (near Petrograd). In August 1917, Lenin secretly departed for Finland, which was part of the Russian Empire at the time.

5 Kaiser Wilhelm II (1859–1941) was the last German Emperor and King of Prussia from 1888 until his abdication in 1918.
6 Vilna is a historical spelling of the name Vilnius, the capital of Lithuania.
7 Dvinsk was the name of Daugavpils, a city in southeastern Latvia, from 1893 to 1920.
8 Jacobstadt was the historical name of Jēkabpils, a town in Latvia.
9 Hotel d'Europe (The Grand Hotel Europe) is a historic luxury hotel opened in 1875 on Nevsky Prospect in Saint Petersburg.
10 *Droshky* was a four-wheeled open carriage used in Russia.
11 Petrograd was the name of Saint Petersburg in 1914–24.
12 The Hotel Astoria was sequestered from its foreign ownership in 1915, fully nationalized by the Russian government in 1916 and converted to the Petrograd Military Hotel.
13 The revolutionary days of February 1917 refer to the February Revolution (February 24–28, [March 8–12], 1917), the first stage of the Russian Revolution of 1917, in which the monarchy was overthrown and replaced by the Provisional Government.
14 The Marie Palace was another name for the Mariinsky Palace, the last neoclassical Imperial residence in Saint Petersburg. The palace housed the Russian Provisional Government after the February Revolution.
15 Grand Duchess Sergey (1864–1918), Princess Elizabeth Feodorovna, granddaughter of Queen Victoria, and the wife of Grand Duke Sergei Alexandrovich of Russia.
16 The Demidov Palace on the Grand Morskaya (Bolshaya Morskaya Street) is a unique eighteenth-century architectural monument and one of the most beautiful buildings in the heart of Saint Petersburg.

Chapter 2

"ALL THE POWER TO THE SOVIET"

About the first thing I saw on the morning of my arrival in Petrograd last spring was a group of young men, about twenty in number, I should think, marching through the street in front of my hotel, carrying a scarlet banner with an inscription in large white letters.

"What does that banner say?" I asked the hotel commissionaire who stood beside me.

"It says 'All the Power to the Soviet,'" was the answer.

"What is the soviet?" I asked, and he replied briefly:

"It is the only government we have in Russia now."

And he was right. The Soviets, or Councils of Soldiers' and Workmen's Delegates, which have spread like wildfire throughout the country, are the nearest thing to a government that Russia has known since the very early days of the revolution.

The most striking parallel between the French and the Russian Revolutions lies in the facility with which both were snatched away from the sane and intelligent men who began them and placed in the hands of fanatics, who turned them into mad orgies of blood and terror. The first French revolutionists rebelled against the theory of the divine right of kings to govern or misgovern the people. They wanted a constitution and a government by consent of the governed. But the mob came in and took possession of the situation, and the result was the guillotine and the reign of terror. Miliukov, Rodzianko,[1] Lvov,[2] and their associates in the Russian Duma,[3] rebelled against a stupid, cruel autocrat who was doing his best to lose the war and to bring the country to ruin and dishonor. They wanted a constitution for Russia, and, for the time being at least, a figurehead king who would leave government in the hands of responsible ministers. But the Petrograd Council of Soldiers' and Workmen's Delegates came in and took possession of the situation, and the result is a country torn with anarchy, brought to the verge of bankruptcy, and ready, unless something happens between now and next spring, to fall into the hands of the Germans.

These councils of workmen are not new. In the upheaval of 1905-6, a man named Khrustaliov,[4] a labor leader, became the head of an organization called the Petrograd Council of Workmen's Deputies. It was made up of elected delegates from all the principal factories in and near the capital, and during the general strike which forced Nicholas[5] to convene the first Duma, the council assumed general control of the whole labor situation, managing matters with rare good sense and firmness. Witte,[6] who became premier in those days, negotiated with Khrustaliov as with an equal. For a time, he and his council were a real power in the empire. A dozen cities formed similar organizations. There were councils of workmen's deputies, peasants' deputies, even, in some places, of soldiers' deputies. The reaction which came in July 1906, swept them all into oblivion, and I never found anybody who knew what became of Khrustaliov. But the tradition of the council of workmen's deputies was unforgotten. Perhaps the council even existed still in secret; I do not know. It was quickly revived in March 1917,[7] and before the political revolution was fairly accomplished, it had added soldiers to its title and had curtly informed the Provisional Government and the Duma that no laws could be made or enforced without first having received the approval of the working people's representatives. No policy in peace or war could be announced or put into practice; no orders could be given to the army; no treaties concluded with the allies; in short, nothing could be done without first consulting the 1,500 men and women—five women—who made up the Council of Workmen's and Soldiers' Delegates.

If the country had been in a condition of peace instead of war, this would not have been at all a bad thing. The working people of Russia, under the electoral system devised by the old regime, had very little representation in the Duma, and they had a perfect right to demand a voice in the organization of the new government. But unfortunately, the country was at war; and more unfortunately still, the Council of Workmen's and Soldiers' Delegates was made up in large part of extreme radicals to whom the war was a matter of entire indifference. The revolution to them meant an opportunity to put into practice new economic theories, the socialistic state. They conceived the vast dream of establishing a new order of society, not only for Russia but for the whole world. They were going to dictate terms of peace and call on the working people of every country to join them in enforcing that peace. After that, they were going to do away with all capitalists, bankers, investors, property owners. Armies and navies were to be scrapped. I don't know what they purposed doing with the constitution of the United States, but "capitalistic" America was to be made over with the rest of the world.

Many members of this council are well-meaning theorists, dreamers, exactly like thousands in this country who read no books or newspapers except those written by their own kind, who "express themselves" by wearing red ties and long hair, and who exist in a cloudy world of their own. These people are honest, and they are capable of being reasoned with. In Russia they are known as Mensheviki,[8] meaning small claims. A noisy and troublesome and growing minority in the council are called Bolsheviki (big claims), because they demand everything and will not even consider compromise. They want a separate peace, entirely favorable to Germany. I talked to a number of these men, but I could never get one of them to explain the reason for this friendship with Germany. Vaguely they seemed to feel that socialism was a German doctrine and, therefore, as soon as Russia put it into practice, the Germans would follow suit. Not all the council members are working people. Some have never done a hand's turn of manual work in their lives. Many of the soldier members have never seen service and never will. The Jewish membership is very large, and in Russia the Jews have never been allowed any practice of citizenship.

Lastly, the council is liberally sprinkled with German spies and agents. Every once in a while, one of these men is unmasked and put out. But it is more than likely that his place is quickly filled. It is a most difficult thing to convince the council that any *Tavarish*, which is the Russian word for comrade, can be guilty of double dealing. The council defended Lenin up to the last moment. Even after he fled the country, the Socialist newspapers, *Isvestiya*, *Pravda* and Maxim Gorky's *Novaya Zhizn*, declared him to be the victim of an odious calumny. It was this Council of Workmen's and Soldiers' Delegates that first claimed a consultative position in the government, and within a few months was parading the streets with banners demanding "All the Power to the Soviet."

I cannot say that I unreservedly blame them. They were people who had never known any kind of freedom; they had been poor and oppressed and afraid for their lives. All of a sudden, they were freed. And when they went in numbers to the Duma and claimed a right to a voice in their own future, men like Kerensky and others, who are honest dreamers, others plain demagogues and office seekers, came out and lauded them to the skies, told them that the world was theirs, that they alone had brought about the revolution and therefore had a right to take possession of the country. The effect of this on soldiers and on the working people was immediate and disastrous.

If Kerensky was not the author of the famous Order No. 1,[9] which was the cause of most of the riot and bloodshed in the army, he at least signed it and defended it. This order provided for regimental government by committees, the election of officers by the soldiers,[10] the doing away with all saluting of superiors by enlisted men and the abolition of the title "your nobility," which was the form of address used to officers. In place of this form the soldiers were henceforth to address their officers as Gospodeen (meaning mister), captain, colonel, general, as the case might be. Order No. 1 was a plain license to disband the Russian army. Abolishing the custom of saluting may seem a small thing. A member of the Root mission expressed himself thus to me soon after his arrival in Petrograd: "This talk of anarchy is all nonsense," he said. "A lot of peacock officers are sore because the men don't salute them any more. Why should the men salute?"

Perhaps I don't know why they should, but I know that when they don't, they speedily lose all their soldierly bearing and slouch like tired subway diggers. They throw courtesy, kindness, consideration to the winds. The soldiers of other countries look on them with disgust and horror. At Tornea,[11] the port of entry into Finland, I got my first glimpse of this "free" Russian soldier. He was handing some papers to a trim British Tommy,[12] who was straight as an arrow, clean cut and soldierly. The Russian slouched up to him, stuck out the papers in a dirty paw and blew a mouthful of cigarette smoke in his face. What the Tommy said to him was in English, and I am afraid was lost on the Russian, who walked off looking quite pleased with himself. In Petrograd, I saw two of these "free" soldiers address, without even touching their caps, a French officer who spoke their language. The conversation was repeated to me thus: "'Is it true that in your country, which calls itself a democracy, the soldiers have to stand in the presence of officers? Is it true that they——.' The interrogation proceeded no further, for the Frenchman replied quickly: 'In the first place French soldiers do not walk up to an officer and begin a conversation uninvited, so I find it impossible to answer your questions.'"

If he had been a Russian officer, he would probably have been murdered on the spot. The death penalty having been abolished, and the police force having been reduced to an absurdity, murder has been made a safe and pleasant diversion. Murder of officers is so common that it is seldom even reported in the newspapers. When the truth is finally and officially published, if it ever is, it will be found that the brutal and horrible butchery of officers exceeds anything the outside world has ever imagined. I met a woman whose daughter went insane after her husband was killed in the fortress of Kronstadt, the port of Petrograd. He, along with a number of officers, was imprisoned there, and some of the women went to the commander and begged permission to see and speak to their men. He grinned at them and said: "They are just finishing their dinner. In a few minutes you may see them." Shortly afterward they were summoned to a room where the men sat around a table. They were tied in their chairs and were all dead, with evidence of having been tortured.

In the beginning of the revolution, the soldiers of Kronstadt killed the old officer commandant. They began by gouging out his eyes. When he was quite finished, they brought in the second officer in command and his young son, a lieutenant in the navy. "Will you join us, embrace the glorious revolution, or shall we kill you?" they demanded. "My duty is to command this garrison," replied the officer. "If you are going to kill me, do it at once." They shot him and threw his corpse on a pile of others in a ditch. The son they spared, and a few nights later, the young man rescued his father's body and brought it home to be buried. This story was related under oath by him, but in the face of it and hundreds more like it, the death penalty was abolished; nor would Kerensky consent to restore it, except for desertion at the front.

At the Moscow congress,[13] held in August, Kerensky said, apologizing for even this small concession: "As minister of justice I did away with the death penalty. As president of the Provisional Government I have asked for its reinstatement in case of desertion under fire." There was a burst of applause, and Kerensky exclaimed: "Do not applaud. Don't you realize that we lose part of our souls when we consent to the death penalty? But if it is necessary to lose our souls to save Russia, we must make the sacrifice."

Petrograd and Moscow are literally running over with idle soldiers, many of whom have never done any fighting, and who loudly declare that they never intend to do any. They are supported by the government, wear the army uniform, claim all the privileges of the soldier and live in complete and blissful idleness. The streetcars are crowded with soldiers, who of course pay no fares. It is impossible for a woman to get a seat in a car. She is lucky if the soldiers permit her to stand in the aisle or on a platform. "Get off and walk, you *borzoi*,"[14] said a soldier to my interpreter one day when she was hastening to keep an appointment with me. She got off and walked. I heard but one person dispute with a soldier. She was a streetcar conductor, one of the many women who have taken men's places since the war. She turned on a car full of these idlers riding free and littering the floor with sunflower seeds, which they eat as Americans eat peanuts, and told them exactly what she thought of them. It must have been extremely unflattering, for the other passengers looked joyful and only one soldier ventured any reply. "Now, comrade," said he, "you must not be hard on wounded men."

"Wounded men!" exclaimed the woman. "If you ever get a wound it will be in the mouth from a broken bottle." There was a burst of laughter, in which even the soldiers joined. But after it subsided one of the men said defiantly: "Just the same, comrades, it was we who sent the Tsar packing." This opinion is shared by the Council of Workmen's and Soldiers' Delegates. They have completely forgotten that the Duma had anything to do with the revolution. At their national congress of Soviets held in July,[15] they solemnly debated whether or not they would permit the Duma to meet again, and it was a very small majority that decided in favor. But only on condition that the national body worked under the direction of the councils.

Notes

1 Rodzianko, Mikhail Vladimirovich (1859–1924) was a Russian statesman of Ukrainian origins. Known for his colorful language and conservative politics, he was the state counselor, chairman of the state Duma and one of the leaders of the February Revolution of 1917, during which he headed the Provisional Committee of the State Duma.
2 Prince Lvov, Georgy Yevgenyevich (1861–1925) was a Russian statesman and political figure, deputy of the First State Duma, president of the All-Russian Zemstvo Union, head of the Provisional Government (2[15] March–7 [20] July 1917).
3 The Russian Duma was an elected legislative body that, along with the State Council, constituted the imperial Russian legislature from 1906 until its dissolution following the 1917 February Revolution. Four Dumas constituted the lower house of the Russian Parliament, and the State Council was the upper house.
4 Khrustaliov-Nosar, Georgy Stepanovich (1877–1919) was a political and public figure, and assistant counselor-at-law in the Russian Empire. From October to November 1905, he served as the first chairman of the St. Petersburg Council of Workers' Deputies.
5 Nicholas II, Nikolai Alexandrovich Romanov (1868–1918) was the last reigning Emperor of Russia from 20 October [1 November] 1894 until his abdication on 2 [15] March 1917.
6 Witte, Sergey Yulyevich, Count (1849–1915) was Russia's finance minister (1892–1903) and the first constitutional prime minister of the Russian Empire (1905–6), who sought to wed firm authoritarian rule to Western-style modernization.
7 Rheta Dorr means the Revolution of February 24–28, 1917 [March 8–12, New Style dates]. The differences in the dating system between the Julian Calendar (Old Style) used in Russia prior to early 1918 and Gregorian Calendar (New Style) used in the West were thirteen days. In her book, Dorr dated events according to the Gregorian calendar except where otherwise noted.
8 Mensheviki was a faction of the Russian Social Democratic Labor Party, which derived its name from the 1903 party congress, when the Mensheviks ('the minority') lost a vote to the Bolsheviks ('the majority') over the membership of the editorial board of the party newspaper *Iskra* (Spark). Popular backing for the Mensheviks vacillated over time, and although they generally enjoyed greater support than the Bolsheviks, they failed to secure a truly massive popular base. Compared to the Bolsheviks, they exhibited greater moderation since in some ways they were more orthodox Marxists: the Mensheviks advocated cementing the bourgeois revolution before a proletarian revolution could take place. The Mensheviks never gained control of the Duma, and after the Russian Revolution of February 1917, they only shared control of the major Soviets (e.g., in Petrograd and Moscow) with the Socialist Revolutionaries.
9 Order No. 1 was the first official decree of the Petrograd Soviet of Workers' and Soldiers' Deputies issued on March 1 [14], 1917 in response to an order of the Military Commission of the Duma calling on the soldiers to return to their barracks and to obey their officers. Order No. 1 instructed soldiers and sailors to obey their officers and the Provisional Government only if their orders did not contradict the decrees of the Petrograd Soviet. It also called on units to elect representatives to the Soviet and for each unit to elect a committee to run the unit. All weapons were to be handed over to these committees "and shall by no means be issued to officers, not even at their

insistence." The order also allowed soldiers to dispense with standing to attention and saluting when off duty, although strict military discipline was to be maintained while on duty. Officers were no longer to be addressed as Your Excellency, Your Honor, etc.; nor were they to execute, corporally punish, or even verbally abuse their soldiers. Soldiers of all ranks were to be addressed formally using the Russian pronoun "*vy*" denoting respect instead of the familiar pronoun "*ty*".

10 In reality, the order made no provision for the election of officers.
11 Tornea is the Swedish name of Tornio, a city in northern Finland.
12 A British Tommy is slang for the rank-and-file soldier in the British Army.
13 Dorr refers to the Moscow State Conference of August 12 [25]–15 [28], 1917. It was composed of members of the Duma as well as representatives of Soviets, local government authorities, trade unions, business interests and the professions. The left-wing parties continued to demand peace without annexations and without indemnities, but admitted that the country had to be defended until peace was obtained. They put their faith in further "democratization of the army" and further proliferation of committees and commissars. The Bolsheviks, who were not represented at the conference, continued to demand immediate peace and to denounce all other parties as warmongers and agents of the Western Allies. On the other side were forces that believed in a restoration of traditional military discipline. They were not reactionaries in the sense of wishing to return to the past, and they were certainly not monarchists. They believed in a democratic Russia, but they insisted that it must be defended. The key difference between them and the non-Bolshevik left was that national defense seemed to them the most urgent task, the precondition for domestic social reforms.
14 *Borzoi*—is Russian slang meaning insolent or maybe the person said "bourzhui" (slang for bourgeois).
15 The first All-Russian Congress of Soviets (Councils) of Workers and Soldiers was held from June 3 [16] to June 24 [July 7]. In total, 1,090 deputies were elected, including 28 Socialist Revolutionaries, 248 Mensheviks, 105 Bolsheviks, 32 Menshevik-Internationalists, etc. Discussions at the Congress largely focused on the issues of public authorities and on the attitudes toward the World War I. The Congress elected a permanent body—the All-Russian Central Executive Committee of the Soviets of Workers' and Soldiers' Deputies (VTsIK). Ultimately, the decision was made to support the Socialist ministers in the government and to continue the "revolutionary war" without annexations and indemnities. The Bolshevik Party argued against it and asked to delegate power to the Soviets.

Chapter 3

THE JULY REVOLUTION

Everyone who has read the old *Arabian Nights* will remember the story of the fisherman who caught a black bottle in one of his nets. When the bottle was uncorked, a thin smoke began to curl out of the neck. The smoke thickened into a dense cloud and became a huge genie who made a slave of the fisherman. By the exercise of his wits, the fisherman finally succeeded in getting the genie back into the bottle, which he carefully corked and threw back into the sea. Kerensky tried desperately to get the genie back into the bottle, and everyone hoped he might succeed. Up to date, however, there is little to indicate that the giant has even begun materially to shrink. Petrograd is not the only city where the Council of Workmen's and Soldiers' Delegates has assumed control of the destinies of the Russian people. Every town has its council, and there is no question, civil or military, that they do not feel capable of settling.

I have before me a Petrograd newspaper clipping dated June 12. It is a dispatch from the city of Minsk,[1] and states that the local soviet had debated the whole question of the resumption of the offensive, the Bolsheviki claiming that the question was general and that it ought to be left for the men at the front to decide. They themselves were against an offensive, deeming it contrary to the interests of the international movement and profitable only to capitalists, foreign as well as Russian. Workers of all countries ought to struggle against their governments and to break with all imperialist politics. The army ought to be made more democratic. This view prevailed, says the dispatch, by a vote of 123 against 79.

This is typical. In some cities, the extreme socialists are in the majority; in others, the milder Minsheviki prevail. In Petrograd, it has been a sort of neck and neck between them, with the Minsheviki in greater number. But as the seat of government, Petrograd has had a great attraction for the German agents, and they are all Bolsheviki and very energetic. Early in the revolution, they established two headquarters: one in the palace of Mme. Kschessinskaya,[2] a dancer high in favor with some of the grand dukes, and another on the Vyborg side, a manufacturing quarter of the city. Here, in a big rifle factory and a few miles down the Neva in Kronstadt, they kept a stock of firearms, rifles and machine guns big enough to equip an army division.

The leader of this faction, which was opposed to war against Germany but quite willing to shoot down unarmed citizens, was the notorious Lenin, a proved German agent whose power over the working people was supreme until the uprisings in July, which were put down by the Cossacks. Lenin was at the height of his glory when the Root Commission visited Russia, and the Provisional Government was so terrorized by him that it hardly dared recognize the envoys from "capitalistic America." Only two members of the mission were ever permitted to appear before the soviet or council. They were Charles Edward Russell[3] and James Duncan,[4] one a socialist and the other a labor representative. Both men made good speeches, but not a line of them, as far as I could discover, ever appeared in a socialist newspaper. In fact, the visit of the commission was ignored by the radical press, the only press that reaches 75 percent of the Russian people.

In order to make perfectly clear the situation as it existed during the spring and summer, and as it exists today, I am going to describe two events that I witnessed last July. Both of these were attempts by the extreme socialists to bring about a separate peace with Germany, and had they succeeded in their plans, they would have done so. Moreover, they might easily have resulted in the dismemberment of Russia.

The 18th of June, Russian style, July 1 in our calendar, is a day that stands out vividly in my memory. For some time, the Lenin element of the Workmen's and Soldiers' Council had planned to get up a demonstration against the non-socialist members of the Provisional Government and against the further progress of the war. The Menshevik element of the council, backed by the government, spoiled the plan by voting for a non-political demonstration in which all could take part, and which should be a memorial for the men and women killed in the February Revolution, and buried in the Field of Mars, a great open square once used for military reviews. As the plan was finally adopted it provided that everyone who wanted to might march in this parade, and no one was to carry arms. Great was the wrath of the Leninists, but the peaceful demonstration came off, and it must have given the government its first thrill of encouragement, for events that day proved that the Bolsheviki or Lenin followers were cowards at heart and could be handled by any firm and fearless authority.

It was a beautiful Sunday morning, this 18th of June, when I walked up the Nevsky Prospect, the Fifth Avenue of Petrograd, watching the endless procession that filled the street. Two-thirds of the marchers were men, mostly soldiers, but women were present also, and a good many children. Red flags and red banners were plentiful, the Bolshevik banners reading "Down with the

Ten Capitalistic Ministers," "Down with the War," "Down with the Duma," "All the Power to the Soviets," and presenting a very belligerent appearance.

With me that day was another woman writer, Miss Beatty of the *San Francisco Bulletin*, and as we walked along, we agreed that almost anything could happen, and that we ought not to allow ourselves to get into a crowd. For once the journalistic passion for seeing the whole thing must give way to a decent regard for safety. We had just agreed that if shooting began, we would duck into the nearest court or doorway, when something did happen—something so sudden that its very character could not be defined. If it was a shot, as some claimed, we did not hear it. All we heard was a noise something like a sudden wind. That great crowd marching along the broad Nevsky simply exploded. There is no other word to express the panic that turned it without any warning into a fleeing, fighting, struggling, terror-stricken mob. The people rushed in every direction, knocking down everything in their path. Miss Beatty went down like a log, but she was up again in a flash, and we flung ourselves against a high iron railing guarding a shop window. Directly beside us lay a soldier who had had his head cut open by the glass sign against which he was thrown. Many others were injured.

Fortunately, the panic was short-lived. It lasted hardly five minutes, as a matter of fact. All around the cry rose that nothing was the matter, that the Cossacks were not coming. The Cossacks, once the terror of the Russian people, in this upheaval have become the strongest supporters of the government. Nothing could better demonstrate the anti-government intention of the Bolsheviki than their present fear and hatred of the Cossacks. So, the *Tavarishi* took up their battered banners and resumed their march. No one ever found out what started the panic. Some said that a shot was fired from a window on one of the banners. Others said that the shot was merely a tire blowing out. Some were certain that they heard a cry of "Cossacks," and some cynics suggested that the pickpockets, a numerous and enterprising class just now, started the panic in the interests of business. This was the only disturbance I witnessed. The newspapers reported two more in the course of the day. A young girl watching the procession from the sidewalk suddenly decided to commit suicide, and the shot she sent through her heart precipitated another panic. Still a third one occurred when two men got into a fight and one of them drew a knife.

The instant flight of the crowds and especially of the soldiers must have given Kerensky hope that the giant could be got back into the bottle, especially since on that very day, June 18, Russian style, the army on one of the fronts advanced and fought a victorious engagement.[5] The town went mad with joy over that victory, showing, I think, that the heart of the Russian people is still intensely loyal to the allies, and deadly sick of the fantastic program of the

Figure 3.1 Typical crowd on the Nevsky Prospect during the Bolshevik or Maximalist risings.

extreme socialists. Crowds surged up and down the street bearing banners, flags, pictures of Kerensky. They thronged before the Marie Palace, where members of the government, officers, soldiers, sailors made long and rapturous speeches, full of patriotism. They sang, they shouted, all day and nearly all night. When they were not shouting "Long live Kerensky!" they were saying "This is the last of the Leninists." But it wasn't. The Bolsheviki simply retired to their dancer's palace, their Viborg retreats and their Kronstadt stronghold, and made another plan.

On Monday night, July 2, or in our calendar July 15, broke out what is known as the July Revolution, the last bloody demonstration of the Bolsheviki. I had been absent from town for two weeks and returned to Petrograd early in the morning after the demonstration began. I stepped out of the Nikolai station and looked around for a droshky. Not one was in sight. No streetcars were running. The town looked deserted. Silence reigned, a queer, sinister kind of silence. "What in the world has happened?" I asked myself. A droshky appeared and I hailed it. When the *izvostchik*[6] mentioned his price for driving me to my hotel I gasped, but I was two miles from home and there were no trams. So, I accepted and we made the journey. Few people were abroad, and when I reached the hotel, I found the entrance blocked with soldiers. The man behind the desk looked aghast to see me walk in, and he hastened to tell me that the Bolsheviki were making trouble again and all citizens had been requested to stay indoors until it was over.

I stayed indoors long enough to bathe and change, and then, as everything seemed quiet, I went out. Confidence was returning and the streets looked almost normal again. I walked down the Morskaya, finding the main telephone exchange so closely guarded that no one was even allowed to walk on the sidewalk below it. That telephone exchange had been fiercely attacked during the February Revolution, and it was one of the most hotly disputed strategic positions in the capital. Later I am going to tell something of the part played in the revolution by the loyal telephone girls of Petrograd. A big armored car was plainly to be seen in the courtyard of the building, and many soldiers were there alert and ready. I stopped in at the big bookshop, where English newspapers (a month old) were to be purchased, and bought one. The *Journal de Petrograd*, the French morning paper, I found had not been issued that day. Then I strolled down the Nevsky. I had not gone far when I heard rifle shooting and then the sound, not to be mistaken, of machine gun fire. People turned in their tracks and bolted for the side streets. I bolted too and made a record dash for the Hotel d'Europe. The firing went on for about an hour, and when I ventured out again it was to see huge gray motor trucks laden with armed men, rushing up and down the streets, guns bristling from all sides, and machine guns fore and aft.

What had happened was this. The "Red Guard," an armed band of workmen allied with the Bolsheviki, together with all the extremists who could be rallied by Lenin, and these included some very young boys, had been given arms and told to "go out in the streets." This is a phrase that usually means go out and kill everything in sight. In this case the men were assured that the Kronstadt regiments would join them, that cruisers would come up the river and the whole government would be delivered into the hands of the Bolsheviki. The Kronstadt men did come in sufficient numbers to surround and hold for two days the Tauride Palace,[7] where the Duma meets and the Provisional Government had its headquarters. The only reason why the bloodshed was not greater was that the soldiers in the various garrisons around the city refused to come out and fight. The sane members of the Soviet had begged them to remain in their casernes, and they obeyed. All day Tuesday and Wednesday the armed motor cars of the Bolsheviki dashed from barrack to barrack daring the soldiers to come out, and whenever they found a group of soldiers to fire on, they fired. Most of these loyal soldiers are Cossacks, and they are hated by the Bolsheviki.

Tuesday night there was some real fighting, for the Cossacks went to the Tauride Palace and freed the besieged ministers at the cost of the lives of a dozen or more men. Then the Cossacks started out to capture the Bolshevik armored cars. When they first went out it was with rifles only, which are mere toy pistols against machine guns. After one little skirmish I counted seventeen dead Cossack horses, and there were more farther down the street. As soon as the Cossacks were given proper arms they captured the armored trucks without much trouble. The Bolsheviki threw away their guns and fled like rabbits for their holes. Nevertheless, a condition of warfare was maintained for the better part of a week, and the final burst of Bolshevik activity gave Petrograd, already sick of bloodshed, one more night of terror. That night I shall not soon forget.

The day had been quiet, and we thought the trouble was over. I went to bed at half-past ten and was in my first sleep when a fusillade broke out, as it seemed, almost under my window. I sat up in bed, and within a few minutes, the machine guns had begun their infernal noise, like rattlesnakes in the prairie grass. I flung on a dressing gown and ran down the hall to a friend's room. She dressed quickly and we went downstairs to the room of Mrs. Emmeline Pankhurst,[8] the English suffragette, which gave a better view of the square than our own. There until nearly morning we sat without any lights, of course, listening to repeated bursts of firing, and the wicked *put-put-put-put* of the machine guns, watching from behind window draperies, the brilliant headlights of armored motors rushing into action, hearing the quick feet of men and horses hastening from their barracks. We did not go out. All a correspondent can do in the midst of a fight is to lie down on the ground and make himself as flat as possible, unless he can get into a shop where he hides under a table or a bench. That never seemed worthwhile to me, and I have no tales to tell of prowess under fire.

I listened to that night battle from the safety of the hotel, going the next day to see the damage done by the guns. A contingent of mutinous soldiers and sailors from Kronstadt, which had been expected for several days by the Leninists, had come up late, still spoiling for a fight; had planted guns on the street in front of the Bourse[9] and at the head of the Palace Bridge across the Neva, and simply mowed down as many people as were abroad at the hour. Nobody knows, except the authorities, how many were killed, but when we awoke the next day, we discovered that, for a time at least, the power of the Bolsheviki had been broken. The next day the mutinous regiments were disbanded in disgrace. Petrograd was put under martial law, the streets were guarded with armored cars, thousands of Cossacks were brought in to police the place, and orders for the arrest of Lenin and his lieutenants were issued. But it was openly boasted by the Bolsheviki that the government was afraid to touch Lenin, and certain it is that he escaped into Sweden, and possibly from there into Germany.[10]

I should not like to believe that the government actually connived at his escape, since there was always the menace of his return, and the absolute certainty that he would remain an outside directing force in the Bolshevik campaign. It is more probable that in the confusion of those days of fighting he was smuggled down the Neva in a small yacht or motorboat to the fortress of Kronstadt, and from there was conveyed across the mine-strewn Baltic into Sweden. Rumor had it that he had been seen well on his way to Germany, but it is more likely that his employers kept him nearer the scene of his activities. He was guilty of more successful intrigue, more murder and violent death than most of the Kaiser's faithful, and deserves an extra-sized iron cross, if there is such a thing. In spite of all that he has done he has thousands of adherents still in Russia, people who believe that he is "sincere but misguided," to use an overworked phrase. The rest of the fighting mob were driven from their palace, which they had previously looted and robbed of about twenty thousand dollars' worth of costly furniture, china, silver and art objects. They were hunted out of their rifle factory, and finally surrendered to the government after they had captured but failed to hold the fortress of Peter and Paul.[11] They surrendered but were they arrested and punished? Not a bit of it. They were allowed to go scot-free, only being required to give up their arms. The government existed only at the will of the mob, and the mob would not tolerate the arrest of *Tavarishi*.

Notes

1 Minsk was the largest city of Belarus on the Svislach River and a part of the territories annexed by the Russian Empire in 1793 during the Second Partition of Poland.
2 Mathilde-Marie Feliksovna Kschessinskaya (Kschessinska) (1872–1971) was a Polish–Russian ballerina who obtained the rank of a Prima ballerina of the Saint Petersburg Imperial Theatres. She was a mistress of the future Emperor Nicholas II of Russia before his marriage in 1894, and later the wife of his cousin Grand Duke Andrei Vladimirovich of Russia. Through her aristocratic connections, she managed to amass much valuable property in the Russian capital.

3 Charles Edward Russell (1860–1941) was an American journalist, columnist, newspaper editor, and political activist. He was part of a group of journalists called muckrakers at the turn of the twentieth century; he took part in founding the National Association for the Advancement of Colored People, and in 1908 joined the Socialist Party of America. Russell was included in the Root mission by Woodrow Wilson. After that he left the Socialist Party, which remained solidly opposed to the war, and joined the Social Democratic League of America.

4 James Duncan (1857–1928) was a Scottish American union leader, influential member of the American labor movement, and co-founder of the American Federation of Labor. Duncan served in a number of capacities for the federal government as well. In June 1917, Woodrow Wilson appointed Duncan Envoy Extraordinary to Russia and included him in the Root mission.

5 Dorr refers to the June offensive, which was called "the Kerensky offensive." On June 18 [July 1], the Russian army launched an offensive, during which the front was cut to a depth of 30 km, Galich and Kalush in today's western Ukraine were taken. However, by July 1–2 [14–15], the advance of the Russian army stopped because of discontent in the Russian troops that were returning to their original positions. Failures at the front and the disintegration of the troops would lead to another Provisional Government crisis. Russia was forced to abandon Galicia; the loss of the Southwestern Front would cost the lives of about 50,000 people, and Lavr Georgiyevich Kornilov would take Aleksei Alekseyevich Brusilov's place as the Supreme Commander-in-Chief.

6 *Izvostchik* was a *droshky* driver.

7 The Tauride Palace is one of the largest and most historically important palaces in Saint Petersburg. After the 1917 February Revolution, the Tauride Palace housed the Provisional Government that was moved to the Mariinsky Palace in early March, and then the Petrograd Soviet.

8 In June 1917, prime minister of Great Britain David Lloyd George agreed to sponsor Emmeline Pankhurst's trip to Russia because she hoped to convince the Russian people not to accept Germany's conditions for peace, which she saw as the defeat of civilization and freedom.

9 The Bourse or the St. Petersburg Stock Exchange became the focal point of the Strelka (or "spit") of Vasilievsky Island. The building had a vital location because it was right in front of the windows of the Winter Palace.

10 Dorr made a mistake. In July 1917, when the Provisional Government outlawed the Bolsheviks and declared Lenin a German spy, he was forced to go to ground in the guise of a Finnish haymaker living in a hut made of tree branches on the banks of Lake Razliv in Sestroretsk. In August 1917, Lenin secretly departed for Finland.

11 The fortress of Peter and Paul built in 1703 on the small Hare Island in the delta of the Neva River became a major political prison of the Russian Empire while the Peter and Paul Cathedral was turned into the burial place of the tsars.

Chapter 4

AN HOUR OF HOPE

There was an hour when the sunrise of hope seemed to be dawning for the Russian people, when the madness of the extreme socialists seemed to be curbed, the army situation in hand, and a real government established. This happened in late July and was symbolized in the great public funeral given eight Cossack soldiers slain by the Bolsheviki in the July days of riot and bloodshed in Petrograd. I do not know how many Cossacks were killed. Only eight were publicly buried. It is entirely possible that the government did not wish the Bolsheviki to know the full result of their murder feast, and for that reason gave private burial to some of the dead. The public funeral served as a tribute to the loyal soldiers, a warning to the extremists that the country stood back of the war, and a notice to all concerned that the days of revolution were over and that henceforth the government meant to govern without the help or interference of the *Tavarishi*, or comrades in the socialist ranks. The moment was propitious for the government. The Council of Workmen's and Soldiers' Delegates was in a chastened frame of mind, caused first by the running amok of the Bolshevik element, the unmasking and flight of Lenin, and next by a lost battle on the Gallician front, and the disgraceful desertion of troops under fire.

The best elements in the council supported the new coalition ministry, although it did not have a Socialist majority, and it claimed the right to work independently of the council. The Cossack funeral was really a government demonstration, and those of us who saw it believed for the moment that it marked the beginning of a new era in Russia's troubled progress toward democracy and freedom. The services were held in St. Isaac's Cathedral, the largest church in Petrograd, and one of the most magnificent in a country of magnificent churches. The bodies, in coffins covered with silver cloth, were brought to the cathedral on a Friday afternoon at 5 o'clock, accompanied by many members of their regiments and representatives of others. The flower-heaped coffins surrounded by flaming candles filled the space below the holy gate leading to the high altar; around them knelt the soldiers and the weeping women relatives of the dead, while a solemn service for the repose of their souls was chanted.

In the Russian church no organ or other instrumental music is permitted, but the singing is of an order of excellence quite unknown in other countries. Part of a priest's education is in music, and the male choirs are most carefully trained and conducted. They have the highest tenor and the lowest bass voices in the world in those Russian church choirs, and there is no effect of the grandest pipe organ that they cannot produce. They sing nothing but the best music, and their masses are written for them by the greatest of Russian composers. Many times I have thrilled to their singing, but at this memorial service to brave men slain in defense of their country, I was fairly overwhelmed by it. I do not know what they sang, but it was a solemn, yet triumphant symphony of grief, religious ecstasy, faith and longing. It soared to a great climax, and it ended in a prolonged phrase sung so softly that it seemed to come as from a great distance, from Heaven itself. The whole vast congregation was on its knees, in tears.

The service in the cathedral next morning was long and elaborate, and it was early afternoon before the procession started for the Alexander Nevsky monastery where a common grave had been prepared for the murdered men. Back of the open white hearses walked the bereaved women and children, bareheaded, in simple peasant black. Thousands of Cossacks, also bareheaded, many weeping bitterly, followed. The dead men's horses were led by soldiers. The Metropolitan of Petrograd and every other dignitary of the church was in the procession. I saw Miliukov, Rodzianko and other celebrities. Women of rank walked side by side with working women. Many nurses were there in their flowing white coifs. There were uncounted hundreds of wreaths and floral offerings. The bands played impressive funeral marches. But there was not a single red flag in the procession.

There was, of course, Kerensky, and his appearance was one of the dramatic events of the day. I watched the procession from a hotel window, and I saw just as the hearses were passing, a large black motorcar winding its way slowly through the crowd that thronged the street. Just as the last hearse passed, the door of the car opened, and Kerensky sprang out and took his place in the procession, walking alone hatless and with bowed head after the coffins. He was dressed in the plain service uniform of a field officer, and his brown jacket was destitute of any decorations. The crowd, when it saw him, went mad with enthusiasm; forgot for a moment the solemnity of the occasion and rushed forward to acclaim him. "Kerensky! Kerensky!"

It was his first appearance as premier, and practically dictator of Russia, and he would not have been human if he had not felt a thrill of triumph at this reception. But with a splendid gesture he waved the crowd to silence and bade them stand quietly back. At first it seemed impossible to restrain them, but the people in the front ranks joined hands and formed a living chain that kept the crowds back, and in a few moments order was restored. There was something fine and symbolic about that action, those joined hands that stopped what might have created a panic and turned the government's demonstration into a fiasco. That spontaneous bit of social thinking and acting restored order better than a police force could have done, and it left in me the conviction that whenever the Russian people join hands on behalf of their country, they are going to work out a splendid civilization. If they had only done it after that day! But the new coalition ministry, with President Kerensky, the popular idol, substituted for Lvov, who had grown wearied and dispirited by the struggle, soon found itself facing the same old sea of troubles that had swamped the former ministries.

The democracy, created largely by Kerensky, in a country which is not yet ready for self-government, had split up into many anarchistic groups. It had become a Frankenstein too huge and too crazy with power to be handled by any man less than a Napoleon Bonaparte, and Kerensky is not a Bonaparte. Perhaps he had the brain of a Bonaparte, as he certainly had the charm and magnetism. It may be that he lacked the iron will or the deathless courage. It may only be that his frail physical health stood in the way of resolution. Whatever the explanation, the fact remains that Kerensky never once was able to take that huge, disorganized, uneducated, restless, yearning Russian mob by the scruff of the neck and compel it to listen to reason. Apparently, also, he was unable or unwilling to let anyone else do it, as the mysterious Kornilov incident[1] seems to prove. The story of the disintegration of the Russian army has been described in many dispatches. Later I am going to tell what I saw of the Russian army, and what I know of the demoralization at the front. The state of things was bad, but it was by no means hopeless, as it is fast becoming. That Russian army, I confidently believe, could, as late as August 1917, have been reorganized, renovated, and made into an effective fighting force. It is very evident that it still has possibilities, because the Germans still keep an enormous number of troops on the eastern front. They know that the Russians can fight, and they fear that they will fight, as soon as they are given a real leader. Military leaders they do not lack, as the Germans also know. Most of the old commanders, the worthless, corrupt hangers-on of the old regime, are gone now. Some are dead, some in prison, some relegated to obscurity. The men who are left are real soldiers, good fighters, true allies of America, France and England. Especially this is true of the once feared and hated Cossack leaders.

The Cossack regiments to the last man had supported the Provisional Government, and were wholeheartedly in favor of fighting the war to a finish.

There are about five million of these Cossacks, and practically every able-bodied man is a soldier. And what a soldier! Except our own cowboys, there never were such horsemen. No troops in the world excel them in bravery and fighting power. They are a proud race and would never serve under officers save those of their own kind. I asked a young Cossack at the front where his officers got their training. He had spent some ten years in Chicago and spoke English like one of our own men. "We train them in the field," he said with a smile. "Everyone of us is a potential officer, and when our highest commander drops in battle, there is always a man to take his place."

The Cossack has no head for politics. He agrees on the government he is going to support, and he serves that government with an undivided mind. When he served the Tsar, he did the Tsar's bidding. When he decided to serve the new democracy, he could be depended on to do it. He has done no fraternizing with wily Germans in the trenches. He has listened to no German propaganda in Petrograd. He wants to fight the war to a successful end, and then he wants to go back to his home on the peaceful Don River,[2] or in the wild Urals[3] and cultivate his fields and vineyards.

Of all Cossack leaders, the most picturesque and the most celebrated as a military genius was Gen. Kornilov. His life and adventures would fill volumes. He fought his way up from a penniless boyhood to a successful manhood. He knows Russia from one end to the other and speaks almost every dialect known to the empire, as well as several foreign languages in addition, especially those of the Orient. He is a small, wiry man with a beard, and the only time I ever saw him he was surrounded by a bodyguard of tall Turkestan Cossacks wearing long gray tunics, huge caps of Persian lamb and a perfectly beautiful collection of silver-mounted swords, daggers and pistols. In a pictorial sense, Gen. Kornilov was quite obscured by them.

Following a series of disasters and wholesale desertions at the front, the late Provisional Government announced that the chief command of the army had been given to Gen. Kornilov. The command was accepted with certain conditions attached to the acceptance. Gen. Kornilov would not be a commander in any limited or modified sense of the word. He demanded absolute power and control over all troops, both at the front and in the rear. He wanted to abolish the committees of soldiers who administered all regimental affairs and who even decided what commands the men might or might not obey. Gen. Kornilov could never tolerate these bodies. Whenever he visited an army division, he asked: "Do your regiments have any committees?" And if the answer was yes, he immediately gave the order: "Dissolve them." One of the principal demands made by Gen. Kornilov on the Provisional Government was the right to inflict the death penalty on deserters, both in the field and in the rear. I have written of the thousands of idle soldiers in Petrograd and of the expressed refusal of many of them to go to the front when ordered. There was no secret about this, nor any concealment of the fact that of many thousands of soldiers sent to the front at various times since the early spring, about two-thirds deserted on the way. They captured trains—hospital trains in some instances—turned the passengers out, left the wounded lying along the tracks, and forced the trainmen to take them back to Petrograd, or wherever they wanted to go.

Kerensky had tried every means in his power to stop this shameful business. He had fixed three separate dates on which all soldiers must rejoin their regiments and must obey orders to advance. He had published manifestoes notifying these cowards and slackers that unless they did report for duty, they would be declared traitors to the revolution, their families would be deprived of all army benefits, and they would not be allowed to share in the distribution of land when the new agrarian policy went into effect. These manifestoes were absolutely ignored. The desertions continued. Army disintegration increased. Anarchy pure and simple reigned on all fronts and in the rear. Soldiers who were willing to fight were afraid to, because there was every probability of their own comrades shooting them in the back if they obeyed their officers. The state of mind of the officers can be imagined perhaps—it cannot be described. Many committed suicides in the madness of their shame and despair.

Gen. Kornilov wanted to deal with this horrible situation in the only possible way, by shooting all deserters. This may sound drastic. No doubt it will to every copperhead and pro-German in this country. But remember, for every man who deserts on that Russian front, some American boy will have to suffer. We shall have to fight for the Russians; we shall have to pay the awful price of their defection. Gen. Kornilov, a true patriot, knew this, and he wanted to save his country from that dishonor. Kerensky apparently could not endure the thought of those firing squads. Or else he did not dare to risk the wrath of the soviet. There is no doubt that he would have courted great personal danger; it may be certain death, but what of it? There is no doubt that Gen. Kornilov, if he saved the situation, would loom larger as a popular hero than Kerensky, but what of it? The whole country, all of it that retained its sanity and its patriotism, looked for Gen. Kornilov to establish a military dictatorship in the army. There was never any question of his assuming the civil power. There was never any indication that he wanted it.

But there was this question—what political party in Russia was going to dominate the constituent assembly, that consummation which has been postponed many times, but which cannot be indefinitely postponed? The Socialist Revolutionary Party, of which Kerensky was a member, seems to have had a clear majority, but there was little organization, and the Socialists were split up into numerous groups. In one city election recently, there were eighteen tickets in the field, most of them separate Socialist parties. The Cossacks, solidly lined up behind Kornilov, announced that in the coming constituent assembly election they would form a bloc with the Constitutional Democrats and the moderate party known as the *Kadets*, of which Prof. Paul Miliukov is the leader. That bloc might dominate the constituent assembly. If it did, the Bolshevik element in the Council of Workmen's and Soldiers' Delegates throughout the country would be overpowered and discredited. The "social revolution" which the councils still insisted must come out of the political revolution might be modified.

Outside of the secret conclaves of the Provisional Government, outside of the inner circles of political life in Russia, there is no one who knows the exact truth of the so-called Kornilov rebellion. It is known that a congress was held in Moscow in late August, in which Kerensky made one of his great speeches, absolutely capturing his audience and once more hypnotizing a large public into the belief that he could restore order in Russia. Kornilov appeared and aroused great enthusiasm, as he always does. Everybody seemed to think that the two leaders would get together and agree on a program. But they did not get together, and the government announced the "rebellion" and disgrace of Kornilov. Two more things were announced: that the Bolsheviki had gained a majority in the Petrograd Council of Workmen's and Soldiers' Delegates, and that Lenin was on his way back to Russia to address a "democratic congress," which had for its objects the abolition of the Duma and the calling of a parliament chosen from its membership. Russia's hour of hope had come and gone. When will it come again?

Notes

1. The Kornilov affair, or the Kornilov putsch, was an unsuccessful attempted military coup d'état by the commander-in-chief of the Russian Army General Lavr Georgiyevich Kornilov (1870–1918), on August 25–31 [7–13 September], 1917, against the Provisional Government headed by Kerensky and the Petrograd Soviet of Soldiers' and Workers' Deputies. Kornilov wanted Kerensky to declare martial law and close down the Soviets. Kerensky refused and called on the Petrograd Soviet to defend the city and allowed them to arm the Red Guard. In return, he freed the Bolshevik prisoners arrested in the July Days uprising. Kornilov was arrested and his revolt weakened the position of the Provisional Government while strengthening the position of the Bolsheviks.
2. The Don is one of Russia's largest rivers, flowing from Central Russia to the Sea of Azov in Southern Russia.
3. The Urals are a mountain range in Eurasia that runs north–south from the coast of the Arctic Ocean to the river Ural and northwestern Kazakhstan.

Chapter 5

THE COMMITTEE MANIA

In writing a plain statement of the condition of anarchy into which Russia has fallen, I am very far from wishing to create a prejudice against the Russian people. I don't want anybody to distrust or scorn the Russians. I want the American people to understand their situation in order that, through sympathy, patience and common sense, they can find some way of helping them out of the blind morass that surrounds them. All the educated Russians I have met like Americans and trust them. They will not soon forget that the United States was the first great power to recognize the new government and to hail the revolution. The American ambassador David R. Francis[1] is easily the most popular diplomat in Petrograd. Everyone knows him, and he rarely appeared in a meeting or convention without being applauded. Over and over again, during my three months' visit to Russia, I was told that it was to America they looked for help and guidance, and after the war they want to enter into the closest commercial relations with us. One businessman said to me just before I left: "Tell your people that we will never trade with Germany again unless the Americans force us to do so. If they will supply us with chemicals, with manufactures and machinery, we will gladly buy them. If they will send us experts for our manufacturing plants, we will be delighted to have them instead of the Germans we used to employ, who never taught our people any of their knowledge because they did not want us to develop."

The Russians want us to help them establish public schools; to show them how to build and operate great railroad systems; to farm scientifically; to do any number of things we have learned to do well. We mustn't despise the Russians; we must help them. And we can't do that unless we understand them. Take, for example, the army situation. It is very bad. The mass of the soldiers are in rebellion against all authority. But consider the past history, the very recent past history of those soldiers. Aside from brutal personal treatment at the hands of some of the officers, they were cheated and starved and neglected by the bureaucracy in Petrograd, and then again by their commanders at the front. The Russian soldier's wants are simple enough. He eats the same food seven days in the week and rarely complains. This food consists of soup made of salt meat and cabbage; kasha, a porridge made of buckwheat; black bread and tea. "Ivan" wears coarse clothes and big, clumsy boots, and he has none of the small comforts we think essential to the fighting man in the field. But slight as the Russian soldier's equipment is, he did not invariably get it in the old days. It was stolen from him by a band of official crooks with which the war department and the army were honeycombed. Every department of the army, from the commissariat to the Red Cross, was full of corruption and graft. The traffic in army supplies and ammunition, even in hospital supplies, that went on constantly beggars' description. Gen. Sukhomlinov,[2] the former minister of war, who has been tried and sentenced to life imprisonment for the part he played in this business, was only one of the big thieves. Under him were myriads more, and among them all the soldiers were often stripped of their overcoats in the dead of winter, and of half of their rations year-round. When a Russian soldier was badly wounded, he might as well have been shot as succored. I have seen these men, pitiful wretches, having lost one or more arms or legs, blind perhaps, or frightfully disfigured, begging in the streets of Petrograd. Clad in tattered uniform, pale and miserable, these poor soldiers stand on the steps of the churches or on street corners and beg a few kopecks from the passersby. There is no such thing as a pension for them, no soldiers' homes. They suffered for a country that knew no such thing as gratitude. Russia sent her men into battle without sufficient arms or ammunition with which to fight. It fed them to the German guns without mercy, that a band of looters in the government might buy sables and bet on horse races. It let them shiver and freeze in shoddy uniforms that army contractors might grow rich. And, after they were wounded, it let them beg their bread.

Small wonder, then, after the revolution, that there was a great popular demand for swift justice for the soldiers. The Provisional Government announced that henceforth each regiment should have an elected committee, an executive body that should have entire charge of regimental affairs. Food, clothing, supplies of all kinds were to pass through the hands of these committees, and they were to hear and pass on all complaints. The committees were the vocal organs of the army. For the first time in Russian history, the soldier was allowed to speak. The plan might have worked excellently had the Provisional Government not made the mistake of too much zeal in democratizing the army. It gorged the soldiers with freedom, gave them such heady doses of self-government that they got drunk on the idea and ran amok like so many crazed Malays. Kerensky decreed that the soldiers need not salute their officers. "Well then, we won't," they said. "And just to show how free we are we won't wash our faces, or wear clean clothes, or touch our caps to women, or stand up straight—" and from that it was an easy journey to: "We won't take any orders from anybody."

The government told the soldiers to elect their own officers, and they did, after butchering a thousand or so of their old ones. They elected them wisely in some instances, but in a great many more they did not. They chose men, not for their capacity to lead in a military way, but for their political views. In a regiment, the best Bolsheviks were elected. If there was a Menshevik majority, the new officers were pretty sure to be Mensheviki. And after they were elected, nobody respected them, nor did they dare give orders. But of all the madness that took possession of the "free" soldiers, the committee madness went farthest. The Russians love to talk. To make speeches, to heckle, and be heckled is the joy of their lives. The committee gave them a new chance to talk, and they got the habit of calling a committee meeting on every conceivable occasion. Petrograd heard with horror last summer that the men in the trenches, when ordered to advance, actually called meetings to discuss the orders and to vote whether or not they were to be followed. They did this at times when the Germans were at the very gates of an important strategic point.

Even in the hospitals it got so that the doctors and the nurses were without authority. If a man was ordered to take a pill, he wanted to call a committee meeting to discuss the thing. It is an actual fact that men refused to

Figure 5.1 Kerensky watching the funeral of victims of the July Bolshevik risings.

take treatment or undergo operations until they had consulted the *Tavarishi* about it. From that to refusing to obey any orders is a short step, and Red Cross nurses have told me some fantastic stories about life in Russian *lazarets*.[3] Some wounded men refused to take their clothes off and insisted on wearing them, boots and all, to bed. Others refused to go to bed at night, preferring to snooze during the day and wander around in pajamas and dressing gowns at night. Some insisted on being discharged before they should be, while others, on being discharged, declined to go.

They were not like that in all hospitals, of course. "Ivan" is a great child, and very often he is a stupid and unruly child. But often he is good, especially when he is sick and suffering and in need of women's care and kindness. I don't want to describe the bad hospital conditions without admitting that they have the other kind, too, in Russia. I remember seeing at the corner of a street below a big *lazaret* in Petrograd a dozen discharged wounded men and a group of nurses and orderlies. They were waiting for the tram that was to carry the men to the railroad station. Some still wore bandages, some were on crutches, some walked with the aid of sticks. Two were blind. But all were wildly happy at the prospect of going home to the old village. The nurses and orderlies shared in the excitement. Some of them were going to the station and had their arms full of bundles, clothes, food and souvenirs of battle. One nurse carried a competent-looking cork leg, the future prop of a pale young fellow on crutches. The car swung around the corner, full of passengers, idle soldiers mostly, but even they, at the command of the energetic sister, vacated their seats for the invalids. They climbed aboard, and those who were most helpless were lifted. The cork leg was handed in through an open window and delivered to one of the more able-bodied men. There had been plenty of time for farewells before, but parting was difficult, and for five minutes after boarding the car the men continued to shake hands with the nurses, shout last messages and kiss their hands to those on the sidewalk. The nurses patted their charges' arms and shoulders and called anxious admonitions. "Take care of that leg, Ivan Feodorovich. You know how to bandage it. Don't try to walk too much and keep out of the sun." You didn't have to know a word of Russian to understand what those nurses were saying.

The streetcar conductor wrung her hands and begged to be allowed to go on. The time schedule had to be observed. "Please, sister, please," she entreated, and at last she was permitted to ring the bell and send her car forward. As it turned the corner the men were still waving and laughing and wiping the tears from their cheeks. I don't believe those men had called any committee meetings before obeying their nurses, or ever reminded the doctors that it was a free country now and they could take medicine or not as they pleased.

You certainly got tired of that overworked phrase "It's a free country now." You hear it on all sides in Russia. "It's a free country," says a man with a third-class ticket taking possession of a first-class compartment. "It's a free country," declares a soldier, tossing a handful of sunflower seed shells on a woman's white shoes in a streetcar. "It's a free country," says a group of men, stripping off their clothes before a crowd of women and children and taking a bath in the Neva. This occurs frequently on the Admiralty quay,[4] a great pleasure resort in Petrograd.

"They called them Sans-Culottes[5] during the French Revolution," said a clever woman writer in one of the newspapers. "Our men will go down to fame as Sans-Caleçons. The difference, perhaps, between a political and a social revolution." The first French phrase means without trousers. The second carries the denuding process to its concluding stage.

In this kind of a free country, nobody is free. Try to imagine how it would be in Washington, in the office of the secretary of the treasury, let us say, if a committee of the American Federation of Labor[6] should walk in and say: "We have come to control you. Produce your books and all your confidential papers." This is what happens to cabinet ministers in Russia and will continue until they succeed in forming a government responsible only to the electorate, and not a slave to the Council of Workmen's and Soldiers' Delegates. Of course, the simile is grossly unfair to the American Federation of Labor. Our organized labor men are the most intelligent working people in the community, and most of them have had a long experience in citizenship. Above all, their loyalty, as a body, has been amply demonstrated. The Council of Workmen's and Soldiers' Delegates has among its members loyal, honest, intelligent men and women. But it has also a number of extreme radicals, people who would dishonor the country by concluding a separate peace with Germany, and who care nothing for the interests of any group except their own. Nobody in Russia has very much experience in citizenship, and the working people have less than others. Yet the soviet, to give the council its local name, deems itself quite capable of passing on all affairs of state, not only in Russia but in the Allied countries as well. The Soviets have had the presumption to announce that they are going to name the peace terms, although Russia has virtually ceased to fight. "No annexations or contributions," is the formula, very evidently made in Germany. I am sure that not one in a thousand knows what this means.

"Have you ever thought," I asked a member of the Petrograd council, "what your program would mean to the working people of Belgium? Don't you think that the farmers and artisans of northern France are entitled to compensation for their ruined homes and blasted lives?"

"Yes, but not from Germany," was the astounding reply. "All countries should contribute."

"If I were a cashier in a bank and stole a million dollars of the depositors' money, do you think I ought to be made to pay it back, or should all the employees be taxed?" To this question I got no answer. There isn't any answer.

In all this confusion of mind, this whirlwind of ideas and theories, are there no Russians who can think clearly? Are there no brave and courageous people left in Russia? None who realize the ruin and desolation that is being prepared for them? There are. Russia has its submerged minority of thinkers. It has at least two fighting elements that are ready to die to restore peace, order and bright honor to their distracted land. These two elements are the Cossacks and the women.

Notes

1 Francis, David Rowland (1850–1927) was an American politician and diplomat. He served in various positions including mayor of St. Louis, the 27th governor of Missouri, and the U.S. secretary of the interior. In 1916, President Woodrow Wilson selected Francis to be the American ambassador to Russia. Francis served in that capacity during the 1917 Russian Revolution.
2 Sukhomlinov, Vladimir Aleksandrovich (1848–1926) was a general in the Imperial Russian Army who served as the chief of the general staff from 1908 to 1909 and the war minister in 1909–15.
3 *Lazaret* was the name of a Russian field hospital.
4 The Admiralty Quay (Admiralty Embankment) is a street along the Neva River in Central Saint Petersburg, named after the Admiralty Board.
5 Sans-Culottes were the common people of the lower classes in the late eighteenth century, a great many of whom became radical and militant partisans of the French Revolution in response to their poor quality of life under the *Ancien Régime*. The name comes from their distinctive clothing: unlike the aristocracy who wore *culottes* (silk breeches), the typical Sans-Culottes wore *pantaloons* (long trousers) as well as the *carmagnole* (short jacket), and the red cap of liberty.
6 The American Federation of Labor (AFL) was a federation of North American labor unions founded in 1886 under the leadership of Samuel Gompers. The AFL focused on the organization of skilled workers and remained the sole unifying agency of the American labor movement for some fifty years.

Chapter 6

THE WOMAN WITH THE GUN

The women soldiers of Russia, the most amazing development of the revolution, if not of the World War itself, I am disposed to believe, will, with the Cossacks, prove to be the element needed to lead, if it can be led, the disorganized and demoralized Russian army back to its duty on the firing line. It was with the object, the hope, of leading them back that the women took up arms. Whatever else you may have heard about them this is the truth. I know those women soldiers very well. I know them in three regiments, one in Moscow and two in Petrograd, and I went with one regiment as near to the fighting line as I was permitted. I traveled from Petrograd to a military position "somewhere in Poland" with the famous Bochareva Battalion of Death. I left Petrograd in the troop train with the women. I marched with them when they left the train. I lived with them for nine days in their barrack, around which thousands of men soldiers were encamped. I shared Bochkareva's soup and kasha and drank hot tea out of her other tin cup. I slept beside her on the plank bed. I saw her and her women off to the firing line, and after the battle into which they led reluctant men, I sat beside their hospital beds and heard their own stories of the fight. I want to say right here that a country that can produce such women cannot possibly be crushed forever. It may take time for it to recover its present debauch of anarchism but recover it surely will. And when it does it will know how to honor the women who went out to fight when the men ran home.

The Battalion of Death is not the name of one regiment, nor is it used exclusively to designate the women's battalions. It is a sort of order that has spread through many regiments since the demoralization began and signifies that its members are loyal and mean to fight to the death for Russia. Sometimes an entire regiment assumes the red and black ribbon arrowhead which, sewn on the right sleeve of the blouse, marks the order. Regiments have been made up of volunteers who are ready to wear the insignia. Such a regiment is the Battalion of Death commanded by Maria Bochkareva (the spelling is phonetic), the extraordinary peasant woman who has risen to be a commissioned officer in the Russian army.

Bochkareva comes from a village near the Siberian border and is, I should judge, about thirty years old. She was one of a large family of children, and the family was very poor. They had a harder time than ever after the father returned from the Japanese war[1] minus one foot, but that did not prevent their number from increasing, and merely made the lot of Maria, the oldest girl, a little more miserable. She married young, fortunately a man with whom she was very happy. He was the village butcher, and she helped him in the shop, as they had no children. When the war broke out in July 1914, Maria's husband marched away with the rest of the quota from their village, and she never saw him again. He was killed in one of the first battles of the war, and the only time I ever saw Bochkareva break down was when she told me how she waited long months for the letter he had promised to write her, and how at last a wounded comrade hobbled back to the village and told her that the letter would never come. He was dead—out there somewhere—and they had not even notified her.

"The soldiers have it hard," she said, when her brief storm of tears was over, "but not so hard as the women at home. The soldier has a gun to fight death with. The women have nothing."

For months Maria Bochkareva watched the sufferings of the women and children of her village grow worse and worse. Winter killed some of them, winter and an unwonted scarcity of food. Typhus came along and killed more. The village forgot that it had ever danced and sung and was happy. Every family was in mourning for its dead. Maria decided that she could not endure sitting in her empty hut and waiting for death. She would go out and meet it in the easier fashion permitted to men. That was the way, she explained to me, she joined the regiment of Siberian troops encamped near the village. The men did not want her, but she sought and got permission, and when the regiment went to the front she went along too.

She fought in campaigns on several fronts, earned medals and finally the coveted Cross of St. George[2] for valor under fire. She was three times wounded, the last time in the autumn of 1916, so badly that she lay in hospital for four months. She got back to her regiment, where she was now popular, and I imagine something of a leader, just before the Revolution of February 1917.

Bochkareva was an ardent revolutionist, and her regiment was one of the first to go over to the people's side. Her consternation and despair were great when, shortly after the emancipation from tsardom, great masses of the people, and especially the soldiers at the front, began to demonstrate by riots and desertions how little they were ready for freedom. The men of her regiment deserted in numbers, and she went to members of the Duma who were going up and down the front trying to stay the tide and said to them: "Give me leave

Figure 6.1 Maria Bochkareva, Mrs. Emmeline Pankhurst and the Women's Battalion of Death.

to raise a regiment of women. We will go wherever men refuse to go. We will fight when they run. The women will lead the men back to the trenches." This is the history of Bochkareva's Battalion of Death, or rather of how it came to be organized. The Russian war ministry gave her leave to recruit the women, gave her a barrack in a former school building and promised her equipment and a place at the front. Many women in Petrograd, women of wealth and social position, took fire with the idea, raised money for the regiment, helped in the recruiting, some of them joining.

In an odd copy of an American newspaper that reached me in Russia, I read a paragraph stating that the schoolgirls of Petrograd were forming a regiment under a man named Butchkareff, a lieutenant in the army. I don't know who sent out that piece of news, but it lacked most of the facts. The women soldiers are not schoolgirls, and Bochkareva's battalion has no male officers. Three drill sergeants, St. George Cross men all of them, did assist in the training of the battalion while it remained in Petrograd. Other men drilled it behind the lines, but Bochkareva and another remarkable woman, Maria Skrydlova,[3] her adjutant, commanded and led it in battle.

Maria Skrydlova is the daughter of Admiral Skrydlov, one of the most distinguished men of the Russian navy. She is about twenty, very attractive if not actually beautiful, and is an accomplished musician. Her life up to the outbreak of the war was that of an ordinary girl of the Russian aristocracy. She was educated abroad, taught several languages and expected to have a career no more exciting or adventurous than that of any other woman of her class. When the war broke out, she went into the Red Cross, took the nurses' training and served in hospitals both at the front and in Petrograd. Then came the revolution. She was working in a marine hospital in the capital. She saw many of the horrors of those February days. She saw her own father set upon by soldiers in the streets and rescued from death only because some of his own marines who loved him insisted that this one officer was not to be killed.

Into the ward of the hospital where she was stationed there was borne an old general, desperately wounded by a street mob. He had to be operated on at once to save his life, and as he was carried from the operating room to a private ward, the men in the beds sat up and yelled, "Kill him! Kill him!" It is unlikely that they knew who he was, but it was death to all officers in those days of madness and frenzy. Half unconscious from loss of blood, still under the spell of the ether, the old man clung to his nurse as a child to his mother. "You won't let them kill me, will you?" he murmured. And Mlle. Skrydlova assured him that she would take care of him, that he was safe.

The door opened and a white-faced doctor rushed into the room. "Sister," he gasped, "go for that medicine—go quickly." Not comprehending, she asked, "What medicine?" But he only pushed her toward the door. "Go, go!" he repeated.

She left the room, and then she saw and understood. Down the corridor a mob was streaming, a wild, unkempt, bloodthirsty mob, the sweepings of the streets and barracks. Quickly she threw herself across the door of the old general's room. "Get back," she commanded. "The man in that room is old and wounded and helpless. He is in my care, and if you harm him, it must be over my body."

Incredible as it seems this girl of twenty was able to hold the mob at bay for forty minutes. When guns were pointed at her, she told the men to fire through the red cross that covered her heart. They did not shoot, but some of the most brutal struck her down, and then held her helpless while others rushed into the room and hacked and beat the old man to death. When the nurse fought her way to his side, he was breathing his last. She had time to whisper a prayer, and to make the sign of the cross above his glazing eyes. Then she went home, took off her Red Cross uniform and said to her father: "Women have something more to do for Russia than binding men's wounds."

When Bochkareva's Battalion of Death was formed, Maria Skrydlova determined to join it. Admiral Skrydlov, veteran of two wars, iron old patriot, went with her to the women's barracks and with his own hand enrolled her in the Russian army service. In the regiment of which this girl was adjutant, I found six Red Cross nurses who were through with nursing and had gone out to die for their unhappy country. There was a woman doctor who had seen service in base hospitals. There were clerks and office women, factory girls, servants, farm women. Ten women had fought in men's regiments. Every woman had her own story. I did not hear them all, but I heard many, each one a simple chronicle of suffering or bereavement, or shame over Russia's plight.

There was one girl of nineteen, a Cossack, a pretty, dark-eyed young thing, left absolutely adrift after the death in battle of her father and two brothers, and the still more tragic death of her mother when the Germans shelled the hospital where she was nursing. To her, a place in Bochkareva's regiment and a gun with which to defend herself spelled safety.

"What was there left for me?" sighed a big Estonian woman, showing me a photograph she wore constantly on her heart. It was a photograph of a lovely child of five years. "He died of want," said the woman briefly. "His father is a prisoner somewhere in Austria."

There was a Japanese girl in the regiment, and when I asked her reason for joining, she smiled and in the evenly polite tone that marks her race, replied: "There were so many reasons that I prefer not to tell any of them." One twilight I came upon this girl sitting outside with the little Polish Jewess with whom she bunked. The two sat perfectly motionless on a fallen tree, watching a group of soldiers gathered around a fire. In their silent gaze I read a malevolence, a reminiscence so full of concentrated loathing that I turned away with a shudder. I never asked another woman her reason for joining the regiment. I was afraid it might be more personal than patriotic.

I do not believe, however, that this was the case with the majority. Mostly the women were in arms because they feared and dreaded the further demoralization of the troops, and they believed fervently that they could rally their men to fight. "Our men," they said, "are suffering from a sickness of the soul. It is our duty to lead them back to health." Every woman in the regiment had seen war face to face, had suffered bitterly through war and finally had seen their men fail in the fight. They had beheld their men desert in time of war, the most dishonorable thing men can do, and they said, "Well then, there is nothing left except for us to go in their places."

Did the world ever witness a more sublime heroism than that? Women, in the long years which history has recorded, have done everything for men that they were called upon to do. It remained for Russian men, in the twentieth century, to call upon women to fight and die for them. And the women did it.

Notes

1 The Russo-Japanese War (27 January [9 February], 1904–23 August [5 September], 1905) was fought between tsarist Russia and Japan over rival imperial ambitions in

Manchuria and Korea. The complete military victory of an Asian and non-Western nation over a European and Western power transformed the global balance of power, with the Empire of Japan emerging as a great power while the Russian Empire's global prestige declined. The war was concluded with the Treaty of Portsmouth mediated by U.S. president Theodore Roosevelt.

2 The Cross of Saint George (St. George Cross) was established by the 1769 decree of Emperor Catherine II as a military order and later restructured in 1807 for lower-ranking soldiers.

3 Skrydlova, Maria Nikolaevna (1898–1940) was a daughter of the Russian Admiral Nikolai Illarionovich Skrydlov and Bochkareva's adjutant during World War I.

Chapter 7

TO THE FRONT WITH BOCHKAREVA

Women of all ranks rushed to enlist in the Bochkareva's battalion. There were many peasant women, factory workers, servants and also a number of women of education and social prominence. Six Red Cross nurses were among the number, one doctor, a lawyer, several clerks and stenographers, and a few like Maria Skrydlova who had never done any work except war work. If the working women predominated, I believe it was because they were the stronger physically. Bochkareva would accept only the sturdiest, and her soldiers, even when they were slight of figure, were all fine physical specimens. The women were outfitted and equipped exactly like the men soldiers. They wore the same kind of khaki trousers, loose-belted blouse and high peaked cap. They wore the same high boots, carried the same arms and the same camp equipment, including gas masks, trench spades and other paraphernalia. In spite of their tightly shaved heads, they presented a very attractive appearance, like nice, clean, upstanding boys. They were very strictly drilled and disciplined, and there was no omission of saluting officers in that regiment.

The battalion left Petrograd for an unknown destination on July 6 in our calendar. In the afternoon the women marched to the Kazan Cathedral,[1] where a touching ceremony of farewell and blessing took place. A cold, fine rain was falling, but the great half circle before the cathedral, as well as the long-curved colonnades, were filled with people. Thousands of women were there carrying flowers, and nurses moved through the crowds, collecting money for the regiment.

I passed a very uneasy day that July 6. I was afraid of what might happen to some of the women through the malignancy of the Bolsheviki, and I was mortally afraid that I was not going to be allowed to get on their troop train. I had made the usual application to the War Ministry to be allowed to visit the front, but I did not follow up the application with a personal visit, and therefore when I dropped in for a morning call, I was dismayed to find the barrack in turmoil, and to hear the exultant announcement, "We're going this evening at eight."

It was an unseasonal day of rain, and I spent reckless sums in *droshky* hire, rushing hither and yon in a fruitless effort to wring emergency permits from elusive officials who never in their lives had been called upon to do anything in a hurry, or even to keep conventional office hours. Needless to say, I found nobody at all on duty where he should have been that day. Even at the American Embassy, where, empty-handed and discouraged, I wound up late in the afternoon, I found the entire staff absent in attendance on a visiting commission from home. The one helpful person who happened to be at the Embassy was Arno Dosch-Fleurot[2] of the *New York World*. "If I were you," he said, "I wouldn't worry about a permit. I'd just get on the train—if I could *get* on—and I'd stay until they put me off, or until I got where I wanted to go. Of course they may arrest you for a spy. In any other country they'd be pretty sure to. But in Russia you never can tell. Shepherd,[3] of the *United Press*, once went all over the front with nothing to show but some worthless mining stock. Why not try it?"

I said I would, and before eight that evening I was at the Warsaw Station, unwillingly participating in what might be called the regiment's first hostile engagement. For at least two-thirds of the mob that filled the station were members of the Lenin faction of Bolsheviki, sent there to break up the orderly march of the women, and even, if possible, to prevent them from entraining at all. From the first, these spy-led emissaries of the German Kaiser had sworn enmity to Bochkareva's battalion. Well, knowing the moral effect of women taking the places of deserting soldiers in the trenches, the Leninists had exhausted every effort to breed dissension in the ranks, and at the last moment they had stormed the station in the hope of creating an intolerable situation. In the absence of anything like a police force, they did succeed in making things painful and even a little dangerous for the soldiers and for the tearful mothers and sisters who had gathered to bid them goodbye. But the women kept perfect discipline through it all, and slowly fought their way through the mob to the train platform.

As for me, a mixture of indignation, healthy muscle and rare good luck carried me through and landed me in a somewhat battered condition next to Adjutant Skrydlova. "You got your permit," she exclaimed on seeing me. "I am so pleased. Stay close to me and I'll see you safely on."

Mendaciously perhaps, I answered nothing at all, but stayed, and every time a perspiring train official grabbed me by the arm and told me to stand back Skrydlova rescued me and informed the man that I had permission to go. At the very last I had a bad moment, for one especially inquisitive official asked to see the permission. This time it was the *Nachalnik*,[4] Botchkareva herself, who came to the rescue. Characteristically she wasted no words, but merely pushed the man aside, thrust me into her own compartment and ordered me to lock the door. Within a few minutes she joined me, the train began to move, and we were off. That was the end of my troubles, for no one afterward questioned my right to be there. At the adjutant's suggestion, I parted with my New York hat and early in the journey substituted the white linen coif of a Red Cross nurse. Thus attired I was accepted by all concerned as a part of the camp equipment.

The troop train consisted of one second-class and five fourth-class carriages, the first one, except for one compartment reserved for officers, being practically filled with camp and hospital supplies. In the other carriages, primitive affairs furnished with three tiers of wooden bunks, the rank and file of the regiment traveled. I had a place in the second-class compartment with the *Nachalnik*, the adjutant and the standard bearer, a big, silent peasant girl called Orlova. Our luxury consisted of cushioned shelves without bedding or blankets, which served as seats by day and beds by night. We had, of course, a little more privacy than the others, but that was all. As for food, we all fared alike, and we fared well, friends of the regiment having loaded the train with bread, butter, fruit, canned things, cakes, chocolate and other delicacies. We had also tea-making materials, and plenty of sugar. So filled was our compartment with food, flowers, banners, guns, tea kettles and miscellaneous stuff that we moved about with difficulty and were forever apologizing for walking on each other's feet.

For two nights and the better part of two days we traveled southward through fields of wheat, barley and potatoes, where women in bright red and blue smocks toiled among the ripening harvests. News of the train had gone down the line, and the first stage of our journey, through the white night, was one continued ovation. At every station crowds had gathered to cheer the women and to demand a sight of Bochkareva. It was largely a masculine crowd, soldiers mostly, good-natured and laughing, but many women were there too, nurses, working girls, peasants. Occasionally one saw ladies in dinner gowns escorted by officer friends.

The farther we traveled from Petrograd, the point of contact in Russia with Western civilization, the more apparent it grew that things were terribly wrong with the empire. More and more the changed character of the station crowds reminded us of the widespread disruption of the army. The men who met the train wore soldiers' uniforms but they had lost all of their upright, soldierly bearing. They slouched like convicts, they were dirty and unkempt, and their eyes were full of vacuous insolence. Absence of discipline and all restraint had robbed them of whatever manhood they had once possessed. The news of the women's battalion had drawn these men like a swarm of bees. They thrust their unshaven faces into the car windows, bawling the parrot phrases taught them by their German spy leaders. "Who fights for the damned capitalists? Who fights for English bloodsuckers? We don't fight."

And the women, scorn flashing from their eyes, flung back: "That is the reason why we do. Go home, you cowards, and let women fight for Russia."

Their last, flimsy thread of "peace" propaganda exhausted the men usually fell back on personal insults, but to these the women, following strict orders, made no reply. When the language became too coarse, the women simply closed the windows. No actual violence had ever been offered to them. When they left the train for hot water or for tea, for more food or to buy newspapers, they walked so fearlessly into the crowds that the men withdrew, sneering and growling, but standing aside.

There was something indescribably strange about going on a journey to a destination unknown, except to the one in command of the expedition. Above all, it was strange to feel that you were seeing women voluntarily giving up the last shred of protection and security supposed to be due them. They were going to meet death, death in battle against a foreign foe, the first women in the world to volunteer for such an end. Yet everyone was happy, and the only fear expressed was lest the battalion should not be sent at once to the trenches.

As for me, when we arrived at our destination, some two miles from the barracks prepared for us, I had a moment of longing for the comparative safety of the trenches. For what looked to me like the whole Russian army had come out to meet the women's battalion and was solidly massed on both sides of the railroad track as far as I could see.

I looked at the *Nachalnik* calmly buckling on her sword and revolver. She had a confident little smile on her lips. "You may have to fight those men out there before you fight the Germans," I said.

"We are ready to begin fighting any time," she replied.

She was the first one out of the train, and the others rapidly followed her.

Notes

1 The Kazan Cathedral was erected in honor of a miracle-working icon of Our Lady of Kazan, discovered in the city of Kazan in 1579. The cathedral was constructed between 1801 and 1811 by the architect Andrei Voronikhin. The cathedral was inspired by St. Peter's Basilica in Rome and intended to be the country's main Orthodox Church.
2 Dosch-Fleurot, Arno (1879–1951) was an American newspaperman who served as a foreign correspondent in Europe since 1914 and reported to Americans about many important world events such as World War I and World War II, as well as revolutions in Russia and Germany.
3 Shepherd, William Gunn (1878–1933) was an American journalist, fiction writer and war correspondent who brought the turbulent scenes of World War I to life. His book *Confessions of a War Correspondent* offered a gripping front-line perspective on the hardships, victories and day-to-day challenges faced by journalists amid the chaos of war.
4 *Nachalnick* means "boss" in English.

Chapter 8

IN CAMP AND BATTLEFIELD

The women's regiment did not have to fight its brothers in arms, however. The woman commander took care of that. She just walked into that mob of waiting soldiers and barked out a command in a voice I had never before heard her use. It reminded me somewhat of that extra awful motorcar siren that infuriates the pedestrian but lifts him out of the road in one quick jump. Bochkareva's command was spoken in Russian, and a liberal translation of it might read: "You get to hell out of here and let my regiment pass."

It may not have been ladylike, but it had the proper effect on the Russian army, which promptly backed up on both sides of the road, leaving a clear lane between for the women. The women shouldered their heavy kits and under a broiling sun marched the two miles that lay between the railroad and the camp. The Russian army followed the whole way, apparently deciding that the better part of valor was to laugh at the women, not to fight them.

Bochkareva must also have decided that the first thing to be done was to give those men to understand that whether the regiment was funny or not, it would have to be treated with respect. As soon as we reached our barracks and disposed of the heavy loads, she made a little speech in which she said that here we were, and while we would be obliged to mingle with the men, relations would be kept formal. The men must be shown that the women were entitled to the same camp privileges as themselves and were no more to be molested or annoyed than any other soldiers. We had had a long, hot journey, she ended, and the first thing we were going to do was to go down to the river and have a nice swim. So, with towels around their necks the 250 women made gaily for the river. I trotted along on the commander's arm. At least a thousand men went along, too, but just before we reached the swimming pool under a railroad bridge, Bochkareva turned around and delivered another of those crisp little commands. The men stopped in their tracks as if she had thrown some kind of freezing gas at them, and we went on.

It was a lovely swimming pool, clear and cold and fringed with sheltering willows. The women peeled off their clothes like boys and plunged in. As we dressed afterward, I looked at them, heads shaved, ugly clothes, coarse boots, no concealments, not a single aid to beauty, but, in spite of it all, singularly attractive. Some of course were homely, primitive types. Purple and fine linen would not have improved them much. But some who would not have been especially pretty as girls were almost handsome as boys. A few were strikingly beautiful in spite of their shaved heads. You observed that they had good skulls, nice ears, fine eyes, strong characters, whereas in ordinary clothes they might have appeared as pleasingly commonplace as the girl on the magazine cover.

Cool and refreshed, the battalion marched back to the barracks, which consisted of two long, hastily constructed wooden buildings, exactly like hundreds of others on all sides about as far as the eye could reach. Some of the buildings were half underground, for warmth in winter, and must have been rather stuffy. Our buildings were well ventilated with many dormer windows in the sharply slanting roof, and they were new and clean and free from the insects which in secret I had been dreading. Inside was nothing at all except two long wooden platforms running the length of the building, about 90 feet. They were very roughly planed and full of bumps and knot holes, but they were the only beds provided by a step-motherly government. Here the women dumped their heavy loads, their guns, ammunition belts, gas masks, dog tents, trench spades, food pails and other paraphernalia. Here they unrolled their big overcoats for blankets, and here for the next week, all of us, officers, soldiers and war correspondents, ate, slept and lived. Two hundred and fifty women in the midst of an army of men. Behind us a government too engrossed in fighting for its own existence to concern itself about the safety of any group of women. Before us the muttering guns of the German foe. Between us and all that women have ever been taught to fear, a flimsy wooden door. But sleeplessly guarding that door, a woman with a gun.

In that first midnight in camp, I woke on my plank bed to hear the shuffling of men's feet on the threshold, a loud knock at the door, and from our sentry a sharp challenge: "Who goes there?"

"We want to come in," said a man's voice ingratiatingly.

"No one can come in at this hour," answered the sentry. "Who are you and what do you want?"

The man's answer was brutally to the point. "Aren't there girls here?" he demanded.

"There are no girls here," was the instant reply. "Only soldiers are here."

An angry fist crashed against the thin wood, to be answered by the swift click of a rifle barrel on the other side. "Unless you leave at once we shall fire on you," said the sentry in a voice of portentous calm.

Down the long plank platform, I heard a succession of low chuckles, and a sleepy comment or two which the retreating men outside would not have found complimentary. That midnight encounter served the excellent purpose of finally establishing the status of the regiment in camp. From that time on we lived unmolested. We stood in line with the men at the cookhouse for our daily rations of black bread, soup and kasha, a sort of porridge made of buckwheat. We performed our simple morning toilets in the open; we washed our clothes in improvised washtubs behind the barracks; we strolled about between drills. The men followed us around from morning until night. They watched us open-eyed, hung in curious groups before the doors. A few were openly friendly, and beyond some disparaging remarks regarding our personal appearance, none were hostile.

The day after we arrived, Monday, it rained. It poured. The camp became a swamp. The women stayed in their barrack, drilling as best they could in the narrow aisles. Sitting on the edge of their plank beds, the only place there was to sit, they listened with deep attention while under-officers read aloud the army code and regulations. In the morning a group of nurses from a hospital train in the neighborhood came to call, and in the afternoon half a dozen officers came from the *stavka*,[1] two miles away. The commander, a charming man, seemed astonished and deeply impressed by the regiment standing at attention to greet him.

"It is beautiful," he said repeatedly, and he was good enough to say to me, "How wonderful for an American woman to be with them. Thank you for coming."

Tuesday it cleared and the battalion had its first open-field drills. The rest of the Russian army stood around and pretended to be vastly amused. Whenever a woman made a mistake in the manual, and better still, when she fell down while charging, or splashed into a mud puddle on a run, the men laughed loudly. Some of that laughter, I feel pretty certain, did hurt pride, for every decent soldier I talked to expressed his sorrow and humiliation that the women had felt the necessity of enlisting. Quite a few men in that camp had been in America and of course spoke English. They said, "Say, sister, what do you suppose they think about this back in Illinois?" One man said, "Sister," (I still wore the nurse's coif, having no other headgear) "back home in the States they used to say women oughtn't to vote because they couldn't fight. I'll bet these women can fight."

The officers in and around that army position were evidently of the same opinion. They came to the drill field every day to inspect and criticize the work, and they sent their best drill sergeants to instruct the women, who worked hard and learned quickly. One day the commander of the Tenth army, whose Russian name is too much for my memory at this distance,[2] came over with his whole staff, a brilliant sight. The commander was plainly delighted and shook hands with a great many of the women. He even went out of his way to shake hands with the American. Kerensky was in the neighborhood one day, but he did not visit us. The *Nachalnik* saw him at Staff Headquarters, and he sent kind messages, promising the women that they should be sent to the front as soon as they were ready.

The impatience of those women to go forward, to get into action, was constant. They fretted and quarreled during the frequent rainy spells which kept them housebound and were really happy only when something happened to promise an early start. One day it was the arrival of 250 pairs of new boots, great clumsy things which it would have crippled me to wear, and in fact all the women who could afford it had boots made to order. Another day it was the appearance of a camp cooking outfit especially for the battalion. Four good horses were attached to the outfit, and the country girls hailed them with delight as something to pet and fuss over.

The women spent much time cleaning and learning their guns. They seemed to love their firearms, one girl always alluding to her rifle as "my sweetheart." "How can you love a gun?" I asked her. "I love anything that brings death to the Germans," she answered grimly. This girl, a highly educated, well-bred young woman, was in Germany when the war broke out. She was arrested and charged with espionage, a charge which, for all I know, may have been true. It was not proved, of course, or she would have been shot. On the mere suspicion, however, she was kept in prison for a year and must have suffered pretty severely. She looked forward to the coming fight with keen zest. I asked her one day what she would do if she were taken prisoner again. She pulled from under her blouse a slender gold chain on the end of which was a capsule in a chamois bag. "I shall never be taken prisoner," she said. "None of us will."

From Thursday on, the weather improved and the regiment worked hard in the field. I had felt the strain of confinement in barracks, and when I was not watching the drill, I was taking long walks down a highway over which went a constant procession of troops and camp supply wagons, moving on and on, nearer the horizon, from which came frequent low mutterings like distant thunder, but which were heavy gunfire. Sometimes I walked as far as a little settlement which the *Nachalnik* told me was not unlike the village she found so unbearable after her husband left it. The village consisted of two rows of log or roughly timbered cottages along a winding, muddy road. Green moss grew on the thatched roofs, and the whole place had a forlorn, neglected look, but surrounding each cottage was a carefully tended garden with beets, cabbages, onions, potatoes, and sunflowers grown for the seeds, which are the Russian substitute for chewing gum. Often the cottages had poppies growing in the rows of vegetables, the bright blooms giving brilliance to the somber and lonely landscape.

Half a dozen miles on the other side of the railroad was another and a larger village, equally dismal, but furnished with a church, a wayside shrine, small shops and other improvements. My special friend the adjutant and I drove over there one day after supplies. We bought chocolate, nuts, sardines and biscuits to relieve the deadly monotony of our daily black bread, soup, and kasha. The regiment bought some supplies at little market stalls near the station. Here one bought butter, sausages reeking with garlic, tinned fish and doubtful eggs. At an officers' store in the vicinity, Bochkareva spent some of the money donated in Petrograd for tea and sugar when they were needed, and for a kind of white bread or biscuits. They were hard and shaped like old-fashioned doughnuts, with a hole in the middle through which a string was run. A yard or two of this bread went well with good butter and hot, fragrant tea. As far as food was concerned, I was better off in the camp than I was a little later in Petrograd. There was even a fairly good hot meal to be had at the station when we chose to go there, which we did several times. But no amount of good food would have kept our regiment happy in camp very long. The women fretted and chafed and demanded to know why they were kept in that hole. The *Nachalnik* coaxed and scolded them along, and Skrydlova, who was easily the most popular person in camp, reminded them that it took six months to train ordinary soldiers and that they were being especially favored by having the time shortened.

Those women went into battle after less than two months of training, as it turned out, for the evening of the ninth day the *Nachalnik* came back from headquarters with orders to march the next morning at five. What an uproar followed! Cheers, laughter, singing. You would have thought they were going anywhere except to a battlefield where death waited for some and cruel suffering for many. I wanted to go with them and would have insisted on going had I known that they were so soon to fight. But orders were merely to advance for further drill under gunfire. I would have been frightfully in the way in the new position, which had no barracks, but only dog tents, just enough to go around. Nothing on earth except the knowledge that I would be depriving someone of those brave women from the comfort of a dry and sheltered bed persuaded me to leave them.

Five days later in Petrograd I read in the dispatches that they had been sent almost directly into action, leading men who had previously refused to advance, and turning a defeat into a victory; a small one to be sure, but Russia was thankful for even small victories those days. A short note from Skrydlova prepared me for the story of losses which I knew was coming. She wrote in French, which she knows better than English, "You have heard already perhaps that we have been in action. I do not know yet how many were killed or have died of wounds, but two of those you knew well were killed. Catherine and Olga, who you remember had won three medals of St. George. Eighteen girls are wounded badly, Nina among them." Nina was the girl who called her gun "sweetheart," and who had been a prisoner in Germany. Skrydlova was badly contused in the head, shoulders and knees, but she remained in command of the remnant of the battalion because the *Nachalnik*, Bochkareva, had suffered so severely from shell shock that she had to be sent to a hospital in Petrograd. She was nearly deaf when I saw her, and her heart was badly affected.

"It was a good fight," she whispered, smiling from her pillow. "Not a woman faltered, not one. The Russian men hid in a little wood while the officers swore at them and begged them to advance. Then they sent us forward, and we called to the men that we would lead them if they would only follow. Some of them said they would follow, and we went forward on a run, still shouting to the men. About two-thirds of them went with us, and we easily put the Germans to flight. We killed a lot of Germans and took almost a hundred prisoners, including two officers." In another hospital I found more than twenty of the battalion, some slightly and others seriously wounded. The worst cases were kept in base hospitals, near the battle front, and I never saw Nina again.

Notes

1 *Stavka* means a Headquarters in English.
2 His name was Lt. Gen. Pyotr Nikolaevich Lomnovskiy.

Chapter 9

AMAZONS IN TRAINING

If the first battle of the first women soldiers in the world had been fought on American soil, imagine what the newspapers would have made of the story. Especially if the women had gone into battle with the object of rallying a demoralized American army and had succeeded in their object. And this is all the space Bochkareva's victorious battalion was accorded in *Novoe Vremya*[1] one of the best newspapers in Russia. After describing briefly the engagement on the Smorgon-Krevo front, in which prisoners, guns and ammunition were taken, the account proceeded:

> The women's battalion made a counterattack, replacing deserters who ran away. This battalion captured almost a hundred prisoners including two officers. Bochkareva and Skrydlova are wounded, the latter receiving contusions and shock from the explosion of a big shell. The battalion suffered some losses but has won historic fame for the name of women. The best soldiers looked with consideration and esteem on their new fighting comrades, but the deserters were not touched by their example, and in this respect the aim was not reached. We must take care of these dear forces, and not give too much consideration to new formations of the kind.

If the press of Russia had been wise, the fact that some of the slackers in the army were not touched by the women's bravery would have been made less conspicuous than the more important fact that many soldiers were touched by it, and that the Russian army was thereby enabled to win a victory. Instead of discouraging new formations, the press should have called for more and more regiments of women to lead the men. They should have kept it up until people got so excited over the tragedy of women being torn to pieces by German shot and shrapnel that they would have risen in wrath, taken hold of their army and their government, and created conditions that would relieve women from the dreadful necessity of fighting.

It could have been done; the people were ready for it. They felt the tragedy. At a memorial service for the dead women, held in Kazan Cathedral the

Sunday after the battle, the presiding priest said: "This is a terrible, and yet a glorious hour for Russia. Sad it is, and terrible beyond expression that men have allowed women to die in their places for our unhappy country. But glorious it will ever be that Russian women have been ready and willing to do it."

After the service a Bolshevik soldier, standing in front of the cathedral, tried to turn the sympathies of the crowd by making insulting remarks about the dead women. He did not have time to say much before a group of working women, with howls of rage, rushed him, and I believe would have killed him if his friends had not gotten him away.

Of the women left alive but wounded, 30 were brought to a hospital not far from the Nikolai station, Petrograd, and there I saw them. When I went into the first hospital ward a wounded girl sat up in bed and, smiling like the sun, held out to me a German officer's helmet, her prize of battle. She had killed him—that was her duty—and had taken his helmet as a man would have done. But when she told me that Orlova, big, dull, kind, unselfish Orlova, loved by everybody, was among the killed, she broke down and wept as any woman would have done.

From this girl and the others I learned that Bochkareva had spoken the exact truth when she said that no woman had faltered or shown fear. "We all expected to die, I think," one girl said. "I know that I did. I said over the prayers for the dying while I was dressing that morning. We all prayed and kissed our holy pictures and thought sadly about the ones at home. But we were not afraid. We were stationed between two little woods. They were full of men, some who openly refused to go forward, some who hesitated and didn't quite know what they ought to do. We shouted at them, the commander shouted at them, called them cowards, traitors, everything we could think of. Then the commander called out: 'Come on, brothers, we'll go first if you'll only follow.'"

"'All right then,' some of them called back, and we ran forward as fast as we could, following Botchkareva. She was wonderful, and Skrydlova was wonderful too. We would have followed them anywhere."

"Did you really capture a hundred Germans?" I asked.

"I don't believe we did it all by ourselves," was the modest reply. "After we got into the fighting, the men and the women were side by side. We fought together and we won the battle together."

Every one of those wounded women soldiers wanted to go back to the front line. If fighting and dying were the price of Russia's freedom, they wanted to fight and fight again. If they could rally unwilling men to fight, they wanted nothing in the world except more chances to do it. Wounds were nothing, death was nothing in the scale of Russia's honor or dishonor. Then too, and this is a strange commentary on women's "protected" position in life, the women soldiers said that fighting was not the most difficult or the most disagreeable work they had ever done. They said it was less arduous if a little more dangerous than working in a harvest field or a factory.

This point of view I have heard expressed by other Russian women soldiers, those who have fought in men's regiments. There are many such women; I have met and talked with some of them. One girl I saw in a hospital, a bullet in her side and a broken hand in a plaster cast, assured me that fighting was the most congenial work she had ever done. This girl had gone to Petrograd from Riga to join Bochkareva's battalion, but for some reason she had not been accepted. She met a young marine who told her of a new Battalion of Death which was being formed out of the remnants of several old regiments and of a number of marines. "Why not join us?" he asked. "We already have four girl comrades." So, she joined.

We were alone except for the interpreter, and I took occasion to ask this girl minutely how it fared with women who joined men's regiments. Were the women treated with respect, let alone? How did they manage about their physical needs? Where did they bathe and change their clothes? Did not the officers object to their presence in the barracks? At first, my young soldier admitted, the men did not treat the women with respect, did not let them alone. She was obliged to give the men some severe lessons. But after a while, they learned. They were considerate in certain respects and arranged for the girls to have some privacy. Of course, one lost foolish mock modesty when in camp.

The officers did not object to their enlisting but were inclined to treat them with a lofty indifference. The men too seemed to assume that the girls could not endure the real hardships of war when they came. "The first thing we had to do in camp was to make a quick march of twelve versts. 'Of course, the girls can't walk that far,' the men said, 'they can ride on the cook wagons.' But we said, 'Not much we don't ride on the cook wagons. We didn't come here to watch you do things. We came to be soldiers like yourselves." So, they said, "Oh, very well! *Harasho!* March if you like." And we did. And when we got back to camp, it was so funny; sailors are not much used to walking, you know, and those men were completely tired out, exhausted. They lay around in their bunks and groaned and called on everybody to look at their feet and their blisters, while we weren't tired at all. Why, any of us had walked as far and worked as hard in one day in the kitchen or the harvest field. So, we laughed at the men and said, "You're just a lot of old women. Look at us. We could do it all over again and not complain." After that I can tell you they didn't patronize us quite such a lot.

When the regiment got into camp near the trenches and the men were given the regulation uniform of the army, the officers decreed that the girls' soldiering should come to an end. The real business of fighting was about to begin, and women were not wanted. They could be *sanitaries*,² said the commander. So, they went back to women's clothes and women's historic job of waiting on men. This girl, however, objected, and finally confided to one of her men friends that the *sanitary*'s work was too distasteful for her to endure longer. "Why should I be obliged to patch up wounds?" she asked. "It is much easier to make them." The soldier found some regimentals for her, and she went out and fought in a skirmish line. When the commander heard of it, he was terribly angry, and to frighten her, he put her on sentry duty in an exposed post. "'He thought he'd cure me of my taste for fighting,' she chuckled, 'but I wasn't frightened a bit,' and so he said, 'Well, be a soldier if you are so bent on it. We need soldiers.' And so, I fought."

She described her first and only battle where she helped storm several lines of trenches and was one of 37 survivors out of a thousand in her regiment who took part in the engagement. Her wounds, she said, did not hurt much at the time, but she was bleeding pretty badly and thought she ought to get to the hospital.

> Just then I saw our captain, and he was badly wounded, almost unconscious in fact, and I had to get him to the rear on my back. It was all that I could do, for about that time I felt that I was growing weak and would soon have to sit down. I managed to get him as far as the first line of Red Cross men, and then I went under. I had been hit in the side by a bullet or a piece of shrapnel and I was pretty sick for a while. By and by I felt better and somehow got back to the rear. The first thing I saw was one of our men who was weeping with his head in his hands. "What's wrong?" I asked, and when he looked up and saw me, he gave a yell. "They said you had been killed," he shouted. And he began to dance a hornpipe. Poor chap, he had been wounded too and before he had danced more than a few steps he began to bleed and fell over in a faint.

The ambulances were pretty full, so this plucky young creature thought she could walk the three or four versts to the hospital. She had to give up before long and a captain of another regiment, himself wounded, took her into his cart or whatever conveyance he had, and carried her to the hospital. "Our captain was there," she finished, "quite out of his head with pain. He kept saying, 'Don't let that girl go back to the field. Don't let her fight again. She is too young.' He did not know then that I had carried him off on my back, and me wounded too."

A great many women who had seen service in men's regiments were leaving them and joining one or another of the women's regiments which were forming all over Russia about that time. The largest of these regiments was being trained for action in Moscow. There were about two thousand women in this battalion, which was formed and recruited by a women's committee, "The Society of Russian Women to Help the Country." Among the women was Madame Morozova, before the war prominent socially, but since the war almost entirely occupied with relief work. She was a very gay and laughter-loving person, but she had fed and clothed and helped on their way thousands of refugees. She had turned her house into a maternity hospital at times, and she had given large sums of money for the relief of women and children. Finally, the women soldiers appealed to her as the most important work to be assisted and her whole energies last summer were devoted to the battalion. Princess Kropotkin,[3] a relative of the celebrated Prince Pyotr Kropotkin,[4] was another member of the society. She had a Red Cross hospital until the army desertions began, and then she closed the hospital and turned to recruiting women. Mme. Popova, vice-president of the society, is one more untiring worker. In August she obtained Kerensky's consent to go to Tomsk, her old home, and organize a battalion there.

The Moscow regiment was being drilled by a colonel and half a dozen younger officers, all of whom seemed immensely proud of their command. Twenty picked women of the regiment were going daily to the officers' school and when ready were to be given commissions in the regular army.

In Petrograd, a regiment of 1,500 women was almost ready for the trenches when I saw them last in August. They too were to be officered by women, two score being a daily attendance at a military school. On August 20 I saw these 1,500 women march out of their barrack in the old Engineers' Palace,[5] to go into camp preparatory to going to the front. This palace was once the home of the mad Emperor Paul,[6] son of Catherine the Great. He was assassinated there, and his restless ghost is supposed to haunt the gusty corridors. I asked Captain Loskov,[7] commander of the regiment, if he had found out what Emperor Paul thought of the women soldiers, and he laughed and promised to report later on that point.

It was not intended to raise many regiments of women, I was told. The intention was to enlist and train to the highest point of efficiency between ten and twenty thousand women, and to distribute the regiments over the various front lines to inspire and stimulate the disorganized army. They would lead the men in battle, when necessary, as Bochkareva's brave band led them, and they would appear as a sign and symbol that the women of the country were not willing that the revolution, which generations of Russian men and women have died for, and have endured in the snows of Siberia sufferings worse than death, should end in chaos and national disintegration.

Notes

1 *Novoye Vremya* was a Russian newspaper published in Saint Petersburg from 1868 to 1917. The newspaper began as a liberal publication, but after Aleksey Sergeyevich Suvorin took it over, it acquired a reputation as a servile supporter of the government, in part because of its antisemitic and reactionary publications.
2 *Sanitaries*—orderlies in English.
3 Kropotkin, Maria Dmitrievna, Princess (1879–1958).
4 Kropotkin, Pyotr Alekseyevich, Prince (1842–1921) was a Russian revolutionary and geographer, the foremost theorist of the anarchist movement.
5 The Engineers' (Mikhailovsky, or St. Michael's) Castle is a former imperial palace built on orders of Emperor Paul I between 1797 and 1801. The Castle was named after its home church of Archangel Michael, the patron saint of the Romanovs.
6 Paul I was Emperor of Russia from 1796 until his assassination in 1801.
7 Loskov, Aleksandr Vasilievich (1888–1920) was a staff captain and a commander of the 1st Petrograd Women's battalion that took part in the defense of the Winter Palace in October 1917.

Chapter 10

THE HOMING EXILES—TWO KINDS

In a great, bare room, furnished with rows of narrow cots like a hospital, but with none of the crisp whiteness of the hospital, nor any of its promise of relief and restoration, a young man, propped with pillows, played on a concertina. He was white, emaciated, near the end of his young life. His eyes were like banked fires. He sat up in bed and in the intervals of coughing made the most wonderful music on that concertina, much more wonderful than I had ever dreamed the humble instrument could produce. The man was a true musician, and he had had many years of practice on his concertina, for it had been the one friend and solace of a solitary confinement that lasted nearly a dozen years. All around him in that bare room men lay in bed and listened to him. Some, however, were asleep. Even music could not break their weary rest. All were sick. Some were as near death as was the musician. Siberia had done its work with them. They had come home to die.

On a soap box, or its equivalent on a corner of the Nevsky Prospect near the Alexander Theater,[1] another young man stood and poured out a passionate speech to the crowd of soldiers, workmen and workwomen and idle boys who had paused to listen. The man was about thirty years old, and his clothes, it was plain to see, had never been purchased in Russia. They were American clothes of fair quality, and of that stylish cut possible to buy for twenty-five dollars in almost any department store. He wore a derby hat, tipped back on his head, a soft collar and a flowing tie. He talked rapidly and with many gestures, and the crowd listened with rapt interest to his speech. I, too, stopped to listen. "What is he saying?" I asked my interpreter.

"I don't like to tell you," she replied.

I insisted, and this is an almost literal translation of what that man said, on that Petrograd street corner, on an August day, 1917:

"You people over here in Russia don't want to make a mistake of setting up the kind of a republic, of the kind of phony democracy like what they've got in the United States. I lived in the United States for ten years, and you take it from me, it's the worst government in the world. They have a president who is worse than the Tsar. The police are worse than Cossacks. The capitalist class is on top there just like they were in the old days in Russia. The working class is fighting them, and they are going to win. We are going to put the capitalists out just like you put them out here, and don't you let any American capitalists come over here and help fasten on you a government like that one they still have in America. It's the capitalists that plunged America into war. The working class never wanted it."

These are two types of exiles which Russia has called back to her bosom since the revolution, both of which constitute another grave problem with which the distracted people are struggling. The sick ones, of whom there are thousands, came back and more of them are coming from Siberia at a time when food suitable for the sick is impossible to obtain. There was almost no milk. Eggs were hard to get and were not very fresh. Food of all kinds was getting scarcer every day. There was a fuel shortage that threatened to make all Russia spend a shivering winter, and what was to become of the sick was and still is a grave question. There is a great shortage of many medicines. If fighting is resumed, the hospitals will be overcrowded. Doctors and nurses will be scarce. Yet the exiles continue to come back, the long stream from the remote villages continues to hold out its longing hands to the people back home, who cannot deny them. And nearly all the exiles come back sick and homeless and penniless. Russia must take care of those freed Siberian exiles, and I don't quite see how she is going to do it, unless the miracle happens and they find a way of restoring peace and order in the land. In that case they can do anything. They can even deal with the kind of exile I heard talking on the Nevsky.

Carlyle[2] says that of all man's earthly possessions, unquestionably the dearest to him are his symbols. They have the strongest hold on us without a doubt. At the time of the French Revolution the sign and symbol of the old regime was the Bastille, that state prison in Paris, which was the living grave of the king's enemies, or of almost anybody who made himself unpopular with one of the king's favorites. When the French people rose up in their might and swept the old regime out, the first thing they did, obeying a common impulse, was to tear down and destroy utterly the Bastille. In Russia, the sign and symbol of the autocracy was the exile system, and particularly Siberia. The first thing the Russian people did when they rose up and dethroned the Romanovs was to send telegrams to every political prison and to every convict village in Siberia that the prisoners and exiles were free. They sent orders to all the jailers and guards that the exiles were to be furnished with clothing and money and transportation to the railroads, and the railroads were directed to bring them back to Petrograd.

There is something to warm the coldest blood in the thought of what it must have meant to those poor, desolate creatures, living in the hopeless isolation of Siberia, to have the door of the cell open one February day and hear the words, "You are free!" Sometimes the announcement was prefaced by words of unheard-of friendliness and courtesy from wardens and jailers who had before been cruel and brutal taskmasters. "Please forgive me if I have been over-zealous in my duties," these men would say, and the prisoner would think that he had gone mad and was dreaming. Then the announcement would come, unbelievable in its wonder; the revolution had actually happened. The Tsar was gone. The prisoner was free. They heard that news in the depths of mines, where men worked shackled and hopeless. They heard it in lonely villages near the Arctic Circle. They heard it in far lands, where homesick men and women toiled in sweatshops among aliens. They were free, and Mother Russia was calling them home again. I should think they would almost have died of joy at the tidings. No generous mind can wonder that Russia called back her children, all of them, without stopping to sort out the good and the bad, the well and the sick, the desirable and the undesirable. Or without stopping to calculate how she was going to take care of them when they got there.

But very early in the day it became evident that Russia was going to face a serious problem in her returned exiles. In the very first days of the revolution, they opened all the prison doors in Petrograd as well as in other Russian cities and let all the prisoners out. Among them were a number of politicals, and many of them immediately became public charges. They had no money, no friends, no home. The revolution had robbed them, in some cases, of all three. In some cases of long imprisonment, the homes and friends had been taken from them by death. There had been a committee working secretly on behalf of political prisoners, and now this committee, with a group in the Red Cross, got together and formed a society which they call the Political Red Cross,[3] the committee in charge of returned exiles. For they saw plainly that what had happened in the case of the Petrograd prisoners would be repeated on a large scale when the Siberian exiles and those from foreign lands returned. Another committee was formed in Moscow. They sprang up in various cities, cooperating with the *zemstvoes* or county councils.

At the head of the work is Vera Figner, one of the most famous of the old revolutionists, almost the last survivor of the nihilism of the 1870s. The Russians are said to lack organizing ability, but the work done by this committee under Vera Figner's direction looks to me that once Russia gets a government that can govern and an army that will fight, the people of Russia will organize a civilization that will teach Europe new things. The committee started with nothing, not even machinery to work with. There is no such thing in Russia as a charity organization society. Charity and benevolence there are, mostly of the old-fashioned type, "Under the patronage of her imperial highness, the

Princess Olga,"[4] or "the empress dowager."[5] There was no well-organized society of any kind to appeal to help take care of some seventy-five thousand exiles hurrying home, an unknown number of them sick, another unknown number poor and homeless, and all of them strangers in a new Russia.

Vera Figner I saw in the Petrograd headquarters of the society. She is a matronly woman, looking less than sixty, although she must be older. She has a handsome face, with the deep, smoldering eyes of the revolutionist, but her smile is quiet and kind. Near her at the long committee table sat Mme. Kerenskaya,[6] the estranged wife of the Minister-President Kerensky. She is an attractive young woman with dark eyes and abundant dark hair, who gives all of her time to the work of the exiles committee. Mme. Gorky is another woman of prominence who works with the committees, and Prince Kropotkin and his daughter, Mme. Lebedev,[7] whose husband was in the government when I left, are also constant workers. The work was done through eight committees, one of which collected money, a great deal of money, too. Hundreds of thousands of rubles have poured in from all over Russia as well as from England, America, France. Another committee collects clothes, and they are much scarcer than money in Russia. A committee on home-finding also collects sanitarium and hospital beds wherever they are to be found. A reception committee meets the exiles and takes them to their various lodgings. A medical and a legal aid committee take care of their own sides of the work. All over Petrograd and Moscow they have established temporary lodgings and temporary hospitals for the cure of the returned sick and helpless. It was in such a refuge that I saw and heard the man with the concertina.

I had come to find Maria Spirodonova, one of the most appealing as well as the most tragic figures of the revolution of 1905-6. She was the Charlotte Corday of that revolution, for like Charlotte she, unaided by any revolutionary society, freed her country of one of the worst monsters of his time. She shot and killed the half-mad and wholly horrible governor of Tambov.[8] And like Charlotte she paid for that deed with her life. She lived indeed to return to Russia, but her span after that was short. Maria Spirodonova was in the last stages of tuberculosis when they brought her back to Russia. Ten years' solitary confinement had done that for her. The first sentence of death, afterward commuted to 20 years' exile, would have been shorter and more merciful. When I saw her, she was in bed, so wasted that she looked like a child. The flush of fever on her cheeks gave her a false look of health, and she looked almost as beautiful as on the day when she stood in the prisoner's dock and told the judges how and why she killed the monster of a governor. Her voice was all but gone now, and it was in a hoarse whisper that she greeted me, and asked news of her one or two friends in America. I could stay only a few minutes; she was so weak. It is hardly possible that she still lives, although no news of her death has reached me.[9]

Until the last breath she must have kept her iron will and indomitable spirit. Ten years in a solitary cell could not break that spirit, as the story of her release shows. When the first telegram came to the distant prison, where she and nine other women were confined, the names of only eight of them were specifically mentioned.

"But what about us?" wailed the two forgotten ones.

The warden of the prison perhaps did not entirely believe in the success of the revolution and wanted to be on the safe side. "You stay," he said.

"Then none of us will go," said Maria Spirodonova, and they all stayed until the next day when another telegram arrived setting them all free. In the same spirit, Spirodonova refused to leave her companions after they reached Petrograd. She was so famous, so sought after, that she could have chosen among a dozen hospitable homes, in the country, in the Crimea or the bracing mountains of the Caucasus. But she said she would not have anything her old prison mates did not have, so Maria Spirodonova, daughter of a general, and the concertina player, child of a peasant, died as they lived, revolutionists, spurning all the comforts of life, all the protection and security of home, all the plaudits of the world. They lived and died for Russia as surely as though they died on the battlefield.

Of the same type is the most celebrated exile of all, Ekatherine Breshkovskaya, the Babushka, or little grandmother of the revolution. They brought Babushka back to Petrograd in the first rush. They gave her a reception at the station such as no crowned head in Europe ever had, and they took her to the Winter Palace and told her that when the Tsar moved out, he left it to her. Babushka lived in the Winter Palace when she was in Petrograd, which was seldom. Most of the time she was touring rural Russia and trying to make her peasants understand what the revolution meant, and that they would make the country a worse place than it ever was before unless they stopped fighting to grab all the land in sight without any regard to right and justice. "I know them," she said in a brief talk I had with her in the palace. "If I can only live long enough to reach them in numbers, I can deal with them. They have listened to a pack of nonsense, but I shall tell them better."

Breshkovskaya is past seventy years old. She is growing very deaf, and her weight makes traveling difficult. Yet her mind is clear and vigorous, and when she makes a speech, she manages somehow to call back the voice and the strength of a woman of forty. Spirodonova, Breshkovskaya, Kropotkin, Tschaikovsky[10] and almost every one of the old revolutionists are eager adherents of the moderate program of the early Provisional Government, before the Bolsheviki crowded in with their cry of "All the power to the Soviets!"

They want the war fought to a finish, and they want order restored in Russia. It is quite otherwise with another type of exile, and I am sorry to say some of this other kind were made in the United States of America.

In the boat in which I crossed the Atlantic last May, there were three Russian men who had spent some years in America and were on their way back to Petrograd. These men were not exiles, but they had found Russia intolerable to live in and had gone to America, which had been so kind to them in a material way that they were able to go back to Russia in the first cabin of an ocean liner. All three were pronounced pacifists and one was a readymade Bolshevik. He was for the whole program, separate peace, no annexations or contributions, no sharing the government with the bourgeois, no compromise on anything. A real Bolshevik. And made on the East Side of New York. This man used to talk to me on deck and in the saloon about how the Soldiers' and Workmen's Delegates were going to dictate terms of peace to the allies, and how the social revolution was going to spread all over the world, and especially all over America, and then he would hasten to assure me that he wasn't nearly as radical as some of the *Tavarishi* I would meet in Russia, and he wasn't. When we reached the Finnish frontier and stopped at Tornea for examination, I had the pleasure of seeing all three of these men taken into custody by some remnant of authority existing in the army and taken down to Petrograd under guard as men who had evaded military duty. My friend declared that nothing would ever induce him to put on a uniform or to fight. Not he. And the others rather less confidently echoed his defiance. Finally, one of them said: "On the whole, I think I will enlist. They need educated men at the front to talk peace to them." Thus at least one emissary of the Kaiser was contributed to poor, bleeding Russia by the United States.

Just one more case, because it is typical of many. This man was a real exile, and for 11 years he had lived in Chicago. Born in a small city of western Russia, he joined, when still a youth, what was known as the Bund,[11] a socialist propagandist circle of Jewish young men and women. The youth's parents, quiet, orthodox people, knew nothing of his activities, nor of the revolutionary literature of which he was custodian and which he had concealed in the sandbags piled up around the cottage to keep out the winter cold. On May 31, 1905, the *Tavarishi*, or comrades, in his town organized a small demonstration against the celebration of the Tsar's birthday. The next day the police began searching houses and making arrests among the youth of the town, and they found the books hidden in the sandbags. The boy fled and found refuge in the next town. Money was raised, a passport forged, and the youth finally got to England via Germany. He didn't like England and in 1906 he crossed to the United States. He didn't like the United States either, and his whole career in Chicago was a history of agitation and rebellion. He was one of the founders of a socialist Sunday school in Mayor Thompson's town, where children of tender years are given a thorough education in Bolshevik first principles.

When the Russian Revolution broke and Russian consuls all over the world advertised for exiles to be taken back to Russia's heart, this man presented himself as one of the returners. He showed me the certificate issued by the Russian consulate in Chicago. It says that it was issued in accordance with the orders of the Provisional Government and records that the said was paid the sum of $157.25 and was given transportation from Chicago to Petrograd, via the Pacific Ocean and the Trans-Siberian railroad. At Vladivostok he received more money, and on his arrival in Petrograd he was given a small weekly allowance in addition to his free lodgings. He had a good time on the journey, he said. There was a band at most of the stations where the train stopped, crowds, flowers and much cheering. It was agreeable to get back to Petrograd also and be met by a committee. But the habit of hating governments was so settled in his system that within a week he was talking against the one that had paid his way back, and he was talking hard against the one which had taken him in and given him a free education and a job and a chance to establish a socialist Sunday school with perfect impunity. He was in with all the Bolshevik activities except one. He had no stomach for fighting. The spirit was willing but the flesh was weak. It got to a point where it was hard to be a Bolshevik in good standing and never do any gun work, so this exile determined to go back to Chicago. When I knew him, he was haunting the committees and various ministries trying to persuade them to give him the money with which to return.

"You don't think they can draft me into the American army, do you?" he asked me anxiously. "I am a Russian subject. I don't see how they could do it legally."

I don't know how many men of this kind went back to Russia from the United States, but there were enough of them to be conspicuous, and the Russian radicals believe them to be far more reliable witnesses than the Root Commission, which made a remarkably good impression on the educated people but none at all on the *Tavarishi*, "Don't you believe that the United States is in this war for democracy," shouted one Nevsky Prospect orator. "The United States is just as imperialistic as England. You ought to read what Lincoln Steffens[12] and John Reed wrote about the United States and Mexico." These men will do Russia all the harm they can, and then they will come back to America and do us all the harm they can. If I had my way they would go from Ellis Island, with all the rest of their kind still remaining here, to some kind of a devil's island in the South Seas and be kept there until they died.

Notes

1 The Alexander Theater (Alexandrinsky Theater) is the oldest national theater in Russia. It was established in 1756.
2 Carlyle, Thomas (1795–1881) was a Scottish historian and political philosopher.
3 The Political Red Cross was the name borne by several organizations that provided aid to political prisoners in the Russian Empire and later in Soviet Russia and the Soviet Union. The first organization using this name was founded in St. Petersburg in 1870 and aided arrested *populists*. In the late 1890s, the Society for Political Exiles and Prisoners was active in St. Petersburg and after the suppression of the 1905–7 Russian Revolution, a political prisoner's bureau of the St. Petersburg organization of the Political Red Cross also offered assistance to prisoners. The already considerable cachet of the Political Red Cross (in its various forms) was further augmented when revered People's Will veteran Vera Figner, having languished for two decades in the notorious Shlisselburg fortress, formed a Paris-based "Committee to Aid Hard Laborers [*kartorzhniki*]" in 1910. This group introduced another generation of dedicated revolutionaries/humanitarians to relief work, including Ekaterina Peshkova, who was soon to become the foremost figure in assisting political prisoners. After the February Revolution, the Political Red Cross aided in the release and repatriation of prisoners and political exiles and created the Society for Released Politicals. Vera Figner led the Petrograd-based Society to Aid Liberated Politicals, while Peshkova ran its Moscow bureau.
4 Dorr refers to the charitable activity of Princess Olga Konstantinovna (1851–1926), a member of the Romanov dynasty. In 1867 at the age of 16, she married King George of Greece. After the assassination of her husband in 1913, Olga returned to Russia. When World War I broke out, she set up a military hospital in the Pavlovsk Palace that belonged to her brother.
5 Dorr refers to the charitable activity of Dowager Empress Maria Feodorovna (1847–1928), Empress of Russia from 1881–94 as the wife of Emperor Alexander III (née Princess Dagmar of Denmark). Her eldest son Nicholas was the last Emperor of Russia.
6 Kerenskaya (born Baranovskaya), Olga Lvovna (1884–1975) was the first wife of Alexander Fyodorovich Kerensky.
7 Lebedeva, Aleksandra Petrovna (Princess Kropotkin) (1887–1966) was a daughter of Russian scientist and anarchist Pyotr Kropotkin and his wife Sophia Kropotkina. In 1910, Aleksandra "Sasha" Kropotkin married Boris Lebedev, a young Socialist Revolutionary Party member; she divorced her husband in 1920. While in Russia, Kropotkin met the newspaper journalist Lorimer Hammond, whom she married in August 1927. Like her father, Aleksandra Kropotkin cared little for her title but used it to establish her American career as a New York-based journalist, writer and translator.
8 Dorr made a mistake. General Luzhenovsky was the governor's advisor.
9 Spiridonova died in 1941. On July 4, 1918, at the All-Russian Congress of Soviets, she accused the Bolsheviks of betraying the cause of the peasantry and of being more interested in abstract theories than in the needs of the poor. On July 6, two members of the SRs entered the German embassy in Petrograd and shot the ambassador. In the chaotic hours following the assassination, the SRs seized the Cheka (The All-Russian Extraordinary Commission) headquarters and held its head, Felix Dzerzhinsky,

hostage. The Bolsheviks counterattacked the following day, retook the Cheka headquarters and arrested many leaders of the SRs, including Spiridonova. In 1937, at the height of Stalin's murderous purges, she was seized from her place of internal exile, the Ural town of Ufa, and, along with 12 other former SR members, accused of plotting against the Bashkir Communist leadership. On December 25, 1937, she was sentenced to 25 years in prison and sent to Orel to serve her time. In September 1941, as the Germans advanced on their location, the prisoners at Orel, including Maria Spiridonova, were murdered by Soviet forces.

10 Tchaikovsky, Nikolai Vasilyevich (1851–1926) was a revolutionary socialist and leader of the early Narodnik movement in Russia. After the February Revolution, he was elected a member of the Petrograd Soviet, where he used his influence to oppose Bolshevik propaganda.

11 The Bund or the General Jewish Labor Bund in Lithuania, Poland and Russia was a secular Jewish socialist party initially formed in the Russian Empire and active between 1897 and 1920. The Bund actively campaigned against antisemitism, defended Jewish civil and cultural rights and rejected assimilation. However, the close promotion of Jewish sectional interests and support for the concept of Jewish national unity was prevented by the Bund's socialist universalism.

12 Steffens, Joseph Lincoln (1866–1936) was a well-known American investigative journalist and one of the leading muckrakers of the Progressive Era in the early twentieth century, as well as a lecturer, political philosopher and reformer.

Chapter 11

HOW RASPUTIN DIED

Looking at these exiles, these wrecks of humanity done to death in the name of the state and reflecting that their number was so great that months had to elapse before they could all be located and brought back to life, it is not to be wondered at that most Russians believed the autocracy a thing too strong to be shaken. But the February Revolution revealed that the autocracy was a tree rotten at the roots. At a touch it collapsed.

The Russian autocracy went down like a house of cards, and within an incredibly short time the whole horde of ignorant and reactionary ministers, grafting generals, corrupt officials, court parasites, vagrant monks, mystics and fortune tellers went down with it and were buried in its ruins. The Tsar—a reed shaken in the wind. The Tsarina,[1] the Empress Dowager, the poor little Tsarevitch,[2] Rasputin, Anna Vyrubova,[3] his sponsor at the court—leaves in the current. They all went. In the dead of night, a group of determined men, led by a nephew-in-law of the Tsar,[4] murdered a monk, and almost the next day the whole Protopopov[5]-Sturmer[6] gang was in the fortress of Peter and Paul and the Romanov family was on its way to Siberia. Rasputin, it is true, was killed in December, and the revolution did not actually occur until February; but two months in the history of a nation is an inconsiderable lapse of time. The story of the killing of Rasputin has been published in this country, and, in its main facts, accurately. In some of its important details the published stories are in error, and I am glad to be able to tell the facts as they were related by Prince Felix Yusupov himself, the man who fired the shot that freed Russia.

Prince Yusupov did not tell these facts directly to me. He told them to Mrs. Emmeline Pankhurst, the English suffragist, with whom he is on terms of warm friendship, and gave her permission to repeat them to me, which she did within an hour of hearing them. Prince Yusupov was willing that I should know the story, but our acquaintance was brief, and I am sure that I heard a more detailed account through Mrs. Pankhurst than I should have had had he talked directly to me, a comparative stranger.

Prince Yusupov did not kill Rasputin, as has been charged, because the monk had cast lascivious eyes on his beautiful young wife, the Grand Duchess Irina Alexandrovna. At least he said nothing about her in connection with the affair, and it is certain that she took no active part in it. She did not lure the monk to the Yusupov Palace on the fatal night. She could not have done so because she was in the Crimea at the time. Prince Yusupov killed Rasputin because of the man's evil influence on the Tsar, his wife's uncle, and his worse influence on the Tsarina. The thing had got beyond scandal. It had become unbearable, and when evidence was presented to him that Rasputin was trying to influence the royal pair to force Russia into a separate peace with Germany, Prince Yusupov decided that the time for Rasputin's death had come. Rasputin had to die. He was invited to Yusupov's house, and he accepted. Then he died.

I have often walked past that great, beautiful, yellow palace on the Moika Canal,[7] the Petrograd town house of the Yusupov family, and tried to reconstruct the ghastly drama enacted there on that December night. Snow burying the black ice of the canal, shrouding the street and silent houses, dimming the streetlights, and in a basement room, a private retreat of the lord of the palace, a young man sweating from every shivering pore, and watching the sinister monk eat and drink deadly poison which affected him no more than water. They had fed one of the poisoned cakes to a dog, just before they sent them downstairs to be fed to Rasputin, and the dog died in a few seconds. Rasputin ate one and lived. Explain it who can but cease to wonder that the Russians firmly believe that Rasputin was something more than human.

Excusing himself on some pretext, Prince Yusupov went upstairs, where the others waited—young Grand Duke Dmitri[8] and two or three other men, and told them the incredible news. When he went back, he had a revolver in his pocket. He and the monk resumed their conversation, which was on general topics. It was the first time Rasputin had visited Yusupov or had any particular conversation with him. The prince was not a favorite at court, the empress especially disapproving of certain alleged episodes in his youthful past. For this reason, young Prince Felix and the monk were on formal terms, and it took a great deal of diplomacy to persuade Rasputin to make that midnight visit at all. They resumed their interrupted conversation, and in the course of it, the prince invited Rasputin to cross the room and look at an ikon, or sacred picture, which hung on the opposite wall. These ikons are frequently rare objects of art, gold or silver, and incrusted with gems. The ikon, which was to be the last on which Rasputin's gaze was to rest, was an antique of almost priceless value. He looked, and the next moment, a revolver shot tore through his side, and he crumpled up on the floor without a groan. Prince Yusupov had shot him.

The prince had never killed a man before, and it was natural that, in his revulsion of nerves after the deed, he should have rushed from the room. He fled upstairs and gasped out that it was over, the thing they had sworn to do was done, Rasputin was dead. The next thing was to get the body out of the house, and this task was rendered the more difficult because a policeman who had passed the house at the moment when the shot was fired rang a doorbell and insisted on knowing what had occurred. He was pacified somehow, and one of the men went out to get a motor car. Prince Yusupov went downstairs to guard the body until the car came. Rasputin lay motionless on the floor

Figure 11.1 Prince Felix Ysupov, at whose palace on the Moika Canal Rasputin was killed, and his wife, the Grand Duchess Irina Alexandrovna, niece of the late tsar.

beneath the jeweled ikon, but as his slayer reached the spot where he lay, the monk's body shot up, the monk's long arms darted forward, and his powerful hands reached and clawed for Yusupov's throat. Half mad with amazement and horror, the young man tore himself loose, leaving one of the epaulets from his uniform in the clawing hands. Rushing with all his might to the room upstairs, he shrieked: "He lives yet! He is the devil himself! We cannot kill him!"

"We must kill him!" they shrieked in return, and the whole band rushed for the stairs. When they opened the door Rasputin was crawling on hands and knees up the stairs. His face was diabolic. What followed does not make pleasant reading. They tried to kill him, crawling toward them, using every weapon they could grasp—revolvers, swords, daggers, clubs, heavy chairs, even their boots. They shot and beat him until he was senseless, but even then he did not die. They tied his hands and feet and regardless of the possible risk of detection they loaded the senseless body into a motor car, drove to the Neva, a considerable distance, and threw the still breathing thing through a hole in the ice. There Rasputin died.

That is the way Prince Yusupov tells it. The world knows how the Tsar had the body embalmed and buried, and how he and all the royal family walked in the funeral procession. It was the intention of the Empress to build a costly tomb over his grave, perhaps a church. They usually built a church to commemorate assassinations of royalty, and the poor, half-demented Empress of Russia regarded Rasputin as greater than royalty. Perhaps if the Revolution of February had not succeeded the church would have been built, loaded with gold and art treasures, as those Russian churches are, and might in time have become a shrine in which the superstitious would pray for miracles. But the revolution did succeed, and one of the first things they did was to unearth the corpse of Rasputin and give it another burial. I heard several accounts of that burial, all of them horrible. One account has it that the body was burned. It doesn't make any real difference. Rasputin had to be killed, and he was. The burial was nothing unless you find something symbolic in the uneasy character of the man even after he was dead. It does indicate, strangely, the sinister nature of the whole Rasputin episode.

No arrests followed the killing of Rasputin, although the men who did it were known almost from the first. Rasputin's family, with whom he lived in Petrograd, knew where he went on his death night, and when he did not return, they telephoned Tsarskoe Selo[9] to ask if he was there. The royal family lived in the Alexander Palace at Tsarskoe, and Rasputin often visited them there. But he did not live at court, as many people seem to think. The Tsarina, frightened half to death, sent for the Petrograd chief of police and the dragnet immediately thrown out drew in the policeman who had heard a revolver shot from the yellow palace on the Moika Canal. The chief of police went in person to the Yusupov Palace and found it a shambles. Prince Felix had been so nearly prostrated by the events of the night—he is really little more than a boy—that he had not even had the place cleaned. The prince at first refused to tell anything of the affair and he steadfastly refused to divulge the names of the men who had helped him do the deed. But little by little the police unearthed the whole story, and the frantic Tsarina learned that at least two of the assassins were of the blood royal. She demanded their punishment, and the Tsar joined with her in the demand.

They would have sent all the men to the farthest Siberian mine if they had had their way. But there was a meeting of the Romanov clan in the Tsarskoe palace, probably more than one meeting. The grand dukes were all there, and the Empress Dowager. They told the royal pair that nobody must suffer for the deed. Horrible as it was, it had to happen sometime, because assassination was the certain end of men like Rasputin. They told the Emperor and Empress plainly that they were fortunate that only one assassination had taken place. Nobody at that time knew that the revolution was close at hand. None of the Romanov family believed that the revolution would ever come. But they knew—all of them except the Tsar and his wife—that the house of Romanov was due to have a thorough cleaning, and they were thankful at heart that Prince Felix and young Grand Duke Dmitri had had the nerve to begin the work. The young Grand Duke was sent to the Caucasus and Prince Felix was banished to his estates. I don't know where the lesser lights were sent, but certainly they were not arrested. The Grand Duke is still in the Caucasus, the Provisional Government wisely considering him well off out there on the Persian border.

Prince Yusupov is not only free, but he is something of a popular hero still. He is very democratic, is openly sympathetic with the revolution, although he detests the Bolshevki, who have turned revolution into riot. The Constitutional Democrats and other conservative revolutionists admire the young man, and there is even a group, I don't know how large, which would like to see him the constitutional monarch of Russia. He is not a Romanov, but his wife is. She is young, rarely beautiful, and a great favorite in society. As for Prince Felix, he belongs if not to royalty, to a family which has intermarried more than once with royalty. On his father's side he is Count Sumarokov-Elston,[10] the latter name indicating British descent, the original Elston coming over from Scotland during the reign of Empress Catherine.[11] He gained her favor and secured the title and estates of Sumarokov. The father of Prince Felix assumed, by imperial decree, the title of Prince Yusupov on his marriage with the beautiful Princess Yusupova, the last of her line, who thus perpetuated the family name. The

Yusupovs are one of the oldest and wealthiest families in Russia. Their origin runs back into the half-fabulous days of Tartar domination, the name Yusupov being Tartar, and not Russian at all. It means Joseph's son. The title, however, dates back only about a century. Prince Felix is the head of the family; his elder brother having been killed in a duel some years ago on French soil. He is barely thirty years old and looks much younger. Nobody would be likely to pick out this man in a crowd for an assassin. He is tall and slender, and almost too handsome. With his fine features, dark, melancholy eyes and ivory skin he might almost be called effeminate in appearance. One sees such men only in very old families where the vigor has begun to run low. There is plenty of vigor left in Prince Felix, however. He has an Oxford education and speaks English perfectly. He speaks many other languages besides, as the highly educated Russians are all supposed to do, but which they frequently do not. French is commonly spoken, of course.

I had a long talk with Prince Felix Yusupov in Moscow, and we talked, most of the time, about the American public school system. He wanted to know what the Gary system[12] was, and fortunately I was able to tell him. As I described the schools, where children spent their days, working, studying, playing, being wholly educated and trained to think as well as to work, the prince's eyes glowed and his face shone with interest and amazement. "It's the finest thing I ever heard of," he exclaimed. "It is exactly what we ought to have in Russia." And then he went on to say thoughtfully: "Mrs. Dorr, my wife and I want to do something for Russia, something really worthwhile. I don't want to be forever remembered for—for just one thing. I want to do something constructive. Of course, as things are now, there is nothing constructive to be done. Besides, my wife is a Romanov, and naturally—" He paused with a graceful little gesture of the hand. Naturally, a Romanov couldn't be conspicuous in any way just then. "But when the time comes, if it ever does, when Russia is normal again, why shouldn't the contribution I make be to the education of children?"

"The salvation of your country lies in the education of its children, all of them, not just the children of the rich," I replied.

"I believe it," was the earnest response. "And I want to help establish the best public school system in the world in Russia. How can I do it?"

I told him, to the best of my ability. And he promised me that he would carry out my suggestions. Prince Felix Yusupov means to spend the next year or two studying the American public school, and especially the Gary system. He doesn't want to be remembered for just one thing.

Notes

1. Tsarina Alexandra Feodorovna (1872–1918) was Queen Victoria's granddaughter and the last Empress of Russia as the consort of Tsar Nicholas II since their marriage in November 1894. Her misrule while the Emperor was commanding the Russian forces during World War I precipitated the collapse of the imperial government in February 1917. In July 1918, she, Nicholas II, and their children were executed by Bolshevik forces in Yekaterinburg.
2. Alexei Nikolaevich (1904–1918) was the last Russian Tsarevich. He was the youngest child and only son of Nicholas II and Alexandra Feodorovna and was born with hemophilia, which his parents tried treating using Grigori Rasputin's methods.
3. Vyrubova, Anna Alexandrovna (1884–1964) was a lady-in-waiting in the late Russian Empire, the best friend and confidante of Empress Alexandra Feodorovna.
4. Dorr is referring to Felix Yusupov, who was a nephew-in-law of the Tsar.
5. Protopopov, Alexander Dmitrievich (1866–1918) was a Russian journalist and politician who served as Minister of the Interior from September 1916 to February 1917.
6. Sturmer, Boris Vladimirovich, Baron (1848–1917) was a Russian lawyer, a master of ceremonies at the Russian Court, and a confidant of Empress Alexandra Feodorovna. He served as the prime minister, minister of the interior and foreign minister during World War I. Under his administration, the Russian Empire suffered drastic inflation and a transportation breakdown, which led to severe food shortages.
7. The Yusupov Palace in Saint Petersburg was owned by the Yusupovs; it was sometimes called the Moika Palace to distinguish it from other palaces the Yusupov family had in the city.
8. Dmitri Pavlovich, the Grand Duke of Russia (1891–1942) was a son of Grand Duke Paul Alexandrovich of Russia, a grandson of Alexander II and a first cousin of Nicholas II.
9. Tsarskoe Selo was a residence of the Russian imperial family since the rule of Alexander I (1801–1825); it is located 24 kilometers (15 mi) south of the center of Saint Petersburg.
10. Sumarokov-Elston, Felix Felixovich (1856–1928), later known as Prince Yusupov following his marriage, was a Russian statesman, nobleman and general. From 1915, he was governor-general of Moscow, a post previously held by Grand Duke Sergei Alexandrovich Romanov.
11. Catherine II (1729–1796), most commonly known as Catherine the Great, was the Empress of Russia from 1762 until 1796.
12. The Gary system (or the Gary Plan) was a new method of building a highly efficient American public school system that was much discussed in the Progressive Era in the 1910s and 1920s. American educator William Wirt, who became superintendent of Gary's schools in Indiana in 1907, developed the Gary Plan, which was also known as the "work-study-play" plan or the "platoon system." It was influenced by the philosophy of John Dewey and the methods of Frederick Taylor, a pioneer of scientific management. Students were split into platoons so that while one platoon was studying core academic subjects (math, science, social studies, English), another platoon was taking art, physical education, and industrial arts courses in specially equipped facilities. Wirt ultimately understood a school as a playground, garden, workshop, social center, library and academic classroom setting, all housed within one facility and under one administration. Reformers tried to copy it across the country.

Chapter 12

ANNA VYRUBOVA SPEAKS

"Let any American mother imagine that her only son, who came into the world a weakling, and whose life had always hung on a thread, had been miraculously restored to health. Suppose also that the person who did this wonderful thing was not a doctor, but a monk of that mother's church. Wouldn't it be natural for that mother to regard the man with almost superstitious gratitude for the rest of her life? Wouldn't it also be natural that she would want to keep the monk near her, at least until the child grew up, in order to have the benefit of his advice and help in case of a return of the illness?"

I had heard the story of the Rasputin murder as told by one of the principals in the gory tragedy, Prince Felix Yusupov, and now I was to hear it again, this time from one of the reputed "dark forces," of which Rasputin had been the head and front, Anna Vyrubova, the intimate friend and confidante of the Empress of Russia, and believed by many to be the chief accomplice of Rasputin. I had heard all sorts of horrible stories about this woman. It was said that she was Rasputin's procuress. It was said that she conspired with him to make the Empress believe that the Tsarevitch would die if the monk were sent away from court, or if he voluntarily withdrew. On the several occasions when he did go, Madame Vyrubova was said to have fed the child with minute doses of poison, so that he sickened, and when that happened of course the frantic mother demanded the return of Rasputin.

As the monk's appetite for power grew and he demanded the removal of this or that metropolitan or bishop, the removal or appointment of ministers, the suppression of newspapers that denounced him, the Tsarina, urged on by her friend Madame Vyrubova, would insist that Rasputin should have his way. Otherwise, he might leave, and the Tsarevitch would surely die. Madame Vyrubova was also said to have conspired with a court physician to poison the Tsar, or rather to put constant doses of some toxic in his food in order to cloud his mind, and thus make him an easier dupe for the pro-German conspirators. They told the most amazing stories about this woman, making her out a sort of combination of Lucrezia Borgia[1] and Jezebel.[2]

Whether the Provisional Government believed these stories or not, the Duma members who forced the revolution evidently believed Anna Vyrubova to be one of the most dangerous of the inner court circle, or camarilla, which was planning a German peace. For when the Tsar was forced to abdicate, and all the accused men of the camarilla were arrested and thrown into the fortress of Peter and Paul, Madame Vyrubova was also arrested and sent to the fortress. She was taken out of a sick bed—there had been an epidemic of measles in the royal family—thrown into an underground cell and kept there for three months. At the end of that time, she was in such a state of collapse that the prison physician recommended her removal to a hospital. To this the Provisional Government consented, but when the order for her release was presented to the governor of the fortress, and he ordered her cell door unlocked, the soldiers on duty refused to obey the order. It was days before they were persuaded to let her go. Madame Vyrubova was sent to a hospital for a month, and then they set her free. That is, they permitted her to go to the home of her brother-in-law, who is a stepson of the Grand Duke Paul,[3] and to live there under strict surveillance. They had searched her house in Tsarskoe Selo, and her rooms in the palace. They had put her through every kind of cross-examination, not once but many times, and they were forced to admit that they could not discover a single incriminating circumstance, or any evidence of poisoning or conspiracy. They had to release her, but she was not allowed to leave the country, or even her brother's house, without permission, which, of course, would not be granted. She was watched all the time and might be rearrested and given the third degree at any time if the least bit of evidence seemed to warrant it.

Anna Vyrubova is considered a very dangerous woman. She is one of two things, very dangerous or very much maligned. She gave me the impression, after two long, intimate talks, of a woman absolutely innocent of any wrongdoing. If she is a criminal she ought to be put in prison for life, for her powers of deceit are simply marvelous. I liked Anna Vyrubova, and I don't think I could possibly like a woman capable of poisoning little boys or handing innocent young girls over into the claws of a lascivious monk.

How I met this woman, how she came to talk confidentially with me, where I saw her and when, are not to be written just now. They could not be published without injuring a number of people, perhaps including Madame Vyrubova herself. I saw and talked with her soon after her release from the prison hospital. She was still a little drawn and haggard from the hardships and the terror of her experiences in Peter and Paul, and she was in the depths of despondency over the plight of her friend the Tsarina. She is a very pretty woman, this alleged Borgia-Jezebel. She has an abundance of brown hair, and her eyes are large and deeply blue. Her features are regular, and her mouth curves like a child's. Two or three years ago the train on which she was traveling between Petrograd and Tsarskoe Selo was wrecked, some say purposely. Madame Vyrubova was desperately injured, both legs being broken and her spine wrenched. She was lamed for life and walks with a crutch, but in spite of that all her movements are singularly graceful. One of the stories about her is that she was a peasant girl brought to court by Rasputin and forced on the Empress as a convenient tool of the conspirators. This is quite untrue. Madame Vyrubova is a patrician by birth, and before she was born, and long before Rasputin appeared in Tsarskoe Selo, her family was attached to the court. The father and the grandfather of Madame Vyrubova were court officials, confidential secretaries to the emperors of their times. Both her parents are living, and I have met them both. They are highly educated and unmistakably well-bred. They are not rich people, but they live in a very beautiful apartment in an exclusive quarter of Petrograd.

For more than a dozen years Mme. Vyrubova lived on terms of closest friendship with the Tsarina. She did not live at court; at least she did not until after the murder of Rasputin, when she went to the palace to be near the frightened and despairing Empress. She had a house of her own in Tsarskoe Selo, and it was at her house that the Empress met the monk who was to have such a sinister influence on her afterlife. The Empress, who was never popular at court and never happy there, liked to have a place where she could go and throw off her imperial character, be a woman among her intimate friends, carefree. Such a refuge was Mme. Vyrubova's home to the melancholy Alexandra, wife of the Emperor of all the Russies. Mme. Vyrubova's husband was an officer in the navy, and gossip had it that he disapproved of his wife's friendship with the Empress and disapproved still more of the people who were invited to meet her in his home. Rasputin was not the only one of the mystics and charlatans she met and talked with, it appears. The Empress was deeply religious, and she was interested in all kinds of strange and mystical doctrines. The husband of Mme. Vyrubova was not, and he feared, as well he might, that almost any kind of political plot might be hatched by that "little group of serious thinkers" who met in his drawing room and in the scented boudoir of his wife. They quarreled. It got to the point where they did nothing but quarrel, and one day Mme. Vyrubova was given a choice between her husband and her friend. She chose the friend, and thenceforth she occupied the house in Tsarskoe Selo alone. The husband went to sea, and after a year or two, he died.

Something of this Madame Vyrubova told me, and the rest a friend of the husband told me. In her story, the husband appears as a jealous, unreasonable, bad-tempered man, almost a lunatic. In her friend's story, he appears a martyr. "I have not had a very amusing life," said Anna Virubova, in speaking of her marriage. She smiled, a little bitterly. "Perhaps that is one reason why I, like the Empress, was attracted to religion, why we both liked and trusted Rasputin. We did trust him, and to the end everything he did justified our confidence. As for the Empress's feeling for him I give you my solemn word of honor it was solely that of a grateful mother, and a devout member of the Orthodox church." And then she spoke the words with which I have opened this chapter.

"Let any American mother imagine that she had an only son who had come into the world a weakling, one whose life had always hung on a thread, and that that child had suddenly and miraculously been restored to health. Let her suppose that the person who did this wonderful thing was not a doctor but a monk of her own church. Wouldn't it be natural for that mother to regard the man with almost superstitious gratitude for the rest of her life? Wouldn't it also be natural that she should want to keep the monk near her, at least until the child grew up, in order to have the benefit of his advice and help in case of return of the illness? Well, that is the whole truth about the Empress and Rasputin."

"But did Rasputin really heal the Tsarevitch, and restore him to health?" I asked.

Figure 12.1 Grigori Rasputin and some of his female devotees.

"Judge for yourself," she replied. "Perhaps you know how ardently the birth of a son was desired by both the Emperor and the Empress. They had four girls, but a woman may not inherit the Russian throne. A boy was wanted, and when at last he came, a poor little sickly baby, the Empress was nearly in despair. The child had a rare disease, one which the doctors have never been able to cure. The blood vessels were affected, so that the patient bled at the slightest touch. Even a small wound would endanger his life. He might bleed to death of a cut finger. In addition to this the boy developed tuberculosis of the hip. It seemed impossible that he could ever live to grow up. He was a dear child, always, beautiful, clever and lovable. Even had less hung on his life than succession to the throne it would have been hard to give him up. Each one of his successive illnesses racked the Empress with such terror and anguish that her mind almost gave away. For a long time she was so melancholy that she had to live in seclusion under the care of nurses. It was not so much assassins that she feared. It was that the child should die of the maladies that afflicted him. And, in addition to all this daily and hourly anxiety and pain she suffered, the poor Empress was torn this way and that by the grand dukes and all the members of the court circle. Each one had a remedy or a treatment they wanted applied to the child. There were always new doctors, new treatments, new operations in the air. The Empress was criticized bitterly because she wouldn't try them all. The Empress Dowager—well—" Vyrubova looked at me and we both smiled. The mother-in-law joke is as sadly amusing in a palace as in a Harlem flat.

"Then came Rasputin," continued Madame Vyrubova. "And he said to the Empress: Don't worry about the child. He is going to live, and he is going to get well. He doesn't need medicine, he needs as much of a healthy, outdoor life as his condition can stand. He needs to play with a dog and a pony. He needs a sled. Don't let the doctors give him any except the mildest medicines. Don't on any account allow them to operate. The boy will soon show improvement, and then he will get well."

"Did Rasputin say that he was going to heal him?" I asked.

"Rasputin simply said that the boy was going to get well, and he told us almost the day and the hour when the boy would begin to get well. 'When the child is twelve years old,' Rasputin told us, 'he will begin to improve. He will improve steadily after that, and by the time he is a man he will be in ordinary health like other men.' And very shortly after he turned twelve years old, he did begin to improve. He improved rapidly, just as Rasputin said he would, and within a few months he could walk. Before that, when he went out it was in the arms of a soldier, who loved him better than his own life, and would have gladly given his life if that could have brought health to his prince. The man's joy when the child really began to walk, began to play with his dog and his pony, was equaled only by that of the Empress. For the first time in her life in Russia she was happy. Do you blame her, do you blame me for being grateful to Rasputin? Whether he cured him, or God cured him, I know no more than you do. But Rasputin told us what was going to happen, and when it was going to happen. Make of it what you will."

Rasputin told the Empress of Russia that her son would begin to improve when he was 12 years old. Almost any doctor might have told her that it was not unlikely that he would begin to improve as soon as adolescence began. Many childish weaknesses, and even some very grave constitutional weaknesses, have been known to disappear gradually from that period. Empresses and ladies-in-waiting are not usually medical experts, but they might have learned that much from ordinary reading, if the doctors failed to enlighten them. But neither Alexandra nor Vyrubova knew it, and when Rasputin threw that gigantic bluff at them, they grabbed it. As a guesser Rasputin was a wonder, for the almost impossible happened and the sick little Tsarevitch lived up to his prediction. That's what I make of it.

When the Tsarevitch grows to manhood, if he ever does, and reads the history of his father's and mother's last years as rulers of Russia, what a subject for reflection this whole Rasputin episode will afford him. He was the pawn shoved back and forth across the chessboard where the destinies of nearly two hundred million Russians, to say nothing of the Romanov family, were being decided. He was the bait with which the biggest game in modern European politics was played. He and a wily monk and two women with a taste for mystical religion.

"This was the beginning of the close friendship between Rasputin and the royal family," Madame Vyrubova continued. "But it was by no means the only tie between them. Whatever anybody says about Rasputin, whatever there may have been that was irregular in his private life, whatever he may have done in the way of political plotting, this much I shall always believe about him, he was clairvoyant, he had second sight, and he used it, at least sometimes, for good and holy purposes. His prediction about the health of the Tsarevitch was only one instance. Often and often, he told us that such and such thing would happen, and it always did. The Emperor and Empress consulted him at several crises in their lives, and he always told them what they ought to do. In each and every case the advice was wise. It was miraculously wise. No one except a person gifted with second sight could possibly have known how to give it."

"Was Rasputin as bad as they say he was?" I asked.

"He couldn't have been," she answered. "But he may have been more or less licentious. Unfortunately, you find men, even in holy orders, who are weak in certain ways. I can only answer positively for myself and the

Empress. The charge that either of us ever had any personal relation with Rasputin was a foul slander. Nothing of the kind ever existed, or ever could have existed. Oh," she cried, a sudden flame dyeing her white cheeks, "how easy, very easy, it is to say that kind of thing about a woman. Nobody ever asks for proofs. Accusation and judgment are joined instantly together. Why, Rasputin was just a wandering monk when we met him. He was dirty, uneducated, uncouth. He did learn to wear a clean shirt and to preserve a sort of cultivated manner when he came to court. That was not very often, by the way. I am sure that the Empress did not see him more than six or eight times a year, and the Emperor saw him more rarely than that."

"Was he a German agent? Was he a part of the political intrigue that threatened a separate peace for Russia?"

Anna Vyrubova was silent for a long minute. She seemed to be pondering. Then she spoke, and her eyes were the candid eyes of a child. "Truly, I do not know. Certainly, I did not believe it in Rasputin's lifetime, but now—I do not know. This much I do know that it was difficult, very difficult, at the Russian court, to avoid being drawn into political intrigues. You know, of course, what a court is like."

"No," I said, "I don't know anything about a court. Tell me what it is like."

"There is only one word in English to describe it," replied Mme. Vyrubova.

"That word is 'rotten.' A court is made up of numberless little cliques, each one with its endless gossip, its whisperings, its secrets and its plots, big and small. There is nothing too big or too small for these cliques to concern themselves with. They plot international political changes, and they plot private murders. They plot to ruin the mind and the morals of an Emperor, and they plot to break up a friendship between two women. They plot to raise this one to power and they plot to bring about the fall of another. They plot in peace and they plot in war. The person who lives at court and is not drawn into some of these plots is an exception to the rule. That is all that I can say. However, Rasputin, as I told you before, never lived at court. He did not even live in Petrograd. Most of his time was spent in Siberia, and he ought to have been in Siberia on the day he was murdered. But he had a home in Petrograd, where his wife and two daughters lived while the girls were being educated. Rasputin was very fond of those girls, and he was visiting them when that Yusupov boy killed him." Mme. Vyrubova usually spoke of Prince Felix Yusupov as "that Yusupov boy."

Notes

1 Borgia, Lucrezia (1480–1519) was an Italian noblewoman and a central figure of the infamous Borgia family of the Italian Renaissance. Daughter of the Spanish cardinal

Rodrigo Borgia, later pope Alexander VI, and his Roman mistress Vannozza Catanei, and sister of Cesare, Lucrezia is often accused of sharing in their many crimes and excesses. In historical perspective, however, she seems to have been more of an instrument for the ambitious projects of her brother and father than an active participant in their crimes. Her three successive marriages into prominent families helped augment the political and territorial power of the Borgias.

2 Jezebel was the daughter of Ithobaal I of Tyre and the wife of Ahab, King of Israel. According to the biblical narrative, Jezebel replaced Yahwism with Baal and Asherah worship and was responsible for Naboth's death. This caused irreversible damage to the reputation of the Omride dynasty, who were already unpopular among the Israelites. For these offenses, Jezebel was defenestrated and devoured by dogs, under Jehu's orders, which Elijah prophesied. Her name became a byword for an impudent, shameless or immoral woman.

3 The Grand Duke Paul Alexandrovich of Russia (1860–1919) was the youngest child of Tsar Alexander II and his first wife Maria Alexandrovna. He was a brother of Emperor Alexander III and uncle of Nicholas II. With the Bolsheviks ascending to power, his palace was expropriated, and eventually he was arrested and sent to prison. In declining health, he and some of his Romanov relatives were executed by the Bolsheviks in the courtyard of the Peter and Paul Fortress in January 1919, and his remains were thrown into a mass grave.

Chapter 13

MORE LEAVES IN THE CURRENT

In an even, passionless voice, Anna Vyrubova went on to tell me the story of the murder in the Ysupov Palace, as it had appeared to the slain man's devotees in Tsarskoe Selo.

"We knew that certain people were plotting to kill Rasputin. His life was attempted, you may know, at least three times. But it never entered our minds that Prince Yusupov was in the plot. He was not a favorite with the Empress, who thought him a very dissolute young man. Still, he was in Tsarskoe once in a while, because his wife, who is a lovely girl, often came, and sometimes he came with her. On one of his last visits, he saw the Empress. I was in the room, and I heard him say, quite casually, that he had invited Rasputin to come to his house. "My wife wants to meet him," he said".

"We thought no more about it, but on the morning after the dreadful thing happened one of Rasputin's daughters called me on the telephone and asked me if I knew where her father was, and if not would I telephone the palace and find out if he was there." Some intuition seemed to tell me that something terribly wrong had occurred.

"Trying not to let my voice tremble, I asked the girl when her father had left the house and with whom. 'He left about midnight,' she answered, 'I don't know whose motor car it was that came for him, but he told us he was going to call on Prince Yusupov.' I did not telephone the palace to ask about Rasputin. I went there as quickly as I could and told the Empress my news. 'He went to see Felix?' she exclaimed. 'Why should he have gone there now, when Irene is in the Crimea?' We looked at each other and the same kind of awful fear looked out of her eyes that had gathered in my heart. 'Send for the chief of police at once,' said the Empress. 'Tell him to come as fast as he possibly can.' It is almost too terrible for me to tell you. The police found the Yusupov house in the most ghastly state of blood and—ugh!" she exclaimed, "it made me sick to hear them describe it, and it makes me sick just to remember it." After a moment she continued, real feeling in her voice. "The thing was not difficult to trace. The Yusupov boy denied everything at first, made up a silly story about a dog that had to be killed."

When Mme. Vyrubova said this, I admit I shuddered. It was evident that she did not grasp the subtlety of that "silly story about a dog that had to be killed."

"While Prince Felix was still insisting that no crime had been committed, the police found the hole in the ice, and around it, on the snow, many bloodstains. And then they found the poor corpse. They had killed him, first by shooting and then by every horrible means in their power. He was shot in the head and in the body, crushed and mangled almost beyond recognition. There was one frightful, ragged wound across his stomach which could only have been made with a spur, the doctors told us. When he had been beaten until he was helpless, those men tied him up with meters of rope and threw him in the river to drown. He must have regained consciousness at the end because he had dragged one arm partially free and by his hand, we knew, that he tried to make the sign of the cross. Yusupov persisted in his denials until Grand Duke Michael[1] and his son drove to the palace and told the Tsar that they were all more or less in it and that it had been a good thing to do. A good thing to murder and mutilate a defenseless man! Well, you asked me what a court was like."

"There was a terrific time at the palace. The Emperor was horrified, and the Empress, I think, was nearer the insanity they accused her of than she had ever been before. They demanded the name of every man and woman connected with the plot and promised that every one of them should be brought to sternest justice. But what power had they, after all? The grand dukes and the whole family stood as one against the Emperor and Empress. They declared that no one should be punished for that atrocious crime. I cannot tell you all they said and did, because that would be revealing confidences. But they held a strong enough club over the poor Emperor when they threatened to desert him in a troubled and uncertain time. He was absolutely forced to agree that only the principal plotters should be banished to their estates, and the others should be left unpunished. Afterward, when we could talk about it at all," Mme. Vyrubova resumed, "reminded the Empress that the day before Rasputin was murdered that Yusupov boy had telephoned to me asking me to arrange for him to see the Empress. She had declined to see him, and we both believe that if she had received him, he would have killed her and then, very likely, me also. We are convinced that there was a great assassination plot all laid. But there is no proof."

This, then, is how the Rasputin murder appears in reverse. Prince Felix Yusupov did not look like a wholesale assassin to me, but then, neither did Anna Vyrubova look like a poison plotter. Evidently, you have to be accustomed to the atmosphere of courts to judge these things. I don't judge anybody in this gruesome drama. I leave that to history.

I asked Mme. Vyrubova why the court cliques plotted against the Empress. "It was inevitable," she replied. "The Empress came there, a stranger, a poor, beautiful, painfully shy young girl. She did not know how to flatter or win favor. She was studious, and she was devoted to her husband and children. They needed her devotion—oh, far more than the ordinary family needs that of the mother. You have heard, I suppose, some of the atrocious slanders that have been circulated about the Empress. One of these had it that she encouraged the Emperor in his weakness for alcohol because she wanted to keep him in a muddled state of mind and herself be the real ruler of Russia. The exact opposite is true. The poor Emperor did drink too much sometimes, but it was not her fault. There were others at that court who were vitally interested in keeping their Emperor in a muddled state of mind, and they constantly played on his weakness. His wife fought for him desperately, did everything in her power to save him from these men."

"Another slander said that the Empress tried to Germanize the court, and that she made her children talk German to her. The children almost never spoke a word of German to her or to anyone else. Of course, they were taught German, along with other languages, but English and Russian were the only two languages spoken in the family circle. The Empress was anxious for all her children to be good linguists, but not all of them were gifted that way. Tatiana, the second daughter, for example, declared that she never would be able to carry on a conversation in French, the easiest of all foreign tongues. But English they all spoke from their cradles."

"As for the Empress's intrigues for a separate peace with Germany," and here Mme. Vyrubova's voice trembled with indignation, "that was the greatest nonsense and the wickedest slander of them all. From the time the war broke out until the revolution last February, the Empress was tireless in her work for the Russian soldiers and their families. She fairly lived in the hospitals at Tsarskoe Selo. Immediately after breakfast every morning, she began her rounds, dressed in the plain cotton frock of the Red Cross nurse. There was no duty too humble, no task too arduous for her to undertake. She stood beside the surgeons in the operating room, seeing the most dreadful amputations. She sat beside the suffering and the dying in their beds. "Stand near me, tsaritza," a poor wretch would cry to her in his anguish and pain, and she would take his rough hand and soothe him, pray for him, that he might bear it for Russia. They loved her then, those men, though they turned against her afterward. We used to motor home for luncheon and then go to more hospitals. It would be 5 o'clock before we reached home, and then the Empress always sent for her children. What time did she have, will you tell me, for German intrigues?"

"The home life of the royal family was happy and harmonious above any I have ever seen," interpolated Mme. Vyrubova.

The Tsar worshiped his wife, and the children worshiped both of them. Would you believe that some of those court parasites tried to break up that happy home? Once when the Emperor was at Livadia, in the Crimea, someone sent each day a great basket of flowers to be placed on his writing table. Attached to the basket was my card. They thought they could make the Empress believe that I was carrying on an intrigue with the Emperor. As a matter of fact, the Empress asked me directly if I sent the flowers. I had not heard a word of it before, and if she had merely sent me away, I should never have known the reason. Against me they plotted ceaselessly. Why? Because the Empress loved and trusted me, and I would have died for her, and they all knew it. They resented our friendship. They hated to see us sitting together hours at a time over our books. We read a great deal. It may interest you to know that we read many American books.

"What American books did the Empress read?" I asked.

"We read Mrs. Eddy's book,[2] of course, and the complete works of the great American author, Miller."[3]

"Miller?" I interrupted. "What Miller?"

"I don't remember his first name," said Mme. Vyrubova. "But you must know who I mean. He wrote many religious and philosophical works. The Empress was very fond of them."

I was obliged to confess that I had never heard of Miller, and Mme. Vyrubova looked her surprise.

Another reason why the Empress, and of course myself, were unpopular was because the children were with us so much of the time. The Empress simply would not allow them to associate with the sons and daughters of the nobility. She wanted to keep them sweet and clean minded and good, and she knew that very few of the children of high society in Russia were fit companions for them. The daughters of our nobility are mostly frivolous, selfish, empty-headed girls, and as for the sons, they are too often debauched in early boyhood. You can imagine that the Empress's poor opinion of them and her refusal to allow her children to know them aroused great resentment. People always think their own children perfect, you know.

The former Empress of Russia is one of the enigmas of history. Mme. Vyrubova, who knew her better than almost any other living woman, makes her out to be a religious devotee and something of a puritan. She does not reveal her as an intellectual woman, in spite of her love of books. A really intelligent woman in her position would not have spent so much of her time in the wards of hospitals in the one small town of Tsarskoe Selo. She would have used her brains, her vast wealth and her almost unlimited power to organize the work of the hospitals all over the war area. I have seen some of those hospitals, and while some of them are modern and well equipped, many are of the crudest description. I never saw such a thing as a fly screen in any Russian hospital. Flies seem to be regarded as harmless domestic pets even in contagious disease hospitals in Russia.

The Empress may or may not have been a German plotter. I heard it said on high authority that the minutest search of all the palace records, after the revolution, failed to unearth any evidence to that effect. Practically everybody in Russia, however, believes that she was a traitor to her country in the war. Those who are charitably disposed toward her say that she was melancholy, mad, irresponsible, and a weak tool in the hands of Russia's enemies. But when the days of revolution burst on the palace at Tsarskoe Selo, and the night of perpetual extinction began to descend on the royal house of Romanov, it was this woman, the Empress of Russia, who alone showed strength of mind and character. She alone of the whole court kept her head and her cool nerve, and kept them to the last.

Much has been made of Alexandra's influence over the weak and yielding Emperor. It is said that the Empress, when arguments failed to move him, resorted to hysterical fits which invariably brought results. But this may be the merest gossip. Alexandra's influence over her husband was probably as strong as the average wife's, but is it not a little curious that, while few countries allow women to inherit a throne and not all countries allow women to vote, when anything happens to a dynasty they always discover that the queen was the only member of the family who had any brains or any strength of character? The troubles of the whole house of Bourbon have been ascribed to Marie Antoinette,[4] and the fall of the Empire and the house of Bonaparte was caused by the malign influence of Josephine.[5]

Rasputin is another actor in the drama who will have to be judged by the historians. I firmly believe that Rasputin as a dark force was very much overrated. I have no doubt that he was a wicked, deceitful, plotting creature, a monster of sensuality, an impostor and an all-around bad lot. That seems to be settled. But I cannot find much evidence that he was anything more than a tool of the German plotters, whoever they were. He exercised great influence, but it seems to me that almost everything he did was out of personal spite. He demanded the suppression of a newspaper that attacked him, the removal of a minister who insulted him. His principal activities were against men in the Orthodox Church. Here he was about as venomous as a rattlesnake. An obscure monk, it filled him with pride and joy to humble a bishop, to unfrock a priest, to influence appointments.

Rasputin had a small, mean mind, and his egotism was colossal. Of course, the women fools at court who flattered and deferred to him, perhaps worse, fostered this egotism until it reached the limit of inflation. But Rasputin, I believe, will live in history more as a scandal than as a menace to Russia. He was a menace also, because a bad, weak man is often even more of a menace than a bad, strong one. The weakling is almost sure sooner or later to fall into the hands of plotters and criminals, and under their directing power he becomes as dangerous as a rabid animal.

Notes

1 Grand Duke Michael Alexandrovich (1878–1918) was the third and favorite son of Emperor Alexander III of Russia and his Danish wife Empress Maria Feodorovna. He was the youngest brother of Nicholas II and de jure Emperor of Russia after his brother Nicholas abdicated in 1917 and proclaimed his brother "Emperor Michael II." But Michael declined to take power a day later. In March 1918, Lenin began his campaign to exterminate the Romanov dynasty. The Grand Duke and his secretary Nicholas Johnson were sent to Perm on the order of the Bolshevik ruling council and later executed in the forest by the members of the Ural Regional Soviet.
2 Eddy, Mary Baker (1821–1910) was a Christian religious reformer and founder of the religious denomination known as Christian Science. She also founded *The Christian Science Monitor* in 1908 and three religious magazines. Eddy wrote numerous books and articles, most notably the 1875 book *Science and Health with Key to the Scripture*, selected as one of the "75 Books By Women Whose Words Have Changed The World" by the Women's National Book Association.
3 Miller, James Russell (1840–1912) was a popular Christian author, editorial superintendent of the Presbyterian Board of Publication, and pastor of several churches in Pennsylvania and Illinois.
4 Marie Antoinette (1755–93) was queen of France and wife of King Louis XVI (1774–93). She is associated with the decline of the French monarchy and the ancien régime, though her courtly extravagance was but a minor cause of the financial woes of the French state in that period. Her rejection of reform provoked unrest, and her policy of court resistance to the progress of the French Revolution finally led to the overthrow of the monarchy in August 1792. Louis XVI was executed in January 1793. She was brought before the Revolutionary tribunal on October 14, 1793, and was guillotined two days later.
5 Bonaparte, Josephine (1763–1814) was the consort of Napoleon Bonaparte and Empress of the French (1804–9).

Chapter 14

THE PASSING OF THE ROMANOVS

I asked Mme. Vyrubova to tell me what happened at the palace during the revolution and how the royal family received the news of its overthrow.

"I can tell you only what I personally know," she replied, "and I was very ill in bed when it happened. All the children had measles and, helping the empress nurse them, I was stricken too. The Empress was an angel. She went from one room to another caring for us, waiting on us, while all the time anxiety must have been tearing cruelly at her heartstrings. Once or twice she said something to me about trouble in Petrograd, food riots."

"The scarcity of food had preyed on the Empress's mind for many months, and one of the last conversations she ever had with Rasputin was on that subject. The winter of 1916 set in early, and the snows were so deep that transportation of all kinds of things, food included, was greatly impeded. I remember that the Empress said to Rasputin that nature itself seemed to be conspiring against poor Russia that year."

"The rioting in Petrograd increased, and even in my bed I could hear echoes of it around the palace. Shots I heard and horrid yells. I tried to get out of bed, but the Empress soothed me. 'It is bad, of course,' she said, 'but it will quiet soon. The poor people are mad with hunger. They will be given food and then all this will be over.' Soon the palace guards, the regiments on duty in Tsarskoe Selo, began to show signs of demoralization. They were afraid for their own lives, and you cannot wonder that they were. The Empress used to go out in the cold and snow in the dead of night and talk to the men, reassure them, comfort them. 'Nothing will happen,' she told them. But for her I believe the last man would have thrown away his gun and fled. Her will and her resolution alone kept them at their posts."

"Do you think that the Empress really believed that it was a riot and not a revolution?" I asked. It was history this woman was telling me, history that will live in libraries a thousand years after we two, and all of us, are dust. I wanted to know the exact truth.

"I am sure she did," said Mme. Vyrubova.

"If she had dreamed that it was a revolution she would have sent earlier for the Emperor, who, you know, was at the front with his army. She was alone and she faced the trouble alone, but if she had known the full extent of the trouble, she would have wanted the Emperor where he would be safer than out there among that murderous gang. She did not know that Russia was in revolution, nor would she believe it at first when she was told that the army had gone over to the revolutionists. The officers of the guard told her, but she simply shook her head. Finally, Grand Duke Paul came tearing out to Tsarskoe in his highest power motor car. He convinced her that it was true. Even then her steel nerves endured. 'Send for the Emperor,' she said calmly and sternly. 'I am going back to my sick children.' And she went."

The iron nerve displayed by the Empress of Russia when she learned that supreme disaster had befallen the house of Romanov was in contrast to the emotion which overcame the deposed Emperor on his return to Tsarskoe Selo. At the time of his abdication, near the army front, he had behaved with dignity and self-command. He scornfully refused the whispered suggestion of one general that he escape in one of the high-power motorcars which always accompanied the imperial train. If the people wanted him to abdicate, he was ready to do so, and ready also to place himself at their disposal. Nicholas also showed himself to be a good Russian and no tool of the pro-German party, if reports are correct. When the news came that the army had gone over to the revolution, someone near the Emperor, it is said, told him that there was one desperate way to avert the catastrophe. He could open up the Dvinsk front, let the enemy in, and thus by the sacrifice of his country save his dynasty. Nicholas refused even to consider such a crime. He committed many sins of cruelty in his time, and many more sins of stupidity. But in the end, he showed himself no traitor. His return to Tsarskoe Selo was intended by Kerensky and the other members of the Provisional Government to be in accordance with his former rank, and orders were given to treat him with all respect and consideration. These orders, if Mme. Vyrubova is to be believed, were disregarded by the soldiers on guard at the Alexander Palace, the home of the royal family.

In my last talk with Mme. Vyrubova, she spoke with deep feeling of the rowdy reception given to the returning Nicholas. "They blew tobacco smoke in his face, the brutes!" she said. "A soldier grabbed him by the arm and pulled one way, while others clutched him on the other side and pulled him in an opposite direction. They jeered at him and laughed at his anger and pain. When he was finally alone with his family and intimate friends, he could not contain his grief but wept unrestrainedly. We all wept, for that matter: we who loved him."

It is to the credit of Kerensky and the ministers that they never would consent to any suggestion that Nicholas be thrown into a dungeon or otherwise harshly treated. As long as the family remained at Tsarskoe Selo, which was until the 1st of August, Russian style, and August 13 in the Western calendar, it lived in its accustomed manner. The servants, most of them, remained at their posts, and while no member of the family was allowed to leave the palace grounds on any pretext, nor the palace itself except when accompanied by armed guards, they had the freedom of their home and the society of a few friends. They were not allowed to telephone, and all letters reaching them had first to be read by the officer in command of the guards. Mme. Vyrubova told me that in spite of Kerensky's good intentions, the deposed royalties were subjected to a number of petty annoyances which must have caused them all the resentment and humiliation their tormentors intended. The electric lights were sometimes turned off early in the evening, leaving the palace in darkness. There were days when the water was turned off and the family was deprived of bathing facilities. The soldiers on guard were not infrequently rude and churlish and openly exultant in the presence of their prisoners.

Kerensky cannot be held responsible for these things, but he was responsible for depriving the former Empress of the society of her most intimate friend, Mme. Vyrubova. I have already told how she was arrested while still suffering from the effects of measles and thrown into a cell in Peter and Paul. The cell was damp and unsanitary, and the sick woman suffered extreme misery all the time she was there. Surrounded constantly by soldiers, who watched her night and day, she was never alone even long enough to dress or to bathe. She is lame, as I have stated, and once she fell on the slippery floor of her cell and was unable for a long time to rise. The soldiers on guard refused to help her, but simply stood and laughed at her efforts to reach her bed. "Twice during the months of my confinement they let my mother visit me," she told me. "But I was allowed to talk to her only in presence of the guard and across a wide table in the governor's room."

A friend of Mme. Vyrubova told me a still worse story concerning her imprisonment. Several times her father was visited by soldiers from Peter and Paul and made to pay large sums of money in order to ensure his daughter from the most horrible indignities at the hands of the men who guarded her. He paid this blackmail. He had to. There was no power in Russia to appeal to, and Kerensky himself could not have prevented the murder or outrage of that lame and helpless woman in the fortress of Peter and Paul. She escaped the last insult men are capable of offering to women, and the government, after vainly trying to fasten the crime of treason on her, set Anna Vyrubova free under military surveillance. But they would not grant the Empress's plea to send her friend back to Tsarskoe Selo.

The first shock of dumbfounded amazement over, the royal family, which had never believed that it could be overthrown, regained its composure and accepted its destiny with quiet resignation. The Emperor became his adored son's tutor, and the Empress her daughters' constant companion. When spring came, the whole family went out and made a garden. The hundreds of soldiers in Tsarskoe and thousands of people from Petrograd made pilgrimages to the palace grounds and watched through the high iron fence the former Tsar spading up the ground and the former heir and his sisters planting and hoeing potatoes. The former Empress, in a wheeled chair or low pony carriage, for she was in feeble health, usually looked on smilingly.

Of course, the *Tavarishi*, or at least the extremists in the Council of Soldiers' and Workmen's Delegates, resented the respectful and considerate treatment accorded the captive royalties. They kept up a constant clamor for the removal of the Emperor and Empress to some dungeon in Kronstadt or Peter and Paul. Every once in a while, the newspapers published a resolution to that effect passed by a committee of the council in Petrograd or Tsarskoe, or a city more remote. A dispatch from Helsingfors[1] said that the crews of three warships lying near there had passed fiery resolutions demanding that the Tsar be turned over to the tender mercies of the ruffians at Kronstadt. The crew of the cruiser *Gangoute* went on record as saying: "This is the third time that we have expressed our will in this matter, and we have not been trifling. This is our last resolution. Next we shall employ force."

The government, however, disregarded all these resolutions and muttered threats. It may very well be, though, that the final decision to send Nicholas and his wife into Siberian exile came as a result of pressure on the part of the Soviets. Kerensky may have feared a bloody tragedy at Tsarskoe Selo, and perhaps he had reason to fear it. At all events, the Provisional Government decided, sometime in July, to transfer the family to one of the remotest spots in the empire, Tobolsk,[2] in eastern Siberia. The government kept this decision an absolute secret, as far as the deposed Emperor as well as the general public were concerned. A few days before the transfer was made, one of the Soviets, I think at Tsarskoe, held a stormy meeting at which great indignation was expressed over the ease and comfort in which the once royal family lived. "We eat black bread, they eat white," complained one impassioned orator. "We drink cold water and Nicholas drinks wine. My wife walks while his rides in a carriage. Where's the justice in that?"

Doesn't it sound like a deliberate plagiarism of one of the speeches made against allowing the sixteenth Louis to remain in the Tuileries?[3] A lot of things have changed since the French Revolution, but some human nature is just as small and mean as ever.

THE PASSING OF THE ROMANOVS

It was not until the Romanov family was well on its way to Siberia that the transfer was mentioned in the newspapers. Many people knew of it, of course, and the news was passed from excited lip to lip in the capital a few hours after the special train left Tsarskoe Selo. In the newspapers of August 3 (16, old style), the carefully censored story of the departure was published. The full story, as far as I know it, reveals that for three weeks beforehand the garrison at Tsarskoe knew, or suspected, that something was about to happen to the captives. Two days before the event, Kerensky went in person to the garrison and asked the soldiers to choose from their ranks a squadron of the most reliable and trustworthy men. They were needed, he explained, for a mission of great importance. Three hundred and eighty-four men were chosen, eight from forty-eight regimental groups. On the 31st of July (August 12) at midnight, Kerensky appeared at the barrack, called the picked men together and told them that their mission was to escort the man who had been their Emperor and autocrat into exile in far Siberia.

The royal family knew its fate before that time, but just when they were told has not been revealed. Kerensky told them, and I feel sure that he did it gently and courteously. But he refused them all information as to where they were going. On July 30 (August 11), the confessor of the family held a service for those about to go on a long journey. Then they went to work to pack trunks and to choose among clothes, trinkets, furs, personal belongings, books, ikons, rugs, and other essential things that would lighten exile and keep them in memory of other days. It is said that neither Nicholas nor Alexandra slept on the night before their departure, but wandered from room to room, hand in hand, mutely and sorrowfully bidding their beloved home goodbye. Many others in Tsarskoe Selo refrained from sleep on that night. The garrison was wildly excited, and the streets of the picturesque little town were full of people. At 3 o'clock in the morning motor vans were driven into the palace grounds, and those near enough the gates could see that the vans were being loaded with trunks and boxes. At 6 o'clock a long train slowly backed into the station of Tsarskoe Selo, the station was surrounded by soldiers, and troops with loaded rifles marched out and lined both sides of the road from the palace to the station, each soldier carrying in his belt 60 rounds of cartridges.

Those who saw the departure differ in minor details, of course, because no two people ever see the same event exactly alike. Especially an important event on which we would like to have all the details. But all the observers agree that Nicholas walked out of the palace and entered the waiting motorcar with the calm manner of a man about to take a pleasure drive. Alexandra did the same. She walked without assistance, having apparently recovered her shattered health. The former Tsarevich, in a sailor suit and cap, danced ahead of his parents, in pleased anticipation of a journey, and the young grand duchesses also appeared in high spirits. They are extremely handsome girls, all of them, and people rather sympathetically observed that during their illness in February, they had all had their luxuriant hair cut short.

Some of the observers say that the former Tsar drove to the station alone, others say Kerensky followed him into the car and still others say that the family went together. Some say that Nicholas wore the uniform of a Russian army officer, others particularly noticed his gray suit. To some he looked dejected and tearful, and to others careless and cold. Some saw tears in his eyes when he entered the train, others marveled at the calmness with which he shook hands with members of the Provisional Government who were on the platform. To this day, we do not know whether Louis XVI laid his head on the block quietly or fought the headsman all over the place, although several thousand Frenchmen witnessed the execution.

It is said that the Emperor left Tsarskoe under the impression that he was being taken to Livadia, the beautiful Crimean estate toward which he yearned at the time of his abdication. He must have been profoundly shocked when he learned that instead he was speeding toward one of the bleakest and dreariest spots in Siberia. Before the train left, the Emperor is said to have asked Kerensky, who accompanied him to the last, if the family would ever be allowed to return to Tsarskoe Selo. If he did, Kerensky's reply must have been evasive, for Nicholas told one of his suite, or is said to have done so, that he expected to return after the war.

The Empress, when told that the family was on its way to Tobolsk, is reputed to have smiled coldly and said: "I am glad we shall see Tobolsk. It is a place that has dear associations." Tobolsk, or its near neighborhood, it will be remembered, was the early home of Rasputin. Women of the French aristocracy mounted the guillotine with exactly such speeches on their lips, a last defiance of the mob.

"Why are there so many soldiers on this train?" asked one of the young grand duchesses. She was used to being escorted by soldiers, but the great number on this occasion excited her surprise. The children all knew that they were going into exile and had been given their choice of remaining with relatives or going with their parents. Mme. Vyrubova's claim that the family bond is strong was borne out by their unanimous decision to go wherever their father and mother went.

Mme. Narishkina,[4] one of the Empress's faithful ladies-in-waiting, went with her, since the Provisional Government would not let her have Mme. Vyrubova or even allow the two friends to bid each other farewell. Prince Dolgorukov[5] was permitted to go with the Emperor. The children retained a governess and the boy a tutor. Twelve servants accompanied the family.

According to the depths of his nature and understanding, one feels a certain pity for the former autocrat of all the Russies or rejoices wildly at his present plight. He had to be exiled, and perhaps Siberia was the best place to send him. But Siberia has a large variety of climates and places to choose among, and it seems to many people that the Provisional Government might have been a little more humane in their choice of a residence for Nicholas and his family. Whatever his shortcomings, however just his punishment, his five children never harmed anybody, and they deserve no punishment. According to accounts, every hour they spend at Tobolsk will be a punishment, and their time there will be short because all of them will probably die owing to the frightful surroundings.

Tobolsk is a town of about 25,000 inhabitants, situated on the Irtysh river, a little sluggish stream that drains, or partially drains one of the great marshes of eastern Siberia. The town is built on a marsh, and the mosquitoes which breed there are said to be of a size and a ferocity unequaled elsewhere. Malaria haunts the miasmas of the marshy forests that stretch for miles around the town and line the riverbanks. The nearest railroad is 300 versts distant. In winter, which endures eight months of the year, the place is shut off from the world. It is as remote from human association as the moon. The Provisional Government apologizes for Tobolsk as a choice on the grounds of the necessity for remoteness.

Notes

1 Helsingfors is the Swedish name of Helsinki, the capital and most populous city of Finland on the shore of the Gulf of Finland. In 1809, Russia planned to annex Finland directly as a province of the Russian Empire, but in order to overcome the Finns' misgivings about Russian rule, Tsar Alexander I offered them the following solution: Finland was not annexed to the Russian Empire but was joined to Russia instead through the person of the tsar. In addition, Finland was made an autonomous state—the Grand Duchy of Finland with its inherited traditions intact.
2 Tobolsk is a town located at the confluence of the Tobol and Irtysh rivers, the second-oldest Russian settlement east of the Ural Mountains in Asian Russia.
3 Louis XVI (1754–93), the last king of France before the fall of the monarchy during the French Revolution, and his family were removed from the Versailles Palace to the Tuileries Palace in Paris, on the grounds that the King would be more accountable to the people if he lived among them in Paris. Louis XVI was tried by the National Convention (which appointed itself as a tribunal for the occasion), found guilty of high treason, and executed by guillotine on January 21, 1793.
4 Narishkina, Elizabeth "Zizi" Alexeevna (1838–1928) was a Russian noblewoman, courtier and memoirist. She served as senior lady-in-waiting to Empress Alexandra Feodorovna from 1910 until 1917.

5 Dolgorukov, Vasily Alexandrovich, Prince (1868–1918) was an advisor to Russian Emperor Nicholas II and Marshal from 1914 to 1917. After the arrest of the Russian Imperial family, he voluntarily accompanied the family into exile in Tsarskoe Selo and later Tobolsk. He was barred from joining them in Yekaterinburg in April 1918 and was executed on orders of the Bolsheviks in July 1918.

Chapter 15

THE HOUSE OF MARY AND MARTHA

On the afternoon of the day when Nicholas II, deposed Emperor and autocrat of all the Rassles, with his wife and children left Tsarskoe Selo and began the long journey toward their place of exile in Siberia, I sat in a peaceful convent room in Moscow and talked with almost the last remaining member of the royal family left in complete freedom in the empire. This was Elizabeth Feodorovna, sister of the former Empress and widow of the Grand Duke Sergei, uncle of the Emperor. The Grand Duke Sergei was assassinated, blown to pieces by a bomb, almost before the eyes of his wife, by a revolutionist on February 4 old style, 1905. He was killed when going to join the Grand Duchess in one of the churches of the Kremlin in Moscow. She rushed out and saw his mutilated remains lying in the snow. The Grand Duchess Sergei had long been known as a noble and saintly woman, and her conduct following the horrible death of her husband perfectly illustrates her character. She besought the Tsar to commute the death sentence passed upon the assassin, and when he refused, she went to the prison where the wretched man waited his death, gained admission to his cell, and almost to the end prayed with him and comforted him. No children had ever been born to her, and after the event which cut the last tie that bound her to the life of royal pomp and glitter she retired from society and gave herself up to religion. As soon as possible she became a nun. Her private fortune, to the last ruble, investments, palaces, furniture, art treasures, jewels, motorcars, sables and other fine raiment were turned into cash and the money used to build a convent and to find an order of which she became the lady abbess. The Grand Duchess Sergei literally obeyed the edict of Christ to the rich young man: "Sell all thou hast and give it to the poor."

The Convent of Mary and Martha of the Order of Mercy in Moscow,[1] is a living token of her great sacrifice. Here for the past eight years, she has lived and worked among her nuns, at least one of whom was a court lady, and many of whom are women from the intellectual classes. Some of the nuns were from humble households, for the order is perfectly democratic. Everyone who enters the House of Mary and Martha does so with the understanding that her life is to be spent in service, spiritual service such as Mary of the Gospels gave, and material service such as the practical Martha rendered her Lord. The somewhat dreamy and passive Russians will tell you that Elisabeth Feodorovna's convent is one of the most efficient institutions in the empire, and they usually add: "They say she makes her nuns work terribly hard."

When the days of revolution came in February 1917, a great mob went to the House of Mary and Martha, battered the gates open and swarmed up the convent steps demanding admission. The door opened and a tall, grave woman in a pale silver-gray habit and white veil stepped out into the porch and asked the mob what it wanted.

"We want that German woman, that sister of the German spy in Tsarskoe Selo," yelled the mob. "We want the Grand Duchess Sergei."

Tall and white, like a lily, the woman stood there. "I am the Grand Duchess Sergei," she replied in a clear voice that floated above the clamor. "What do you want with me?"

"We have come to arrest you," they shouted.

"Very well," was the calm reply. "If you want to arrest me I shall have to go with you, of course. But I have a rule that before I leave the convent for any purpose I always go into the church and pray. Come with me into the church, and after I have prayed, I will go with you."

She turned and walked across the garden to the church, the mob following. As many as could crowd into the small building followed her there. Before the altar door she knelt, and her nuns came and knelt around her weeping. The Grand Duchess did not weep. She prayed for a moment, crossed herself, then stood up and stretched her hands to the silent, staring mob.

"I am ready to go now," she said.

But not a hand was lifted to take Elizabeth Feodorovna. What Kerensky could not have done, what no police force in Russia could have done with those men that day, her perfect courage and humility did. It cowed and conquered hostility; it dispersed the mob. That great crowd of liberty-drunk, blood-mad men went quietly home, leaving a guard to protect the convent. It is probably the only spot in Russia today where absolute inviolability may be said to exist for any members of the hated "*bourju*," as the Bolsheviki call the intellectual classes.

On the August day when I rang the bell of the convent's massive brown gate, I did not really know that I was to see and speak with the Grand Duchess. Mr. William L. Cazalet,[2] of Moscow, the friend who took me there, doubted very much whether I could be received thus informally, without a previous appointment. The gravity of the times, and especially the situation of the Romanov family, placed the Grand Duchess Sergei in a position of extreme delicacy, and Mr. Cazalet said frankly that he expected to find her living in strict retirement. The best he could promise, he said, was that I should see the convent, where one of his young cousins was a nun.

The convent, which is situated in the heart of Moscow, is a group of white stone and stucco houses built around an old garden and surrounded by a high white wall, over which vines and foliage ramble and fall. A key turned, the brown gate swung open to our ring and we stepped into a garden running over with the richest bloom. I remember the pink and white sweet peas against the wall, the white Madonna Lilies that nodded below and the carpet of gay verbenas that ran along the pathway to the convent door. There were many old apple trees and a forest of lilacs, purple and white.

In her small room, a combination of office and living room, we were received by the executive head of the convent, Mme. Gordeeva,[3] for many years the intimate friend of Elizabeth Feodorovna. Like the Grand Duchess, she had had a life full of tears and tribulation, in spite of her rank and wealth, and when the Grand Duchess took the veil, she followed her example and became a nun. The business of the convent is transacted under her direction, and most ably, I was told. Efficiency and ability are written in every feature of Mme. Gordeeva's fine face, in her crisp, clear voice, and quick though graceful movements. Her enunciation was a joy to hear, an especial joy to me, for I have difficulty in understanding the rather indistinct French spoken by the average Russian. Mme. Gordeeva's French was of that perfect kind you hear spoken in Tours more often than in Paris or elsewhere. I understood every word. A woman of the world to her fingertips, Mme. Gordeeva wore the picturesque habit of the order with the same grace that she would have worn the latest creation of the ateliers. She smiled and chatted with Mr. Cazalet, who is very well known in the convent, and was most kind and cordial to me. After a few minutes' conversation, my friend said to her that I had told him some extremely interesting things about public schools in America, and he wanted me to repeat them to her.

So, I told her something about the extraordinary experiments that have been worked out in Gary, Indiana, and the work that was being done in New York and elsewhere to give children, rich and poor alike, the complete education they merit. As I talked, she exclaimed from time to time: "But it is excellent! I find it admirable! The Grand Duchess should hear of this!"

I said hopefully that I would like very much to meet the Grand Duchess, and she replied she thought it might be arranged. Not today, however, as the Grand Duchess's time was completely filled. How long did I expect to remain in Moscow? A week? It could certainly be arranged, she thought. Meanwhile, what would I like to see of the convent? Everything? She laughed and touched a little bell on the desk beside her. A little nun appeared, and Mme. Gordeeva handed me over to her with orders that I was to see everything.

Figure 15.1 The Grand Duchess Elizabeth Feodorovna, sister of the late Tsarina, and widow of the Grand Duke Sergei, who was assassinated during the Revolution of 1905, is now abbess of the House of Mary and Martha in Moscow.

I saw a small but perfectly equipped hospital, with an operating room complete in all its details. The hospital had been devoted to poor women and children before the war. Now most of the wards are filled with wounded soldiers. I saw a room filled with blinded soldiers who were being taught to read Braille type[4] by sweet-faced nuns. Blindness is bitter hard for any man, but for illiterates, it must be blank despair. I saw a house full of refugee nuns from the invaded districts of Poland. I saw an orphanage full of slain soldiers' children. I lingered long in the lovely garden where nuns were at work, some with their habits tucked up among the potato rows, some pruning trees and hedges, some sweeping the gravel paths with besoms made of twigs, some teaching the orphan girls to embroider at big frames, to knit and to sew. They made a fascinating picture, and I could hardly leave them even to see the church, which is one of the most beautiful small gems of architecture to be found in Europe. I never really saw that church at all, as it turned out, for just as we entered and I was getting a first impression of its blue and white and gold beauty, a messenger hastily opened the door and said that the Grand Duchess wanted to see me.

We went back to the convent, and I was taken to a tiny parlor, which is the private retreat of the lady abbess. It is not much bigger than a hall bedroom, and it gave the same general impression of blue and white and gold that one sees throughout the place. There were many books bound in the lapis blue which seems to be the Grand Duchess's favorite color; a few pictures, mostly of the Madonna and Child; some small tables, one with Stephen Graham's book, "The House of Mary and Martha,"[5] held open upon it by a piece of embroidery carelessly dropped. There were easy chairs of English willow with blue cushions, and a businesslike little desk crammed with papers. Everywhere, in the window, on tables and the desk, were bowls and vases of flowers. Every room in the place, in fact, was filled with flowers.

The door opened and the Grand Duchess came in with a radiant smile of welcome and a white hand outstretched. "I am so glad to find that I had time to meet you to-day, Mrs. Dorr," she said, in a rarely sweet voice.

"Your highness speaks English?" I exclaimed in surprise, and she replied, waving me to a comfortable armchair: "Why not? My mother was English."

I had forgotten for the moment that the Grand Duchess and her younger sister, the former Empress of Russia, were daughters of Princess Alice of England and granddaughters of Queen Victoria. Russia seemed to have forgotten it also and to have remembered only that the father of these women was the Grand Duke of Hesse and the Rhine. The Grand Duchess added when we were seated that when she was a child at home, they always spoke English to their mother, if German to their father. "I welcome an opportunity to speak English, because if one is wholly Russian, as I am, and especially if one is orthodox, he hears little except Russian or French." Then she said, with another radiant smile: "Tell me what you think of my convent."

I told her that I felt as though I had stepped back into the glowing and romantic thirteenth century.

"That is just what I wanted my convent to be," she replied, "one of those busy, useful medieval types. Such convents were wonderfully efficient aids to civilization in the Middle Ages, and I don't think they should have been allowed to disappear. Russia needs them, certainly, the kind of convent that fills the place between the austere, enclosed orders and the life of the outside world. We read the newspapers here, we keep track of events, and we receive and consult with people in active life. We are Marys, but we are Marthas as well."

The Grand Duchess's interest in the outside world is patent. She asked me eagerly to tell her how things were going in Petrograd, and her face saddened when I told her of the riotous and bloody events I had witnessed during the days of the July Revolution, scarcely past. "Times are very bad with us just now," she said, "but they will improve soon, I am sure. The Russian people are good and kind at heart, but they are mostly children—big, ignorant, impulsive children. If they can find good leaders, and if they will only realize that they must obey their leaders, they will emerge from this dreadful chaos and build up a strong, new Russia. Have you seen Kerensky, and what do you think of him?"

I replied rather cautiously. Like everyone else, I still hoped that Kerensky would succeed in getting his released giant back into its bottle, and I did not want to unsettle anyone's confidence in him even to the extent of an expressed doubt. Kerensky, I told her, was greatly admired and liked, and I hoped he might prove the strong leader Russia needed in her trouble.

"I hope so," replied the last of the Romanovs, "I pray for him every day."

The bells of the little church chimed the hour softly, and the Grand Duchess paused to cross herself devoutly. "I want to hear about those wonderful public schools of yours," she said, "but first tell me what America is doing in war preparation."

As I talked, she listened, nodding and smiling as if immensely pleased. The great airplane fleet in the course of construction seemed to amaze and delight her, and when I told her of the conservation of the food supply and the restriction of the manufacture of alcohol, she fairly glowed. "America is simply stupendous," she exclaimed. "How I regret that I never went there. Of course, I never shall now. To me the United States stands for order and efficiency of the best kind. The kind of order only a free people can create. The kind I pray may be built some day here in Russia." And then she made her one allusion to the deposed Tsar. I did not know that at that minute the Tsar was on his way to Siberia, but it is very probable that she knew it. She said: "I am glad you are going to protect your soldiers from the danger of the drink evil. Nobody can possibly know how much good the abolition of vodka did our soldiers and all our people. I think history should give the Emperor credit for his share in that act, don't you?" I agreed that the Emperor should receive full credit for what he did, and I spoke with all sincerity.

Elizabeth Feodorovna kept me for nearly three-quarters of an hour talking to her about the Gary schools, which she is eager to see in Russia; about American women and their part in the war, and about welfare work for children, especially for tubercular and anemic children. "It is wonderful," she said with a sigh. "I can scarcely help envying you sinfully. Think of a great, young, hurrying nation that can still find time to study all these frightful problems of poverty and disease, and to grapple with them. I hope you will go on doing that, and still find more and more ways of bringing beauty into the lives of the workers. How can you expect workmen who toil all day in hot, hideous factories or on remote farms, with nothing in their lives but work and worry, to have beauty in their souls?"

She wanted eagerly to know about the women soldiers and said that she greatly admired their heroism. What was their life in camp like, and were they strong enough to stand the hardships? The Grand Duchess Sergei is a good feminist, and she agreed with me that in Russia's crisis, as in the situation in all countries created by the war, it had been completely demonstrated that women would have henceforth to play a role equally important and equally prominent as that of men.

They would have to share equally with men in the successful operation of the war whether on the battlefield or behind the lines. She had always had a special devotion to Jeanne d'Arc[6] and believed her to have been inspired by God. Other women also had been called by God to do great things.

"I am glad you like my convent," she repeated as we parted. "Please come again. You know that it does not belong to me anymore, but to the Provisional Government, but I hope they will let me keep it."

I hope they will. The House of Mary and Martha, with the beautiful woman in it, is one of the things new Russia can least afford to lose.

Notes

1. The Martha and Mary Convent of Mercy in the Possession of Grand Duchess Elizabeth Feodorovna or the Marfo-Mariinsky Convent was founded in 1908 by Grand Duchess Elizabeth Feodorovna. This convent was intended to assist sick, wounded, and maimed soldiers in their recovery, and to provide for the needs of the poor and orphans. Grand Duchess Elizabeth Feodorovna became its abbess. Her vision was to begin a religious community made up of women from all social strata that would merge the ideals of saints Martha and Mary, dedicated both to prayer and to serving the needs of the poor.
2. Cazalet, William Lewis (1862–1953) was a businessman born in Saint Petersburg whose British family lived in Russia until the 1917 October Revolution and held a major share in the Muir & Mirrielees trading company.
3. Gordeeva, Valentina Sergeevna (1863–1931) served as a lower-rank lady-in-waiting at the Russian Court and later became a nun at the Marfo-Mariinsky Convent. After the arrest of the Grand Duchess in 1917, she took the post of the abbess. She died in 1931 in exile in Turkestan (today's Kyrgyzstan).

4 Braille is a tactile writing system for the visually impaired. This system is named after its creator Louis Braille, a Frenchman who lost his sight as a result of a childhood accident.
5 Graham, Stephen (1884–1975) was a British journalist, travel writer, essayist, and novelist. His best-known books recount his travels around pre-revolutionary Russia and his journey to Jerusalem with a group of Russian Christian pilgrims. He published *The Way of Martha and the Way of Mary* in 1915.
6 Jeanne d'Arc (1412–31), anglicized as Joan of Arc, is a patron saint of France, honored as a defender of the French nation for her role in the siege of Orléans and her insistence on the coronation of Charles VII of France during the Hundred Years' War. Claiming to be acting under divine guidance, she became a military leader who transcended gender roles and gained recognition as a savior of France.

Chapter 16

THE *TAVARISHI* FACE FAMINE

The Romanovs gone, the Soviets apparently yielding to Kerensky's demand for a coalition government, and finally voting to give him almost supreme power, what then stood in the way of restoring order in the army and civil life? Readers of the dispatches in the daily press last September and later must have puzzled over this question. The fact is that while there were indications that the last convention held in Petrograd by the Russian Socialists, the so-called Democratic Council, ended in a partial victory for Kerensky, there remained every evidence that the Bolshevik element was still very strong. Kerensky succeeded in forming a coalition ministry, but the Petrograd Council of Soldiers' and Workmen's Delegates at the same time succeeded in electing a Bolshevik central executive committee with the notorious Leo Trotsky[1] as chairman, displacing N.C. Chkheidze,[2] the Georgian Duma member, prominent in the Council, but against whose sincerity and honesty I never heard a word.

Trotsky was elected because the Bolsheviki couldn't then get Lenin back. There were not enough bold spirits in the Democratic Council to force from the government a promise of immunity from arrest for Lenin, should he appear at a meeting, so he was kept in the background and Trotsky was made chairman of the Petrograd executive committee in his stead.

Lenin is the real leader of the Bolsheviki today, exactly as he was during the fateful days of July when he sent mutinous soldiers and idle workmen out on the streets of the capital with machine guns to murder the populace. Trotsky, however, is an able and faithful lieutenant. He is a Jew, and his real name is Bronstein. He is one of those Jews, unhappily too prominent in Russian affairs just now, who are doing everything in their power to prejudice the people of Russia against the race, and to check the movement for the full freedom of the Jews of the empire.

Trotsky, or Bronstein, is known to many in New York City. He gained some newspaper publicity when he arrived in New York from Spain a short time before the February Revolution. He posed as a martyr to socialist principles, one who had been persecuted by the governments of four countries—Russia, Germany and Spain. All four had expelled him, he said, for the crime of editing really successful socialist newspapers. Trotsky's story was founded on fact. At least four countries did find him as a citizen too undesirable to retain. Banishment from Russia, under the old regime, is no stigma, so we may begin Trotsky's saga in August 1914, the early days of the World War. He was editing a Jewish paper in Berlin. He was given a few hours to leave, he says, and with his family fled across the Swiss frontier to Zurich. From there he went to Paris, where he was miraculously able, poor as he had always been, and high as the price of white paper was soaring, to establish a socialist newspaper in the Russian language. When the Russian contingent of the Allied armies reached France in April 1916, *Our Words*, which was the name of Trotsky's spicy little sheet, was circulated free among the 65,000 soldiers. The motto of the paper was "Down with the War" far more than it was "Up with Socialism." It was filled from page one to page four with the sort of pro-German stuff that has done its deadly work with the men at the Russian front, inducing them to refuse to fight and thus opening their country to the German army.

The French government, which had its hands full with its own pet sedition raisers, had never before heard of Trotsky, but now it told him to move on. He did. He went to Spain, where he was arrested as an extreme troublemaker, and after a short time expelled from the country. He came to the United States, where he remained until the Russian Revolution of late February 1917, when he flew back to Petrograd. Trotsky always had money to make these long journeys. At Halifax he was halted, for the English government knew his record. The English authorities considered interning him for the duration of the war, but a lot of people interceded for the poor Russian exile, and he was allowed to go on to Russia. Poor Russia!

Trotsky was elected a member of the Petrograd Council of Workmen's and Soldiers' Delegates, being a pacifist and never having done any manual work. Last summer when I was in Russia I used to read almost daily in the accounts of the National Council of Soviets, or councils, burning speeches of Trotsky's in which he urged a separate peace with Germany, or what would amount to exactly the same thing, Russia's immediate cessation of fighting. Trotsky ridiculed the idea that abandonment of the allies would in any way injure Russia in a material way or soil the national honor. His ideas of economics and finance were simply and frequently reiterated. Arrest all capitalists and force them to disclose the secret of how they got rich and hang all the bankers—presumably as the first step toward seizing the contents of the banks. With this man as chairman of the central executive committee of the Petrograd Council of Workmen's and Soldiers' Council, and with the October revolt of the German naval men on five ships for him to point to as evidence that the social revolution is at hand in Germany, the life of the last coalition government was not likely to be peaceful.

But the end of the Bolsheviki is in sight in spite of Lenin, Trotsky and the entire majority in the Council of Soldiers' and Workmen's Delegates. It has been coming on stealthy feet for many months, and now the messengers' hands are on the latch. The messengers' names are Hunger and Cold.

When I went down to my first dinner in Petrograd last May, I was amazed to see the price on the menu card placed at five rubles fifty kopecks, about $1.80. In a previous visit to Petrograd I had eaten an excellent dinner in this same hotel and had paid for it one ruble seventy-five kopecks, or about seventy-five cents, as the ruble was then valued. The one offered for more than twice this amount consisted of a watery soup, a small piece of not very fresh fish, a thin slice of veal with peas and a water ice flavored with cherry juice. One piece of black bread without butter was served. If I wanted water to drink with the meal, I had to pay two rubles for bottled water, for one drink of plain water in Petrograd is an attempt at suicide by the typhoid route. If I wanted coffee, I had to pay one ruble sixty-five kopecks more, and after I added the customary 10 percent for the tip, my check was ten rubles and six kopecks. Three dollars and thirty-five cents.

This was bad enough, but before I left Russia the price of that meager meal had advanced to thirteen rubles and the quality of the dinner had sensibly declined. Also, the tip had advanced, for after a strike of waiters a system was adopted all over Russia, as far as I traveled, whereby tips were abolished and 15 percent was added to the bill by the hotel and restaurant proprietors.

You now pay an additional 15 percent of your entire hotel bill in Russia, which is distributed in tips to all the servants except the lift boys and the gorgeous individual who stands in front of the hotel door, who assists you to alight from your droshky when you arrive, and touches his peacock feather trimmed hat to you when you go in and out. He is called the Swiss, denoting the origin of his earliest predecessor, I imagine, and why he and the elevator men do not share in the general distribution, I never found out.

Walk down the Nevsky Prospect, or the Grand Morskaya, which begins in fine shops and ends in palaces, like Fifth Avenue. Wander through the maze of little shops in the huge arcade called the Gostiny Dvor. Go far out on the Nevsky, cross the beautiful Anichkov Bridge, with its four groups of rearing horses, and turn in at the Liteyny, where the cheaper shops are to be found, and try to buy something. It doesn't matter what, just try to buy something to eat, drink, wear or use. When the waiter brought in the coffee that morning, he said cheerfully, "Net moloko," no milk. Try to buy a few cans of condensed milk against a similar experience. I walked all over Petrograd trying to buy condensed milk, for the shortage of fresh milk was grave when I arrived and grew steadily worse. I found one can, for which I paid two dollars. Shortly afterward a friend arrived from Japan and gave me two cans, which she spared out of her store.

Russian illiteracy is so general that the shop signs are not written but illustrated. Brilliant signboards on the outside show pictures of what the shopkeeper has to sell. A dairy shop will have a picture of a cow, crocks of butter, chickens, ducks, geese, baskets of eggs, cheese of many varieties, and so forth. A greengrocer's signboard is decorated like a seed catalog cover, while a clothing store is advertised by pictures of clothes and hats that were fashionable perhaps ten years ago. It once added to the gay appearance of the streets, but just now it increases their anxious and ominous air. Hundreds of the shops are empty, the doors are locked, and the brilliant signboards alone remain to indicate that business was ever conducted there. One of the most mournful sights in Petrograd to me was an abandoned shop where they once sold French bread and pastry. I used to turn my head away from the mocking poster, picturing crisp white bread in yard-long loaves, delicious breakfast crescents, pâtés and cakes. The standard bread served in Russia at the present time is black, soggy, sour and indigestible. It is sold by weight, hence loaded with water and baked as little as possible to be bread and not dough. Someone has suggested that that bread was meant for food and drink together, and it is certain that it is so wet that it quickly mildews. But bad as it is scarce and expensive. A bread ticket calls for three-quarters of a pound, the daily allotment per person when I left at the end of August. This costs at the rate of ten kopecks a pound. It used to be three and a half kopecks a pound, and good bread, too.

Butter, when it can be bought at all, was three rubles a pound, about a dollar. Excellent butter a year or two ago was less than fifty kopecks a pound, for Russia was rapidly becoming a dairy country. And veal is about the only meat to be had, was nearly a dollar a pound. Feed for cattle is so scarce and so expensive that cows are not allowed to grow into beef size; hence the prevalence of veal. Chickens may vary the menu if you can afford to pay from three dollars upward. You could buy only a short weight half pound of meat a day per person, except for the Sunday dinner, when a pound was allowed.

Even at the Hotel Militaire, where I lived most of the time, and where the food supply came from government sources, we had veal or its derivatives, hash, croquettes, and so on, five days a week. Sometimes they offered what they called beef, but it wasn't. It was horsemeat, coarse and strong. Once a week or so we had chicken, a welcome change. When August came, we began to have game, grouse of various kinds mostly. Game is very plentiful in Russia and Finland this year because, since the war, men have hunted only one another. But game, which is a treat when you have it occasionally, is a punishment when you have it more than once or so a week. You detest it when it appears on the table three times a week, and if it appears more often, you choose a meatless day as an alternative.

Coffee was about a dollar and a half a pound, not so bad, and tea was even more moderate in price. What the Russian people would do if the tea gave out, I cannot imagine. Everybody drinks tea, scalding hot, several times a day. Even the babies drink tea, and it is a fact that in the best babies' hospital I saw in Russia, the head nurse proudly showed me, in a hot water table, a whole row of nursing bottles full of tea for the sick babies' evening repast. Tea they still have, but they are almost out of sugar to go with it. In a hotel or restaurant, they serve you with three very tiny lumps of sugar with each glass of tea, and that is all you can have. If for any reason you do not use all your sugar, you put it in your pocket. You do this whether you keep house or not, because you can't buy much candy, and when meat is scarce everybody craves sweets.

Sugar is not the only leftover one takes home. One day I went into the Vienna restaurant on the Gogol for dinner, sitting down at a table just vacated by a very smart young officer. He left behind him on the window ledge a little parcel neatly wrapped in white paper with a pink string. It might have been a jeweler's parcel. I picked it up with the impulse to hand it over to the waiter, but first as a matter of precaution, lest it should be really valuable, I opened a corner of the paper and examined the contents. A piece of fairly white bread as big as a small turnip, the remains of luncheon, perhaps, at the house of a rich friend. I went into a fashionable tea place in Moscow just before I left, and they served with the tea, in lieu of sugar, a kind of sticky preserve. I had with my sugarless tea a cake made without flour or sugar. It tasted like almond paste and the whole thing cost me a dollar and ten cents.

Most of the shops are closed, but before most of those that remain open you may see, at any hour of the day or night, a queue of people, men, women and children, waiting to get in and buy. The people often wait in line 24 hours or more. They wait days to buy some things. Go home from a visit or get in from a journey at any time of night, midnight, 3 a.m., any hour, and you see these long, patient, waiting lines of people. They curl up on the stones of the pavement and sleep; members of a family relieve one another at intervals, but everyone desperately hangs on to his place in the line.

Not only do all the small shopkeepers and the street peddlers have to replenish their poor little stocks by standing thus for days, but housekeepers have to feed and clothe their families that way. People who can afford servants, of course, send their servants to wait in line. The daily newspapers often contain the advertisement, "Wanted a queue maid," meaning a woman whose sole duty it is to sleep on the sidewalk and bring home next day's dinner.

It was summer when I was in Petrograd and Moscow. Sleeping on the sidewalk left something to be desired even in warm weather. The first hint of autumn was in the air when I left on August 30. By the first of October it was cold, and by the end of November it was frigid. When the storms and the driving snows of winter set in in earnest, people will not be able to sleep on the sidewalks. Where will they get food, and when starvation stares them in the face, what will they do? Russia's real crisis, political and economic, will come then, and the Bolsheviki will not be the people to overcome it.

Notes

1 Bronstein, Lev Davidovich better known as Leon Trotsky (1879–1940) was a Russian revolutionary and political theorist, a central figure in the 1905–1907 Revolution, the 1917 October Revolution, and in the Russian Civil War. In the early years of the Soviet government, Trotsky and Lenin were widely considered its two most prominent figures, and Trotsky was Lenin's de facto second-in-command from 1917 to 1923. Ideologically, Trotsky was a Marxist and a Leninist, and his ideas inspired a school of Marxism known as Trotskyism.
2 Chkheidze, Nikoloz (1864–1926) was a Georgian politician and statesman. In the 1890s, he promoted the Social Democratic movement in Georgia. From 1907 to 1917, Chkheidze was a member of the Russian State Duma and gained popularity as a spokesman for the Menshevik faction of the Russian Social Democratic Party. He was a key figure in the 1917 February Revolution as the Menshevik president of the Committee of the Petrograd Soviet.

Chapter 17

GENERAL JANUARY, THE CONQUEROR

After Napoleon Bonaparte's defeated legions had fled from Russia to freeze and starve and die by thousands in a frenzied attempt to get back to France,[1] the victorious commander of the Russian army said that his two greatest aides had been General January and General February. The relentless cold and storm of a Russian winter were foes too strong for Bonaparte to conquer. They sent him to St. Helena, and the same strong foes this winter are going to rout and banish the Bolsheviki. The Russian Revolution began with a bread riot, and it will culminate in a bread riot. When the people of Russia get hungry enough, they are going to stop talking about "no annexations or contributions," "all the power to the Soviets," and the rest, and demand a government that shall govern, and as soon as possible put the country back on a normal basis. When the thermometer falls to 45 degrees below zero, and a fifty-miles-an-hour wind is driving sleet and snow in their faces, people can no longer stand 24 hours in line to buy food for their children. Especially when their clothes are thin and worn and their boots are dropping off their feet.

I have told something about the food situation in Russia. The clothing situation and the fuel situation are, if anything, worse. If you want to buy a pair of shoes in Petrograd, you must take two days to do it and you must put a lot of money in your purse. There is an American shoe store on the Nevsky Prospect and every day the line of people trying to get in and buy shoes was so great that it blocked traffic, and the city authorities finally had to close the street entrance. The line now forms in a court or lane in the rear of the store and the customers are admitted, a few at a time, through the back door. This American shoe store is very popular because the shoes are of excellent quality and the prices are regarded as reasonable. A woman can buy a pair of boots there as low as $25. Men's shoes are somewhat dearer. But the stock was running low when I was there in the summer, and when it gives out I don't see how they are going to replenish it. On a corner of the Grand Morskaya there was another shoe store, in front of which a crowd stood all day long and all night. The queue extended around the corner, and I have seen it when it stretched to the Moika Canal a very long block away. This is a store where cheaper shoes were sold. It represented an attempt on the part of one of the fleeting ministries to relieve the shoe shortage. Large quantities of shoes and leather were purchased and were then being distributed through authorized channels in the shop on the Morskaya.

In order to buy a pair of those shoes, a man or a woman went there and got a place in line. Each stood in line until his or her turn came to be admitted to the shop, a long and weary business. When he gained admission to the shop and the clerk got around to waiting on him, he received—a pair of shoes? Not a bit of it. He got a ticket with a number on it. The ticket enticed the customer to come back at some future date, stand in line and claim a pair of shoes that were probably at the time being made—provided he could afford to pay a minimum of ten dollars for them.

When I was in Poland with the women soldiers, the Botchkareva's Battalion of Death, the regiment was delayed in its further progress toward the fighting line by a dearth of boots in which to march. About half the women soldiers received boots along with their other equipment before they left Petrograd, but the other half wore, with their khaki uniform, the women's shoes, often worn and tattered, in which they had enlisted. One day there was great rejoicing in the barracks. The boots had come, and the rest of the afternoon was spent in sorting out from the pile a pair to fit each girl. I was interested in those boots, for they were mute but eloquent witnesses of the poverty of life in Russia. Not a pair was new. They were all second-hand, remade and mended boots, and I strongly suspect that most of them had been taken off the feet of dead soldiers. They had, in many cases, new feet or new soles, but the majority of them were merely mended and patched. Coarse, stiff, malodorous and badly put together as these were, the girls were only too glad to get them. The Adjutant, Skrydlova and one or two of the well-to-do soldiers had their boots made to order, and they paid ninety dollars a pair for them. Seventy-five dollars for a pair of women's boots is not an unheard-of price.

What is true of boots and shoes is true of almost every other clothing commodity. I ran out of gloves while I was in Russia, but, after hearing what gloves cost in Petrograd, I went without. You could get cotton gloves as low as a dollar and eighty cents a pair. They were ugly and shapeless, but people bought and wore them. If you wanted a pair of kid gloves and you knew where you could find them and had time, you could buy them for three to five dollars. They were the kind that an American department store might put on a table in the center aisle and sell for fifty cents to attract customers in the dull season. A man pays a dollar for a fifteen-cent collar in Petrograd. He pays several dollars for a decent pair of socks. What he pays for a suit of clothes staggers the imagination. There are only two things that are cheap to buy in Russia just now: cats and dogs. You can buy a magnificent wolfhound or other thoroughbred dog, or a pure-bred Persian or Angora cat for a song in Petrograd, because people can't afford to feed pet animals. Mr. Basil Miles, attached to the Root mission, took home with him two Russian wolfhounds that are going to make him the most envied man in the next dog show in his town, and the song he sang to get them was too short to mention.

Russia is a very cold country and almost everyone, rich and poor alike, wears furs. The rich wear sable, mink and ermine, and the poor wear rabbit and sheepskin. But furs just now are as difficult to buy as other clothing indispensables. There are several special reasons for this shortage of fur in a fur country. There are not so many people hunting furs since the war, and the pelts are scarcer; and besides, the Russians have never cured and dyed their own furs. They sent them to Germany to be prepared for market, and, of course, the war put a stop to that. Aside from these special reasons, the fur shortage and all the food, clothing and other shortages are caused by two main obstacles. There is plenty of food in the empire, plenty of raw materials for clothing. But the transportation system has almost broken down, and they cannot distribute food or raiment. Also the factory system has all but broken down, and they cannot produce the clothing. There are besides minor and contributory obstacles, some of which I shall describe. The main reason why Russia will starve and freeze this winter is that the people of Russia have allowed their railroad system to go to pieces, and because they have, to an almost incredible extent, ceased to do any work.

I cannot speak as an expert about the railroad situation, nor would mere figures and statistics give the reader any adequate picture of the railroad demoralization. To say that on May 15, 1917, the then Minister of Ways and Communications[2] reported to the Duma that more than 25 percent of the total number of locomotives in the empire were laid up for repairs wouldn't begin to express the thing. The average reader does not know that 5 percent of "sick" locomotives is considered high by competent railroad managers. I might go further and say that the number of freight cars loaded from May 15 to May 31, 1917, was 87,000 poods less than the number loaded between those dates in 1916, but that would not mean much. Few outside of Russia know what a pood is. As a matter of fact, it is thirty-six pounds. But figures cannot adequately describe the situation.

What told the tale of railroad demoralization to me was the constant anxiety I heard voiced on all sides by people trying to buy their winter stock of wood and coal. There is an endless quantity of wood in Russia. Great forests of pine and cedar and birch—beautiful forests. I had often marveled at them from the windows of my railway carriage passing through Finland and the country between Petrograd and Moscow. Plenty of this wood has been cut. I saw thousands and thousands of cords of it piled up along the railroad tracks, and of course there must have been much more elsewhere. Petrograd is built on a marsh and the ground is drained by picturesque if rather badly smelling canals which run through the city and empty into the Neva. Down one of the widest of these—the Moika, which I crossed every day—a constant line of barges, loaded with wood, floated slowly, drawn by horses and sometimes by men walking along a towpath beside the canal. I used to watch those bargeloads of wood and wonder why, with such an almost unparalleled means of distributing wood after it got there, the people of Petrograd should be troubled about the winter fuel supply. Not nearly enough of it was getting there last summer; that was all. The quantity that floated down the Moika and the other canals and got stacked up in woodyards and in the courtyards of apartment houses, hotels, hospitals, factories and even palaces, was not half the normal quantity. There weren't enough flat cars and locomotives running to get the wood as far as the city limits.

I tried the experiment of keeping house with the wife of the *Outlook* correspondent after he left Russia on a mission. We had a charming little apartment offered to us rent free, with a maid thrown in, if we would live in it and keep it from being looted. Everyone who knew a Cossack or other reliable soldier, or an American, did that when they went to the country from Petrograd. We gave up housekeeping after a week and went back to hotels, partly because the maid could not get us enough to eat, and partly because we never had any hot water. The landlord of the apartment house had cut off the wood. He said that he couldn't get enough wood to warm the house next winter, much less provide warm baths for the tenants in summer.

The railroad situation was visualized for me on a dreadful two days and nights' journey I took on a Russian railroad last July. Miss Beatty, of the San Francisco *Bulletin*, was with me, and the train was so small and so crowded that the only berth we could get was an upper one three feet wide. The two of us slept in that berth. Miss Beatty's head one way and mine the other. Every time the train struck a rough place on the rails, the *Bulletin* came near losing its star reporter, for she had the outside, just above an open window. That railway carriage could have seated, by close crowding, eleven passengers. On the last night of the journey, 25 people were packed into it. They took turns sitting down.

Every railroad train you get on is about as crowded as that, and one of the most difficult things to buy at present is a railroad ticket. To buy one, you usually have to bribe the ticket agent or the hotel manager. You go to the office of the International Wagons-Lits[3] and tell them that you want to go to Moscow or Kazan. You want to go tomorrow or in three days, some near date. The clerk shakes his head. "I might be able to get you a ticket and a berth in three days," he will say. "Of course, you will have to pay a supplement; say, sixty rubles." Pressed for particulars he will explain that someone will have to be paid to stand in line for the ticket. I paid forty rubles extra to Bennet's, which is the Cook's[4] of Petrograd, for a ticket to Moscow, and that was considered a bargain. When I wanted to return, I asked the hotel management in Moscow how much they would charge to send to the station and get me a ticket, and they said one hundred rubles. The ruble was then about thirty cents, so I would have had to pay, in addition to the cost of the ticket, which had just been raised about 50 percent, thirty dollars. I got the ticket in almost the only other way possible. I acted as a courier carrying confidential papers from a foreign consulate in Moscow to an embassy in Petrograd, and the consul used his official influence to get me a ticket for the regular price only.

On the 21st of July, the minister of ways and communications ordered a reduction of 50 percent in the number of travelers passing between Petrograd and Moscow. In view, he explained, of the shortage of fuel and rolling stock, soon it will be next to impossible to buy, for love or money, a ticket or a sleeping berth between the two points in Russia.

This is nearly true now on the Trans-Siberian Railroad. Every Tuesday evening at 8 o'clock, the weekly express on that famous line leaves the Nikolai station, Petrograd, and every berth is filled every week. What those passengers paid extra for their tickets forms one of the principal topics of conversation during the long trip over Siberia. The passengers beguile the weary journey, swapping experiences of how they came to be there at all. I have known people who waited weeks for a chance to pay the extortionate supplement. The Trans-Siberian post train, which leaves every night and makes stops along the way, is a sight to behold before it leaves. The people crowd the train platform and fight for a place near the edge. As the train backs slowly into the station shed, the travelers run to meet it, climb in the windows, drag their women and children in, rush the platforms and fight like tigers to get in the doors. The number of carriages to each train has been reduced gradually until now the train is too short to hold the travelers.

But didn't we send a railroad commission to Russia, and didn't the papers say something about some 5,000 locomotives and 23,000 freight cars sent to Vladivostok? We did send a railroad commission, headed by John Stevens,[5] of Panama Canal fame, one of the greatest organizers and executives in the United States. This commission has done good work. It has shown the Russians how they could immediately increase the efficiency of their railroads by 60 percent. We have sent many locomotives and freight cars to Russia. Nevertheless, the transportation problem remains unsolved.

Notes

1 The French invasion of Russia (June 24–December 24, 1812) was initiated by Napoleon with the aim of compelling the Russian Empire to comply with the continental blockade of the United Kingdom. Snowfall and frost complicated Napoleon's retreat from Moscow. Shortages of food and winter attire for the soldiers and provisions for the horses, combined with guerrilla warfare from Russian peasants, resulted in significant losses.
2 The minister of ways and communications (Minister of Transport) from March to July 24 (August 6), 1917 was Nikolai Vissarionovich Nekrasov (1879–1940), an engineer, a Russian liberal politician (a Constitutional Democrat – *kadet*) and the last governor-general of Finland.
3 The International Wagons-Lits was a Belgian-founded French company known for providing and operating luxury trains with sleepers and dining cars during the late nineteenth and the twentieth centuries.
4 Thomas Cook & Son was a travel agency in London that also published a series of travel guidebooks for tourists in the nineteenth to twentieth centuries.
5 Stevens, John Frank (1853–1943) was an American civil engineer who built the Great Northern Railway in the United States and was the chief engineer on the Panama Canal from late 1905 to April 1907. When leaders of the Provisional Government appealed to the U.S. president Woodrow Wilson for help with their transportation systems and overall ability to stay in the war, Stevens was selected to chair a board of prominent U.S. railroad experts sent to Russia to rationalize and manage the transit system that was in disarray.

Chapter 18

WHEN THE WORKERS OWN THEIR TOOLS

John Stevens, head of the railroad commission sent to Russia from the United States, has shown the Russian government how to increase its transportation facilities 60 percent. In a report made public in mid-August, Mr. Stevens said that the chief cause of the railroad crisis was bad management. Locomotives traveled 2,800 versts a month when they could be made to travel 5,000 versts. A verst is about three-quarters of a mile. Twice as much freight as was being hauled could be carried, said Mr. Stevens. Freight cars were constantly being sent out only half loaded. Mr. Stevens recommended government dictatorship of all railroads, both publicly and privately owned. That was rather naive, considering that the government was powerless to control, much less to dictate to, any department of activity in the empire. A little earlier, Mr. Nekrasov, then minister of ways and communications, issued a circular in which he outlined his plan for coping with the railroad crisis. He advised turning the entire railroad system over to the workmen, the engineers, firemen, conductors and machinists. A shriek of protest went up from the engineering profession and a howl of laughter arose from the press of Russia. But the fact of the matter is that the railroads were and are still, for all practical purposes, in the hands of the working people, and so is every other industry in Russia.

One of the great dreams of the socialists and philosophical anarchists is of the day when the worker shall own his tools, as they put it, when all industry shall be owned by the people who operate the machines, and all profits shall be shared by them. It really is a great dream and will probably be realized in some measure someday. But not now. The human race is not yet educated to such a utopia. The strongest proof that the capitalistic system is not yet ready to pass is the well-known fact that the secret ambition of almost every human being in every walk of life is to become a capitalist, large or small. This has just been proved on an enormous scale in Russia. The workers have seized the factories, shops, department stores and offices, and in no instance of which I could learn, and I searched diligently, have they used their great opportunity wisely or unselfishly for the common good. They have used it to get all the money possible out of the employers and to render back the minimum of service.

This is what is the matter with the transportation system in Russia. It is the reason why the people of Petrograd, Moscow and other cities will go cold and hungry this winter, one reason why the death rate of children and old people, already appallingly large, will grow more appalling within the next few months; one reason, and a very strong one, why order has not been restored in Russia. High as are the prices of all food and manufactured articles, the working people, as a class, have enough money to pay for them, and not until the merchants' stocks are completely gone and the weather gets too cold to stand in line for long hours in order to buy will the purblind workers realize their situation. Not until then will they realize what their selfishness and cruel folly have done to themselves and the entire working class of the country.

So struck was I by the scarceness of goods in the shops and the soaring prices of almost every article that I went to the minister of labor[1] and asked him to tell me something of industrial conditions of the country. I was not entirely ignorant of those conditions. I knew, for example, that Russia is not exclusively an agricultural country, that, on the contrary, her development as a manufacturing country has been going on by leaps and bounds, especially in the last dozen years. Russia has a proletariat and a factory system, although not quite as large proportionately as those of the United States. Her iron industry, her cotton mills, her machine shops are enormous and in normal times they are wonderfully productive. After the suppressed revolution of 1905-06 important reforms in the land laws were enacted, and for the first time the peasants were given their lands in fee simple. That is, they were given an opportunity in certain circumstances to take title to their share in communal lands. This gave them an opportunity to sell if they chose, and a large number of peasant artisans did sell their lands, moved into the cities and became factory workers. Before this time the factory workers had more or less alternated between town and rural life.

The leaders of the Social Democratic Party encouraged by every means in their power the selling of lands by peasant owners, because they wanted the workers to move to town, organize in labor unions and become a political power. In their own words, they wanted to create a landless working class, one which, having no stake in property, would the more easily revolt against the government and more heartily support the movement to create a cooperative commonwealth. It was good reasoning up to a certain point. A man with a piece of land thinks twice before he puts that land in danger of being absorbed by his neighbors. He hesitates before he takes a course of action which might turn even a bad government out at least. The bad government protects his title. But the leaders of the Social Democrats left an important human element out of their reasoning. A landless man makes a good revolutionist, it is true, but he does not necessarily make a good cooperator. Nine and three-quarters times in ten, he is just as strong for number one as the real estate owner. When he gets a chance to grab power and money, he does it, and he divides up just as little as the others let him.

A story is told in Russia which illustrates this trait of character. Someone asked a peasant of Little Russia what he would do if he were made czar. "I'd steal a hundred rubles and run away," was the prompt reply. In a word, that is virtually what the working people of Russia did as soon as the Revolution of February 1917 made them into individual tsars of Russia.

When I called on the minister of labor and asked him what was the matter with industry, his face assumed an expression of mingled amusement and despair. "If you really want to know," he said, in effect, "go and look at some of our factories."

I was given an official document, elaborately stamped and signed, authorizing me to enter and inspect any factory in Petrograd, and I began, bright and early the next morning, with one of the largest munitions factories in the Vyborg district[2] of the city. I showed my pass to the man at the gate, who read it doubtfully, and said he didn't think it was good. "What right has the Minister of Labor to give you permission to visit this plant?" he inquired. "If anybody had a right to give you such permission, I should think it would be the minister of war, for only war materials are manufactured here. Anyhow, I don't think you can get in."

I asked him mildly if he was sure that he had the power to keep me out, and I suggested that he put the case up to a higher authority, the manager, for instance. He turned to a wall telephone in his little gate house and conversed with someone at the other end of the line. Then he said: "The committee is in session and will see you."

A long walk through the enormous yard and past many shops brought me to the office building of the plant, and there, in a small room, I found the committee, that is, the group of workmen elected by the entire working force of the factory to manage the industry and to fix all conditions of labor. Every industry in Russia is thus managed. I had a long talk with this committee, but I did not get into the factory. The man would not permit me to get in. They wouldn't even allow me to see anyone connected with the office force. Kindly but firmly they gave me to understand that they were all the power there was in that plant, and they could give me all the information I could possibly need. So, I sat there for an hour or so, and, through my interpreter, learned how manufacturing is carried on when the workers own their tools.

Because I could carry but few notes out of the country, I am not certain how many delegates per thousand workers make up a committee of management in a Russian factory, but I think each unit of one hundred men elects a representative. Perhaps there are two hundred men to the unit. My memory for numbers is not always reliable. At all events, the committee members, who are usually the intelligent and highly paid workers, do no work except committee work. But they draw their full pay. The employer has no voice in the conduct of his own business. The committee tells him how much he pays his employees, what their hours of work are, when they arrive and when they depart and how much they produce. And the employer pays the committee for its kind words and deeds. I asked the particular committee which thus informed me if this seemed fair to the employer. Mostly the men said they thought it did. One man asked me who in my opinion ought to pay the committee members. I told him I thought the workers might pay at least a part of their salaries, and perhaps also give the employers a casting vote in case of a tie, or something like that. They seemed to find the idea humorous, all except one fine, thoughtful young fellow, who said: "There may be an element of unfairness in some of the present conditions, but time will adjust them. There is no question but that the workers should own the industries, and they will. The working class has never had a square deal and now that they have seized the powers of government, nothing less than confiscation of industries will satisfy them."

The working class in Russia has had rather less of a square deal than any other in the modern world, it is true. The factory system being comparatively new in Russia, there has not been time for the workers to organize closely, and under the autocracy there was little or no chance to obtain enlightened factory legislation. There was hardly a chance for the Russian workman to attain a very high degree of skill in many industries. He could not, as a rule, learn the finest processes of his trade, because until the war broke out most of those processes were in the hands and under the control of Germany. When I was in Russia in 1906, one of the most striking things to me was the prevalence of German shopkeepers, German managers, German foremen. You hardly ever saw a Russian in command of any industry. I spoke of this to a Russian friend and told him that I should not like to see in my country all the business controlled by foreigners, for these Germans were not even Russian citizens. He shrugged his shoulders and said "*Nichego,*" which means almost anything and is a general expression of indifference or resignation to the inevitable. "We have no heads for that sort of thing, we Russians," he apologized.

"But what if you should ever go to war with Germany?" I asked. And he, sobered a little, said: "We should have to learn to be businessmen and skilled mechanics, in that case, and we should have a devil of a time doing it."

Eight years later, almost to a day, they did go to war with Germany, and they did have a devil of a time adjusting their industries to meet the crisis caused by the exodus of thousands of highly skilled German managers and department heads in hundreds of factories and shops throughout the empire.

One story told to me in Moscow is representative, I believe. A very large factory taken over by the government for the fine toolmaking facilities its machines afforded was found to be managed exclusively by German foremen and managers. Not only had they drawn large salaries for years in that factory, but they had insisted on hiring for the last processes and the most highly skilled jobs workmen from Germany. They didn't want, or rather the German government didn't want, the Russian people to know how to do skilled work. They wanted to keep Russia in exactly the right condition for permanent commercial exploitation by the fatherland.

I go into this because I think it is only fair to the Russian working class to explain that they have not been allowed to develop the intelligence and skill which the English and American working classes have done. Because of this ignorance, the Russians of the working class have, in their few months' debauch of liberty and the control of industry, wrecked their country industrially and have brought themselves and their own people to the verge of starvation. They have done to their class approximately what the mutinous soldiers at the front did to the men who wanted to go forward and fight—shot them in the back. I know this because I have seen it. The next factory I approached the committee let me in.

Notes

1 The minister of labor from March to September 25 (October 8), 1917 was Skobelev, Matvey Ivanovich (1885–1938), a Russian Marxist revolutionary (Menshevik) and politician.
2 The Vyborg district of Saint Petersburg became the city's largest industrial center in the late nineteenth century. It had, among others, New Arsenal, Rosenkrantz's copper-rolling and piping mill, Phoenix metal works, Ludvig Nobel and Gustav Lessner's machine-building factory, Ericsson's electrotechnical companies. During World War I, it was home to the city's largest munitions factory. The February Revolution of 1917 broke out in that district when female factory workers went on strike to protest against chronic food shortages. Other workers joined the rallies, which culminated in a garrison revolt and eventually the abdication of Nicholas II as the crisis spread nationwide.

Chapter 19

WHY COTTON CLOTH IS SCARCE

When I got on the train to leave Russia for the United States, the first familiar face I saw was that of Mr. Daniel Cheshire, mill owner and operator of Petrograd. "I'm going home to England to enlist," he said, as we shook hands.

"What have you done with your mills?" I asked.

"I have left them to the *Tavarishi*," replied Mr. Cheshire, "I thought I might as well."

Daniel Cheshire is not the only large manufacturer who has abandoned his business after a vain struggle to cope with the situation created by the Russian Revolution, and the taking over by the working people of the control of industry. Others have given up the struggle, and many more will probably follow their example. But Mr. Cheshire's story I know at first hand. His abandonment of his mills is full of significance, partly because of the importance of his branch of manufacturing and partly because his act may hasten the day when, through sheer lack of the necessities of life, the Russian people will cease pursuing their utopian dream and will content themselves with a government which, although still capitalistic, will rescue them from starvation and ruin.

Those who think of Russia as a land of snow and ice will be interested to learn that in Turkestan and Transcaucasia as well as in other provinces of the south and east, they raise millions of pounds of very good cotton, the seeds of which originally came from America. Those who think that every Russian peasant does nothing but farm will be surprised to hear that over a million Russians work in textile mills, principally cotton textiles.

When cotton spinning and weaving began in Russia the mill owners, in most cases, sent to England for their foremen and managers, and the descendants of some of these Englishmen still live and still manage cotton mills in Russia. The Cheshire family is a case in point. The original Cheshire went out from Manchester in the 1840s to manage a small cotton spinning factory in Petrograd. He saved money, bought a partnership and enlarged the business. His sons enlarged it still more, and today his grandchildren own and operate ten large cotton mills in and around Petrograd. Daniel Cheshire, a keen young man of thirty-something, is head of the family and chief owner of the mills. That is, he was up to February 1917. After that, he wasn't. The *Tavarishi*, or "comrades," whose wages he paid, became the virtual owners then, and on August 30, 1917, they became, temporarily at least, the sole owners.

It was in one of the Cheshire cotton mills that I got the most intimate view of what becomes of industry when the workers own their tools. Perhaps it would be fairer to say, when the workers seize their tools. Someday, perhaps, they will find out how to own them honestly and then they will use them wisely and for the common good.

It was a happy accident that first led me into a Cheshire cotton mill. After being refused permission to inspect the big munition works to which I applied—refused by the workers' committee, not by the proprietors—I wandered through the Vyborg district of Petrograd until I found another large factory. This time the permit given to me by the Minister of Labor worked better, and I was shown into the general office of the plant. It was a big, modern, up-to-date office, furnished with the usual desks, files, safes and the like, but to remind me that I was in revolutionary Russia, the walls were decorated with many red flags and banners inscribed with white-lettered mottoes and declarations. The head of the workmen's committee, who came forward to meet me, looked a little doubtful about letting me go through the mill, but just then the door opened and a strapping young Englishman came in. "See the works?" said he. "Of course you may. I'd like nothing better than to show my mills just now to newspaper people. I call them my mills yet, but only for a joke."

He said something in Russian to the workman, who shrugged his shoulders and stood aside, and Mr. Cheshire and I went into the nearest mill room. It was a storeroom, as a matter of fact, the receiving room for the huge bales of coarse yarn spun in another mill. The bales were soft and made excellent beds, a fact that was not overlooked, for two tired Russian millworkers reposed blissfully on a pile of bales as we passed through, sleeping the sleep of the just. They were not the only sleepers I saw in that mill. Several women were taking naps on piles of cloth near their machines, and a great many of the workers, men and women, might as well have been asleep, for they were doing no work. One woman was displaying a new pair of shoes to a group of other women, who stopped their machines to look. Shoes are so expensive in Russia at present that a new pair is worth looking at, I admit, but they might have postponed the exhibition until closing time. These women stood and discussed the shoes, from every point of view, apparently, nor did they go back to their machines when we stopped and discussed the women.

"Do you mean to tell me that you cannot order them back to their work?" I asked.

"Oh, I can order them," was the reply. "But if they choose not to go that would make me look rather foolish, wouldn't it?"

"You could discharge them, couldn't you?" I countered.

"I certainly could not," declared Mr. Cheshire. "Nobody can discharge an employee until the shop committee has sat on the case and decided that it does not want the man or woman in the mill. All I can do is to make my complaints to the committee and ask it to act."

Mr. Cheshire was born in Russia and has lived there all his life except for a few years spent in an English school. Yet he speaks the English of his grandfather, the same unmistakable little Lancashire burr. He has the Lancastrian's sense of humor also, and he laughed even when he told me of the demoralization and ruin in which the fantasies of the revolution had plunged his business. The utter absurdity of it was as present in his mind as the disaster.

"Look at that man," he said, pointing to a machine at which a man sat and wound cotton cloth into huge round cylinders. "He and the others at his particular job have had their wages raised to sixteen rubles (about $5.25) a day. Yes, of course. The committee decides on the wage scale. I am not consulted. Even if I were, I should have nothing except a complimentary vote, one against hundreds. That chap gets sixteen rubles a day, and in addition I must hire a girl at four rubles a day to lift the roll of cloth off the machine."

We passed into a print room still discussing the committee. I asked Mr. Cheshire if it was true that these workmen committees were highly paid men who performed no service to their employers and still received their regular pay.

"It is true," he replied. Then he went on to tell me the following story: "The work we do in this room is something a little unusual in Russia. Few mills have these machines as yet, and our product is almost the only cotton goods of the kind possible to buy in Russian markets since the war. Before that a great deal of it was imported from England and Germany. Naturally it is scarce at present, and not long ago one of our men complained that he couldn't buy it at all. 'Of course you cannot,' I told him, 'because these mills are turning out very little of it. Go into the print room and see for yourself how many machines are idle for lack of workers.' And then I made him this offer, for he was a member of the committee: 'Let me have four men of your committee back to work on these machines, and I will guarantee that you will soon be able to buy the goods you want.' Well, he agreed, and he got the rest of the committee to agree, and I got the men back. But what do you think those four men demanded? They said that they had been doing hard mental work on the committee for two months, and they thought before they went back to the machines, they ought to have a month's vacation with pay. I did draw the line there. I told them I'd close the works first. But since then, I understand that the committee has begun to discuss the two months on and one month off as a future policy. They say that mental work—they call committee meetings mental work—is much harder than physical labor."

"I'm glad they are finding it out," I remarked. "Perhaps after a while they will discover that even you belong to the proletariat."

"If they raise the wages again," said Mr. Cheshire, "I mean to ask them to give me a job. I'll have to. Then they'll have some real mental work finding out how to pay me or themselves either. This factory and all the others in our name have been running farther and farther behind for months. Soon we shall have to close. We should have been closed before now except that we hoped that a strong government would be formed and industry as well as the army and navy would be placed under a dictatorship."

The committees have created an eight-hour day in this particular industry. Some industries have a six-hour day, and I was told that numbers of working people claimed that a two-hour day was the ideal toward which they aspired. I heard also, on good authority, that certain groups favored a complete cessation of all factory work during the three hot months of summer.

Mr. Cheshire's mills were supposed to run eight hours a day, but he declared that he would be satisfied, in present circumstances, to get a good, solid five hours' work out of his people. If they would stay on the job and actually produce for five hours every working day, he thought he might avert bankruptcy. "We close at five," he told me. "But along about 4 o'clock you watch them begin to go home."

I watched and they did. Man after man and woman after woman stopped all work and began to put on their shoes. Many millworkers work barefoot. They gathered in little knots at a window and looked out, talking aimlessly. They strolled about the rooms. Some just stopped work and went out. At half past four in the rooms through which I walked, not half the machines were running.

"Is it really like this in all the mills and factories of Russia?" I asked, "or is this mill an exception to the rule? Is it worse than the average?"

"It is no worse than most," was the reply. "It is better than some. Industrial Russia has completely broken down in some places. It is rapidly breaking down everywhere."

What I saw afterward absolutely confirmed this statement. The industrial world is as much in the hands of the Bolsheviki or extremists as are the councils of workmen's and soldiers' delegates. While the Provisional Government of the early weeks of the revolution discussed ways and means whereby the workers in mills and factories might gradually acquire an interest in their industries and a voice in the councils of the managers, the workers settled the whole thing by turning the employers out and taking over the industries themselves. They have voted themselves enormous salaries, short hours and little work. But they have done little or nothing to ensure the permanence of the salaries. Soon there will be, instead of an eight-hour day, no working day at all. All the shops and factories will close.

In Moscow is the largest and finest department store in Russia. It is an English concern, the Muir & Mirrielees,[1] managed and largely owned by Mr. William L. Cazalet. I know him well, and his testimony, when I saw him in August, bore out this statement. The committee in the Muir & Mirrielees voted that they found it inconvenient to have clerks and other employees go home for lunch at different hours. They therefore ordered the store closed every day from 12 to 2 o'clock. The store was accordingly closed.

"I don't mind," said Mr. Cazalet cheerfully. "My stocks are running low, the transportation system is on the verge of collapse, and I can't get any more goods. As each line of goods is exhausted, I shall close the department. When the time comes, I shall close the store and go home to England for a vacation."

He will go, as Daniel Cheshire went, others will follow, and the workers will own their tools. They won't own anything else.

Notes

1 Muir & Mirrielees was an iconic and pioneering shop in Moscow at the end of the Imperial Era. Founded by two Scotsmen in St. Petersburg in 1857, it moved to Moscow in the 1880s and was the country's first department store, selling everything from furniture and perfume to cuddly toys.

Chapter 20

MRS. PANKHURST IN RUSSIA

Emmeline Pankhurst, the English militant suffrage leader, known to thousands in this country, went to Russia in late June of this year to organize the women of the country and help them to support the Provisional Government and to oppose the Bolsheviki or extremists. She succeeded in organizing a group of strong and influential women leaders, and she might have accomplished great good had not Kerensky frowned on the movement. Mrs. Pankhurst's project, in my opinion, was one of Kerensky's many lost opportunities.

This will answer a natural curiosity on the part of the reader as to why Mrs. Pankhurst came to be in revolutionary Russia. She went of her own initiative and under the auspices of her suffrage organization, the Women's Social and Political Union,[1] but her plan had the warm approval of the English premier, Mr. Lloyd George,[2] who personally issued her passport and that of her secretary, Jessie Kenney.[3] Mr. Lloyd George also gave directions that Mrs. Pankhurst and Miss Kenney should be allowed to travel on the only passenger boat that plies regularly between Great Britain and Norway. This boat is strongly convoyed, and it is used by very few people not in the service of the English government. No one in England has a higher esteem for Mrs. Pankhurst than Lloyd George, and since the beginning of the war the two erstwhile enemies have become friends and allies. Mrs. Pankhurst's suffragettes fired a house that Mr. Lloyd George was building in the country, and Mrs. Pankhurst was sentenced to three years' penal servitude for the deed. She had served several weeks of the sentence, in hunger strike intervals which extended over a year or more, when the war broke out and all internal feuds were declared off in England. The Pankhurst at once called a truce of militancy and ever since have done yeoman service in recruiting for the army, collecting money for war sufferers, especially in Serbia, and in many other lines of patriotic work.

The whole world admired the statesmanship of this policy, but only a few people know how really statesmanlike it was. Among those who do know is the English premier, for without it he might not have become premier. In abandoning militancy, Mrs. Pankhurst and her daughter Christabel[4] were actuated by two motives: they wanted England and the allies to win the war, and they saw in the war an opportunity to further the cause of woman suffrage. They were under no delusion that a grateful country would bestow the vote on its women as a reward for their unselfish war services. Women have rendered the noblest kind of service in all the wars that have ever been fought, but no country ever showed its gratitude by making them citizens for it. Witness our civil war. Mrs. Pankhurst and Christabel knew that suffrage would come in England when the political situation suffered certain changes, and it would come in no other way.

They were in France in July 1914, Mrs. Pankhurst out of prison under the famous the Cat and Mouse Act[5] and resting up for another bout with the Holloway jailers.[6] Christabel lived in Paris and edited there the British suffragette weekly newspaper. They watched with deep emotion the mobilization of the French army and saw the French women drop all their other activities and mobilize for hospital and relief work. They agreed that they must go back to England and organize their women for the same work, and they said: "At last! A chance to get rid of Asquith[7] and Sir Edward Grey!"[8]

These two men, especially Mr. Asquith, were the arch enemies of the women's cause. Mr. Asquith had consistently blocked the woman suffrage bills in Parliament, even when a large majority of the House of Commons wanted to vote favorably on them. Mr. Lloyd George, on the other hand, was, theoretically at least, a suffragist. He wanted the women to have votes, but he wanted something else a great deal more. He wanted, with an earnestness amounting to a cosmic urge, to be prime minister of England. His whole soul being set on that ambition, he was not going to take people's minds off of his candidacy by getting into the woman suffrage controversy. So, he put the whole subject one side for future reference.

Mrs. Pankhurst, great and wise stateswoman that she is, perfectly understood this. She knew that, if Mr. Lloyd George became premier, he would probably put a suffrage bill through Parliament, and she and Christabel knew that the new war cabinet, which they trusted would come, would probably have Lloyd George at its head. So, they bent all their energies to ousting Mr. Asquith and boosting Mr. Lloyd George. They criticized caustically, with pen and voice, the cabinet's war policies; they turned a whole volume of scorn on England's Serbian blunders and the Dardanelles failure. They went all over England talking about Mr. Asquith and his ministers, and their work told. So, when Mrs. Pankhurst decided to go to Russia and do what she could to rally the women of that distracted country, Mr. Lloyd George knew that she would do it if anyone could. He gave her a passport and a safe conduct, and she went. A little later, Ramsay MacDonald,[9] leader of England's "little group of wilful men" opposing the war, thought he would go to Russia and undo any good Mrs. Pankhurst might do.

Mr. Lloyd George at first refused to give Mr. MacDonald a passport, but his refusal so angered the Bolshevik element in the Petrograd Council of Soldiers' and Workmen's Delegates that Kerensky was actually forced to ask the English premier to allow Mr. MacDonald to visit Russia. The English premier therefore consented to issue the passport, but the Seamen's Union, which was not in the least afraid of the Petrograd soldiers and workmen, or of any international misunderstandings, refused point blank to allow Mr. Ramsay MacDonald to travel on any boat crossing to Norway. The union served notice that the moment Mr. MacDonald stepped foot on any boat leaving England the sailors on that boat would step off. Mr. Ramsay MacDonald accordingly never stepped on a boat.

Mrs. Pankhurst was very well received in Russia. The newspapers published columns about her, statesmen and ambassadors called on her, almost as on a visiting royalty, and the finest women in Petrograd came to her and welcomed her proffered aid. Which is certainly discouraging to those suffragists who always try to be good and well-mannered and never picket the White House or disturb a congressman's afternoon nap. A series of meetings were arranged for Mrs. Pankhurst, but they were neither well-arranged nor well-managed. Some of them got into the hands of women who had movements of their own to push, and who were willing to use Mrs. Pankhurst's drawing capacity to fill a room but were not willing to turn the meeting over to her when she got there.

I was present at such a meeting, which had for chairman a lady of title who had a scheme of some kind, and the speakers were mostly women who had other schemes, and they all talked and talked about their schemes, until I feared that Mrs. Pankhurst would never be given a chance to talk at all. One woman spoke for over an hour about the food situation. Her remedy was to send a commission to America and beg that a shipload of food be sent via Archangel to Petrograd. It was pointed out to her at some length by Mr. MacAlister-Smith, an American businessman living in Petrograd, that there was plenty of food nearer home than America, and that it didn't need to be begged for.

Through it all Mrs. Pankhurst sat quietly, but I who knew her well saw a suspicious little color creep into her cheeks and a light of battle flash into her gray eyes. I don't know what might have happened, but what did happen was dramatic. A tall, fine-looking woman in the back of the room sprang to her feet and burst into a passionate speech of protest. While the women in that room were wasting time in inconsequential talk the Germans were steadily advancing, the Russian troops were retreating, and ruin and desolation were at their very doors. She begged them for the sake of bleeding Russia to drop all controversy and let Mrs. Pankhurst, if she could, tell them what to do.

As she sat down, or rather dropped exhausted into her seat, Mrs. Pankhurst stood up. She is a small woman, but when she is in certain moods, she manages somehow to look tall. She looked tall on this occasion. She spoke in French and her talk lasted no longer than 15 minutes, but when she finished, half the women in the room would have gone into the trenches after her. The others looked frightened. Mrs. Pankhurst told the women that 250 Russian women had gone out of their homes, donned soldiers' uniforms, and were prepared to give their lives for their country and the democracy of the world. Mrs. Pankhurst was naturally an admirer of Bochkareva and her Battalion of Death, and had a few days before this meeting reviewed the regiment. She told these women of leisure that if working women were willing to risk their lives on the battlefield for the freedom of Russia, the women who remained at home ought to be willing to risk their lives on the streets. Whenever a Bolshevik street orator preached separate peace or a cessation of fighting, a woman of education and ability ought to stand up and tell that same street crowd the truth. The women ought to storm the Soviets all over Russia and force the men to support Kerensky and the Provisional Government in their effort to rally the army and defeat the Germans.

The movement, she told them, must be a Russian women's movement only. No foreigners should appear in it at all. They must do the work, but she was there to give them the full benefit of her experience as an organizer. She would show them how to do the work, how to train speakers, how to manage politicians, how to arrange demonstrations. One of the first things she advised them to do was to establish a headquarters in a conspicuous place, and to get up a great demonstration of women to march in a body to the Winter Palace or the Tauride Palace, wherever the Provisional Government was holding its meetings at the time. They should offer their services to the government, and let the country see that women were in the field to support the war. That speech and that program swept the women off their feet. Immediate steps were taken to organize, and a few women, without waiting for the organization, actually did go out into the streets and talk against the Bolsheviki.

Then came the days of the July Revolution when all street speaking ceased, and that interfered with the women's plan. What discouraged it most of all was Kerensky's cynical attitude toward it. A woman of rank and of great ability, knowing Kerensky well, went to him and told him what they proposed to do, and asked for his cooperation. To her astonishment he refused point blank, and he told her that the women would not be allowed to make a demonstration or to march to the palace. Naturally she asked him why, and he replied evasively that there had been too many demonstrations already.

Ambassador Francis shared the women's disappointment to the extent of calling on Kerensky and trying to make him see the value of their assistance in an hour of crisis, but Kerensky persisted in his refusal.

I do not understand why he acted in this manner. His own domestic affairs were in a sad state at this time, a rumor stating that Mme. Kerenskaya was divorcing her famous husband. It may be that Kerensky was in a state of mind of general prejudice against all women. Perhaps he has the Napoleonic conception of the position of women in the state.[10] I do not know. But if he is an anti-suffragist, he is almost alone in his opinion in Russia. Mrs. Pankhurst did not have to convert the country to suffrage. There is no spoken opposition to it anywhere, as far as I could discover. It is taken for granted that women will vote under the new constitution. They have voted already in municipal elections, and in many cities they have been elected to the town dumas. Fourteen women were elected to the Moscow town Duma last summer.

Neither is Russia opposed to militant suffragism. Mrs. Pankhurst was a guest of honor one night at the great congress of Cossacks in Petrograd. When she appeared on the platform, she received an ovation and Prof. Miliukov's introduction of the famous Englishwoman was a high eulogy. Mrs. Pankhurst's autobiography has been translated into Russian and is widely circulated. Her mission failed because Kerensky killed it. That is all. Her visit to Russia was not a complete failure, however, for she succeeded in awakening at least one group of Russian women to a keen sense of their political responsibilities. They have begun to work, and when order is restored in the country, their work will be heard of.

They told her in my hearing that they had never before realized what was before them, and they did not intend that the new constitution should be written by any but the best men in Russia. Much can be expected of Russian women in the future, in my opinion.

Among the working people, the women have shown themselves to be at least as ready for citizenship as the men. They appear among the Bolsheviki, of course, and they are seen among the slackers in industry. But one group of women workers played a loyal part throughout the February Revolution and in the after troubles. This was the telephone force, especially the girls in the big central office in the Morskaya. These girls, without any direction or orders, joined in an absolute refusal to connect the headquarters of the Bolsheviki in the dancer's palace on the Neva, or the munitions factory, which was their other stronghold. Cut off from using the telephone, the mutinous soldiers and workmen were severely handicapped, and the government was materially assisted.

Women of the educated classes will play an important part in the reconstruction of Russia. They will hold office and may sit in the ministry. Already one woman has been appointed adjunct Minister of Public Welfare. This was the well-known and efficient Countess Panina,[11] whose civic work is famous throughout the empire. Countess Panina held office for a short time only, because no ministry held together long. That she will be returned to office when stability is secured, there seems to be no doubt.

Notes

1. The Women's Social and Political Union (WSPU), the militant wing of the British women's suffrage movement, was founded in Manchester in 1903 by Emeline Pankhurst; its motto was "Deeds not words." Along with the more conservative National Union of Women's Suffrage Societies (NUWSS) founded in 1897, the WSPU sought to enfranchise women in a country that had expressly denied women suffrage in 1832.
2. Lloyd George, David (1863–1945) was prime minister of Great Britain from 1916 to 1922. A Liberal Party politician from Wales, he was known for leading Great Britain during World War I, for social-reform policies, for his role in the Paris Peace Conference, and for negotiating the establishment of the Irish Free State.
3. Kenney, Jessica "Jessie" (1887–1985) was an English suffragette who was jailed for assaulting the prime minister and home secretary on September 5, 1908, in a protest to gain suffrage for women in Great Britain. In June 1917, Kenney accompanied Emmeline Pankhurst on a trip to Russia.
4. Pankhurst, Christabel Harriette (1880–1958), daughter of Emeline Pankhurst and sister of Sylvia Pankhurst, advocated the use of militant tactics to enfranchise women in Great Britain. With her mother, she founded the Women's Social and Political Union in 1903.
5. In its attempts to deal with the problem of suffragettes going on hunger strikes, the government of Great Britain passed the 1913 Prisoners (Temporary Discharge for Ill-Health) Act commonly known as the Cat and Mouse Act. This Act allowed for the early release of prisoners who were so weakened by hunger striking that they were at risk of death. They were to be recalled to prison once their health was recovered, where the process would begin again.
6. Before World War I, Holloway prison, opened in 1852 as a mixed-sex prison, was used to imprison those suffragettes who broke the law.
7. Asquith, Herbert Henry (1852–1928) was a British statesman and Liberal politician who was prime minister of Great Britain from 1908 to 1916.
8. Grey, Edward, 1st Viscount Grey of Fallodon (1862–1933), better known as Sir Edward Grey, was a British statesman and Liberal Party politician who served as foreign secretary from 1905 to 1916.
9. MacDonald, Ramsay (1866–1937) was Great Britain's first Labour Party prime minister in the Labour governments of 1924 and 1929–31 and in the national coalition government of 1931–5.
10. Historians generally describe Napoleon Bonaparte's regime as one that placed severe limits on women's public and political roles. Although this interpretation is true on

the level of legal discourse, official celebrations continued to bring women into politicized public spaces.

11 Panina, Sofia Vladimirovna, Countess (1871–1956) was the last member of the aristocratic Panin family. After the 1917 February Revolution, she was elected to the Kadet Party Central Committee and in May became the first woman in world history to hold a cabinet position as assistant minister in the newly created Ministry of State Welfare. In August, she was made assistant minister of education.

Chapter 21

KERENSKY, THE MYSTERY MAN

It is unfortunate that nothing has ever been written about Kerensky except eulogies. However, deserved they may be, eulogies have the fault of not being informative. Who is Kerensky? What kind of a man is he? Why hasn't he restored order in Russia? If he cannot restore order, discipline the army and make it fight, why doesn't he step aside and let somebody else try? These questions have been asked on all sides.

I may not be able to answer all or any conclusively. But I was in Russia for three months, and I watched Kerensky progress from minister of war to minister-president of the Provisional Government and virtual president of the Russian Republic. I can tell my own observations of the man, and I can present the evidence of events, allowing the reader to draw his conclusions. I saw Kerensky frequently, heard him speak several times, and, like almost everyone else, I went through a period of extreme enthusiasm for him. A certain enthusiasm I have retained. I still think he has achieved marvels in keeping a government together and remaining for nearly six months at the head of that government. In fact, Kerensky, whatever else is said of him, for a time at least kept before the wild-eyed, liberty-mad masses of the Russian people the certain fact that governments must be, that the state cannot exist without leaders.

There was apparently no other man in Russia who could do this thing. The old theory that great events always produce great men seems to have failed in this case. The most stupendous event in modern history, the Russian Revolution, has as yet produced no great, or even, when Kerensky is left out, no near-great men. The first Provisional Government contained able men like Lvov and Miliukov. But they could no more cope with the situation created by the fall of autocracy in Russia than so many children could operate a railroad system.

These men thought that they had helped to bring on a political revolution. They little knew their Russia. There was just one man of ability in that first ministry who knew the truth, and he knew only part of it. Alexander Fyodorovich Kerensky, the socialist who was appointed minister of justice, knew that what the world was about to witness in Russia was a social revolution. But he, too, was blind to the task before him. At the very outset of his career as minister of justice, Kerensky insisted on abolishing the death penalty. "I do not wish that this shall be a bloody revolution," he declared. In one sentence he showed how little he, too, knew his Russia.

There was some excuse for ignorance on the part of most of the other ministers. Prince Lvov, for example, was a large estate owner, a man who lived in the country a great deal of the time, one who had been active in the affairs of his zemstvo or county council, a friend and adviser of peasants, but always the great gentleman, the aristocrat. Miliukov was a university professor, a man of books, an amateur of music, and so on through the list.

But Kerensky was no aristocrat. He was an obscure lawyer, one who specialized in cases of men and women accused of political offenses. He defended with fiery zeal young students whose revolutionary activities drew them within the tiger claws of the autocracy. He was the friend of the poor. He was one of the Executive Council of the Social Revolutionary Party, largely made up of peasants. Why did he not know and understand his countrymen? Why could he not have known that the abolition of the death penalty at that hour of supreme crisis would drench the revolution in blood?

Kerensky was in the beginning an extreme idealist, a preacher, a prophet. He changed a great deal between February and November 1917. But events, I think, on the whole, prove him an extreme idealist, a dreamer instead of a doer. Such men and women are never really great as leaders. They can stir up an enormous enthusiasm, send the crowd to the highest pitch of inspiration, even make it do monumental things for a time. But the dreamer's usefulness stops there.

Somewhere in Russia, in one of the universities perhaps, in some farmhouse or on some lonely steppe, there lives a big, hard-fisted, strong-brained, ruthless boy who can and will someday do the kind of ruling and guiding Kerensky talks about and would have enforced if he could. Perhaps that boy got his inspiration from hearing Kerensky talk. But the boy is a real leader. He will stretch out his hand to the mob, and the mob will obey his indomitable will.

Did the mob ever obey Kerensky's will? Take the army situation, for example. The day I arrived in Petrograd, May 28, I had a talk with the then American consul, Mr. North Winship.[1] He told me what he had seen of the revolution and spoke gravely and apprehensively of the future. The sedition in many regiments at the front was, to his mind, the most sinister single menace that had yet developed. "Kerensky, the new war minister, has just been sent down to the front," he told me. "He will save the situation if any living human

Figure 21.1 Alexander Fyodorovich Kerensky.

being can. His influence over the Russians is enormous. He can sway them like the tides with his eloquence."

Kerensky, who all the world knows is a sickly man, spared himself no whit during those critical days. He tore all over the front in motor cars. He made scores of speeches, thrilling speeches. Everyone reading in the newspapers of his wonderful speeches breathed more freely and whispered, "We are saved." But were they?

One incident. It may have been cabled to the American newspapers. On one front where Kerensky was speaking, a soldier, doubtless deputed by the less brave in the regiment, stepped forward and said: "It is all very well to urge us to fight for liberty, but if a man is killed fighting what good is liberty to him?" Instantly Kerensky's wrath poured out in a torrent of eloquence. He denounced the man for a traitor and a disgrace. The man who would think about his miserable skin when the freedom of his mother country was threatened was unfit to live with brave men. Turning to the colonel of the regiment, he demanded that the soldier be degraded and immediately turned out of the army, sent home a branded coward.

The colonel replied that there were others in the regiment who might, with justice, receive the same treatment. But no, said Kerensky, one man disgraced was enough. He would be a symbol of dishonor. The Russian army needed nothing more. The unfortunate man is said to have fallen in a swoon. I wouldn't be surprised if this was so. But he was probably glad enough after he recovered that he was sent home. Nor was the symbol of dishonor enough for the Russian army. It continued to desert.

Often after one of Kerensky's speeches, he would call on the troops to declare whether or not they would fight. Always they roared out that they would, to the death. Sometimes they did. It is true, but sometimes also they didn't. At present, no one can tell whether any soldiers, except the Cossacks and the women, are going to go forward when commanded.

When the army demoralization, fraternization and desertions began to assume recent frightful proportions, Kerensky issued a manifesto telling the soldiers what he was prepared to do to deserters. They would not be shot— no, the death penalty was for all time abolished in Russia. But deserters would be treated as traitors. Their families would receive no soldiers' benefits, and they would not be allowed to participate in the redistribution of land. The minister-president, for by this time Kerensky was at the head of the Provisional Government, would give the deserters time to get back to their regiments. He named a date about three weeks in advance. But on that day, at the extreme limit, all soldiers must be back in their regiments. This manifesto was issued not once, but three times, as I have stated. Three separate dates were given, three ultimata pronounced. But none of them was even noticed by the demoralized soldiers. On one date, June 18, it is true, Kerensky's order to advance was obeyed. At all events, the troops advanced on that day and fought a victorious fight. It may have been in response to Kerensky's order, or it may have been a coincidence.

Kerensky's idealism began to suffer. He began to see his people as an unruly, unreasoning, sanguinary mob. But he loved the mob and could not bring himself to do it violence even for its own good. In July he agreed that Kornilov should be made commander-in-chief of the army, with power to shoot deserters in the face of battle. Kornilov's demand for full command of the army, both at the front and in the reserve, with power to shoot all slackers, Kerensky would not agree to. However, in that same month of July 1917, Kerensky had progressed so far that he told the world that he was prepared to save Russia and Russian unity by blood and iron if argument and reason, honor and conscience, were not sufficient. Apparently, they were not sufficient, but where was the blood and iron? Beating Russia into submission would be a big job for anybody just then, and it would be interesting to know just how Kerensky thought he could do it. He was the only man of first-rate ability in his ministry, the only strong force. He would have had to have some backing, and where could he get it?

The Soviets? They have over and over, after fierce fighting, voted to give Kerensky support. Once they voted to give him supreme power. But they were never in earnest about it, and Kerensky knew it very well. They proved that they were insincere, it seems to me, by their action in October in refusing to support any ministry not made up exclusively of Socialists, and then making such a body subject to criticism and control.

"The Germans are at our very gates," Kerensky told those men. "While you sit talking here and are refusing to listen to words of reason from your commander-in-chief, your revolution is in danger of destruction. Are there no words of mine to make you see it?"

Words, words, words! Hurled passionately from a burning heart into a whirling void. That seems to me to typify Alexander Fyodorovitch Kerensky talking to the Russian revolutionary mob.

The French Revolution offers no parallel to this. Each one of the successive leaders of that mob accomplished something good or bad. Mirabeau[2] led the mass as far as a constituent assembly. Marat and Danton[3] got rid of the king. Robespierre[4] imposed his will on Paris until the end of the reign of terror. Robespierre, "the sea-green incorruptible," is the nearest parallel to Kerensky that the French Revolution offers. He led the mob in the direction it wanted to go. Kerensky followed it in a direction it wanted to go, begging it with all his eloquence to turn around and follow him. The mob applauded him, adulated him, wove laurels for his brow, but it would not follow him.

He could not turn the mob. Perhaps nobody could have done so. Perhaps what had happened in Russia was inevitable, the only possible reaction from three centuries of Romanov rule. To have it otherwise Kerensky has all but laid down his life. He suffers from some kind of kidney disease, and shortly before the February Revolution he underwent an operation that nearly finished him. His right hand is incapacitated and is usually worn in a sling or tucked inside his coat. He is thin, hollow of chest and walks with a slight stoop.

A man of 37, Kerensky is about five feet eight in height. He has thick brown hair, which bristles in pompadour all over his finely shaped head. His myopic eyes are blue, or gray, according to his mood. You see those eyes in Russia, deep, beautiful blue at times, steel gray at others. Kerensky's eyes look straight at you and give you confidence in his candor. Sometimes when he is suffering physically, the eyes seem to sink in his head and lose all their brightness. When he is tired or discouraged, they burn like somber fires. His face is pale, and even sometimes an ashen gray, and the face is deeply lined and scarred with troubled thought. The nose is big and strong, the mouth deeply curved, and the strong chin is cleft, with a deep line rather than a dimple.

Kerensky's speeches, to my mind, read better than they sound. He is intensely nervous on the platform, jerking, moving from side to side, striding up and down, thrusting out his chin—a kind of delivery I especially dislike. His gestures are all jerky and nervous. His voice is rather shrill. But in spite of all this, he is a really eloquent speaker, and he rouses his audiences to a point of enthusiasm I have seen only one man equal. Of course, I mean Theodore Roosevelt.[5]

Kerensky was formerly a model family man, I heard, but something went wrong, and last summer Mme. Kerenskaya and her two small sons, nine and seven, lived alone in the modest home. Kerensky lived in a suite in the Winter Palace and drove in the Tsar's motorcars and was waited on by a whole retinue of faithful retainers. No disparagement to him is intended in the statement. The Winter Palace was his headquarters, and as for the motorcars he had a right to drive in them, and every right in the world to be waited on and cared for.

The parents of this fated child of revolution were well-educated and fairly well-circumstanced. The elder Kerensky was a school inspector and was able to give his son a university education. Rumor persistently states that Kerensky's mother was a Jewess, but I do not know whether this is true or not.

Notes

1 Winship, North (1885–1968) was a career foreign service officer who served as U.S. consul in Tahiti, Owen Sound, Petrograd, Milan, Bombay, Fiume and Cairo. He was the U.S. consul general in Copenhagen and Montreal and held the post of the U.S. minister to South Africa—later upgraded to Ambassador in 1949—before retiring.
2 Mirabeau, Honoré Gabriel Riqueti, Count (1749–1791) was a leader of the early stages of the French Revolution. An aristocrat, he had been involved in numerous scandals before the start of the Revolution in 1789 that had left his reputation in ruins. Nonetheless, he rose to the top of the French political hierarchy in the years 1789–91 and acquired the reputation of a voice of the people.
3 Danton, Georges Jacques (1759–1794) was a leading figure in the French Revolution, often credited as the chief force in the overthrow of the monarchy and the establishment of the First French Republic on September 21, 1792. He later became the French minister of justice and the first president of the Committee of Public Safety, but his increasing moderation and eventual opposition to the Reign of Terror led to his own execution by guillotine.
4 Robespierre, Maximilien (1758–1794) was a French lawyer who became one of the primary leaders of the French Revolution (1789–99). From his initial rise to stardom in the Jacobin Club, Robespierre went on to dominate the powerful Committee of Public Safety and oversee the Reign of Terror. He was arrested and guillotined in July 1794.

5 Roosevelt, Theodore (1858–1919) was the 26th president of the United States (1901–9) and a writer, naturalist and soldier. He expanded the powers of the presidency and of the federal government with a view to supporting the public interest in conflicts between big business and labor and steered the nation toward an active role in world politics, particularly in Europe and Asia. He won the Nobel Peace Prize in 1906 for mediating the end to the Russo-Japanese War (1904–5). He secured the route for the Panama Canal; its construction was also started during his presidential tenure (1904–14).

Chapter 22

THE RIGHTS OF SMALL NATIONS

One of the main contentions of the extremists of the Russian Revolution concerns the self-governing rights of the states, large and small, which make up the empire. I met no one in Russia who did not agree that each one of the states had a right to local autonomy, but I met many who feared greatly lest the empire should be dismembered and should fall apart into a number of small, weak states. Especially disastrous would this be, both to Russia and to the Allies, if it happened during the war. That Germany is doing everything in her power to bring about this end is proof enough that it would be disastrous to the Allies. Germany's army and navy and German diplomacy are working overtime to separate the Russian states. The enemy forces are working now to isolate the Baltic states and Finland, and German agents are busy all over the empire spreading the propaganda of secession.

"The right of small peoples to govern themselves" is one of the easiest gospels in the world to preach. As a principle it is not even debatable. In practice, however, it very often is far from expedient or practicable. But the recently liberated Russians, each separate language and racial group smarting from remembered wrongs inflicted by the old government, took fire with the idea of self-government, and in every corner of Russia are found provinces, governments, even cities, repudiating the central government and setting up republics of their own. Provisional governments were created last summer in provinces of Siberia, in the rich province of Ukraine, in the town of Kronstadt, in the Siberian towns of Tomsk and Tsaritsyn,[1] and in a number of other localities. Finland very early started an agitation for a separate government, and only the closing of the Diet[2] and the prevention by armed force of the convening of a new Diet stood in the way of a socialist manifesto of separation. The Socialists are the majority party in the Diet, and they counted on the support of enough people in the three "bourgeois" parties—the Swedish, old Finnish and young Finnish parties—to carry their measure through.

Everyone of these attempts at secession was marked by riots, murders and excesses of every kind. A report from Kirsanov,[3] a city that wanted last June to be a republic all by itself, told of a garrison of soldiers who broke loose, fell on the inhabitants of the town, robbed and murdered them, outraged women, burned houses, looted shops and generally behaved like maddened animals. There seemed to be no reason why the soldiers, who had previously behaved like decent men, should have been seized with sudden criminal mania. Liberty simply acted on their systems like a deadly drug.

It was the same thing in Kronstadt, only in Kronstadt they developed a drug habit, so to speak. This fortified town of some 60,000 inhabitants is situated at the mouth of the Neva on the Gulf of Finland. The fortress of Kronstadt, which dominates the town, in normal times constitutes one of the chief defenses of Petrograd, a few miles up the river. The Gulf of Kronstadt, on which the fortress stands, is the chief station of the Baltic fleet. With a strong garrison, a fleet of battleships and a well-organized Bolsheviki, Kronstadt was able for many weeks to defy the Provisional Government, to maintain what it called a government of its own, and to commit more horrible crimes and more stupid excesses than almost any other place in Russia. Murder on a wholesale scale marked the progress of the revolution in the fortress and on the battleships. More than a score of young officers in training were killed in the fortress in one day last spring. They were not even arrested and tried on any charges. They were just butchered. A number of other officers were killed, including the commandant and vice-commandant of the fortress, and other officers were thrown into cells and kept there for months without even the farce of a trial.

Kronstadt set up a republic in late May and by mid-June the orgy was in full swing. The civil population looted and robbed, and the soldiers and marines aided and abetted them heartily. Once a band of looters sacking a warehouse were arrested by the militia police after a lively shooting match and put in jail. Cases where the militia actually arrested thieves were so rare in Russia last summer that this one received considerable newspaper publicity. The papers were obliged to record that, a few hours after the men were arrested, a crowd of armed soldiers and sailors demanded the liberation of the prisoners. Of course, their demands were honored.

The Provisional Government was able to keep Finland in partial check by threatening to withhold cereals and other provisions from her in case of secession. But Kronstadt, being a fortress, had plenty of provisions, as plenty goes in Russia these days. Kronstadt had more food and fuel than Petrograd. That is why her orgy was able to last so long. It lasted until the days of the July Revolution, when thousands of loyal troops were recalled from the front to restore order, many of the ringleaders of the mutinous troops were expelled from the army and several regiments were disbanded in disgrace. The orgy still goes on to a certain extent in the fortress, and no one knows yet how far disaffection among the naval forces went.

The Kronstadt Soviet, or Council of Workmen's and Soldiers' Delegates, covered itself with glory during the existence of the republic. The Soviet, or one of its committees, undertook the solving of the housing problem as follows: The committee went all over the town and inspected houses and apartments. They inquired in each case at the different places the amount of the rent, and then they proceeded to cut down the rent, one-third to one-half. They didn't say anything about the reduction to the landlord, but they passed the word around to the *Tavarishi*. A perfect exodus of renters out of their apartments into bigger and better ones ensued. Everybody moved, and when rent day came around and the landlords or their agents called on the new tenants they were calmly told: "Not on your life is my rent thirty rubles a month. It is fifteen rubles, and if you don't take that you will get nothing."

The landlords appealed to the Soviet, but all the satisfaction they got there was a threat of confiscation. "You've robbed the working class long enough," said the Soviet. "We ought not to pay you any rent, and perhaps after a while we won't."

From one point of view, not the least outrage the Soviet perpetrated on the helpless population of Kronstadt was an attempt to talk it to death. There is a fine cathedral in Kronstadt and in front of it, as is customary in Russia, a large open square. In this square, the Soviet erected a speaker's stand and every day the population, or as much of it as could get into the square, assembled and listened for hours to fervid oratory. The people had to come because the Soviet ordered them to, and very likely they enjoyed themselves at first. Even in Russia, however, a continual political meeting, carried on for three months at a time, every day at 5 p.m., must be a trial.

Tomsk was another city where the right of small peoples to govern themselves was demonstrated last summer. In the newspapers of June 8, old style, appeared a telegram from Tomsk to Minister-President Kerensky, the minister of justice[4] and the all-Russian Council of Deputies, Workmen and Soldiers, then in session in Petrograd. The telegram was sent by the commanding general of loyal regiments, and it read in part thus: "Criminal and mutinous soldiers in company with other criminal elements of the population have organized themselves into bands and have set themselves systematically to pillage and assassination. Under the flag of anarchy, they have looted the banks, the shops, business houses of all kinds. They were prepared to murder all heads of public organizations and declared that they would next move on to other towns and cities and continue their robberies there."

The telegram went into more particulars of these outrages and closed by saying that martial law had been established in Tomsk on the 3rd of June,

2,300 persons had been arrested and the city, thanks to the presence there of a few brave and loyal troops, was now in order.

Thus the tale could be continued. Finland, usually a peaceful, orderly, law-abiding, and intelligent country, by far the most enlightened in Russia, lost its head completely over the right of small peoples' idea. Helsingfors has seen days of violence in the old years of rule by fire and sword. But Finland has never answered with fire and sword, but by the most intelligent kind of passive resistance. With the revolution, passive resistance became violence. Most of this, it is true, came from soldiers and sailors of Sveaborg,[5] the island fortress of Helsingfors. Murder of officers went on there and in the town also. Marines pursued their hapless officers through the streets, cutting them down with swords and knives, shooting them and killing them by torture before the eyes of women and children. The townspeople did no such shocking deeds as that, but there were bloody strikes and many riots, and finally the attempt to open an illegal diet and to force a separation from the empire. Kerensky handled that situation very well, sending the best men in the government to Helsingfors, where some kind of a truce, temporary no doubt, but a truce, was patched up.

Kerensky's fiercest battle last summer was with Ukraine, where a real government was established. It was real enough at all events to force a kind of recognition from the central Provisional Government. Ukraine is an enormous territory in the south of Russia. It extends into southwestern Siberia and southward to the Black Sea. Odessa is its principal port, and within its borders are many important cities. Kiev is one of the largest of these. About 35,000,000 people inhabit Ukraine, as it is called in Russia. The people are not Russian, strictly speaking. They are Slavs, but they have a language of their own, a literature, a culture. They have been Russian subjects for nearly 300 years.

Ukraine is a self-contained country and could be made a very rich one. It is rich already in agricultural resources, the "black earth" of certain regions producing the most splendid crops of wheat and other grains. The fruits of Ukraine are the best in Russia, and the vineyards furnish grapes for excellent wines. Russia would be poor indeed without this country.

Last June the Ukrainian Rada, or local diet, voted to establish a republic, restore the old language and customs and cut themselves off absolutely from the Russian empire. They actually created a Provisional Government on the spot. Some of the more moderate members of the Rada favored remaining in the empire as a federated state having complete autonomy, and this was finally accepted, I believe, by the majority. But immediately the Bolsheviki of the south began to clamor for separation, and the Ukrainians in the army began to show dangerous signs of unrest. A congress of Ukrainian armies was held in Kiev in the middle of June, in which it was decided that the armies of the south and southwest ought to be completely and exclusively made up of Ukrainians. If this had been done, the Rada would have been in a perfect state to dictate terms of any kind to the Russian Provisional Government.

As it was, there was considerable dictating done. The military Rada, meeting in June in Odessa, served notice on the Provisional Government that unless the Ukrainian soldiers were prevented from forming their own regiments, no more soldiers of their force would be sent to the front. The Ukrainian regiments were formed, some of them in Petrograd, and the strains of the national hymn, "Ukrania is not dead," were heard on the streets, played by military bands or sung by soldiers, almost as often as the classic "Marseillaise."

Kerensky made a frantic dash to Odessa, to Kiev and other cities of Ukraine. He took with him Tereshchenko,[6] minister of foreign affairs, and one or two other ministers, and they met the new Provisional Government in parley. The result was that Kerensky made a complete surrender, recognized the Provisional Government—at least informally—and agreed that Ukraine should be a separate state. There was a perfect tempest of protest when the ministers returned to Petrograd. The rest of the ministry declared that Kerensky had overstepped his authority in committing the entire government to a policy which ought to have been left to the constituent assembly to decide. They said that his act, entered into without the knowledge or consent of the full government, was illegal. Perhaps it was; but it stood, and all the most aggrieved ministers could do about it was to resign.

The greatest task ahead of Russia is federation, and she probably will in the end learn how to give autonomy to her states and establish a central government that will bind all the states together in happy union. But she has years of strife and monumental effort ahead of her before the task is done. The wisest men in Russia—even Prof. Miliukov, who lived for years in the United States—appear to be in a complete fog on the subject of federation. Half the wise men want an empire like Great Britain or Germany, with practically all the power in one central governing body. The other half see nothing ahead but dismemberment of the empire. Nobody apparently can see Russia as another United States.

I believe that part of our responsibility, after the war—perhaps before that time comes—will be to teach Russia how to establish a peaceful federation on republican lines. Russia perhaps does not need to be taught democracy. When she emerges from this present anarchy, she may be trusted to establish a safely democratic civilization.

Notes

1 Tsaritsyn (1589–1925), Stalingrad (1925–1961) and Volgograd (1961–) is a city that lies on the western bank of the Volga in the southeastern part of European Russia. Dorr made a mistake here; Tsaritsyn was not considered a Siberian city.
2 The Diet of Finland was the legislative assembly of the Grand Duchy of Finland from 1809 to 1906.
3 Kirsanov is a town in Russia on the Vorona River 95 kilometers (59 miles) east of Tambov.
4 The minister of justice at the time was Pereverzev, Pavel Nikolaevich (1871–1944), a member of the Trudovik (Labor) Party. He was later forced to resign by Kerensky. Pereverzev emigrated after the Bolshevik takeover and settled in France.
5 Sveaborg (today's Suomenlinna) is a sea fortress off the coast of Finland, 4 km (2.5 miles) southeast of Helsinki (Helsingfors).
6 Tereshchenko, Mikhail Ivanovich (1886–1956), a major Ukrainian landowner, owner of several sugar factories and a financier, was the foreign minister of Russia from May to November 1917.

Chapter 23

WILL THE GERMANS TAKE PETROGRAD?

Will the German army get to Petrograd and Moscow? The answer to this question is, they probably can if they want to, but it is hardly possible that they do. If they have that objective, and if they succeed in taking Moscow, it will simply add one more to the psychological blunders committed by the German government since the war began. The disorganized Russian army might not pull itself together and fight for Petrograd, but the army and the people would fight to the death for Moscow. It is their holy city, their crown of glory, their dream. Moscow is Russia, and one who has never seen it knows not the Russian people.

Petrograd is a modern European city, built by Peter the Great[1] in the early part of the eighteenth century and by Catherine II, also called "the Great," in the latter half of the same century. Peter, who would have been a master man in any century and in any country, whether born in a palace or a farmhouse, was all the more a marvel because he was a Russian, born at a time when the Russian people were still medieval and still oriental. Peter didn't allow the fact that he was heir to an oriental autocracy to interfere with his ambitions or his activities. He left the golden palace in the Kremlin, left Moscow, the capital, and sacred heart of the empire, left Russia altogether, and went off to become a day laborer in the shipyards of England and Holland. Peter learned what he could in a short time and went back to establish Western civilization in Russia. He chose the site of his new capital much as the United States Steel Company[2] chose the site of Gary, Ind., for its nearness to a good harbor, its easy access to trade routes and its fine front view of the best commercial centers. Peter called his city "a window toward Europe."

Petersburg, as it was styled by the half German Peter, was a more stupendous piece of engineering than Gary, Ind., although the steel town is one of the greatest triumphs of engineering this country can boast. It was built on a marsh which nowhere rose above the muddy waters of the Neva more than two or three feet, and in most places was partially or wholly submerged.

That marsh never has been completely drained. When, in 1765, St. Isaac's Cathedral[3] was built to replace a small wooden church of Peter's time, they first had to drive over twelve hundred huge piles into the soft ground. Of the 40,000 workmen who toiled under Peter's direction to create the first Petrograd a majority died from exposure and cold, and of fevers bred in the miasmas of the bogs.

Catherine, who became Tsarina a little more than half a century later, vastly improved the city. She enlarged it, erecting many splendid palaces and public buildings, and bringing in a vast amount of Western culture in the way of libraries, art galleries and theaters. The monuments of Peter and Catherine are the most conspicuous objects in the capital. The ghosts of Catherine and Peter may be said to walk in every street in Petrograd. But the Russians, for all their admiration for their greatest monarchs, have little real love for the city they built.

The ghost of Ivan the Terrible[4] walks through the streets of Moscow; nevertheless, the Russians love the place as the Mohammedans love Mecca. It is one of the most beautiful cities in the world, and one of the strangest. It has hundreds of churches, so gorged with art treasures and with gold, silver and jewels that it dizzies the mind to contemplate them. It has the ancient wall, foliage-hung, that enclosed the Moscow of the thirteenth century, and it has the Kremlin, or fortress, which antedates the town. Inside the Kremlin is the old palace of the rulers of Russia built, in part, centuries before they became czars. The first Kremlin palaces were built by the dukes of Moscow in the twelfth and thirteenth centuries.

Some of the most beautiful of the treasure churches of the Kremlin were built by Ivan the Terrible in the sixteenth century. One of these, just outside the walls, the Cathedral of St. Basil's,[5] is a gem of such radiance supreme that the half-mad Ivan determined that it should never be surpassed. When it was finished, he called the architect to him and asked him if he thought he could ever design a better church. The architect, in the pride and joy of his achievement, modestly said that he thought he might. "You never will," said the terrible Ivan, and he had the man's eyes burned out with red-hot irons.

In the great square in front of the Kremlin still stands the high place of execution where Ivan and the other almost as terrible tsars tortured and slew their victims. In a side street still stands the wonderful golden house which was the home and seat of the Romanov boyars, and where the first (or second) tsar of Russia was born.[6] Moscow is the very symbol of tsardom; nevertheless, the Russians love it as their heart. Germany might send her armies there, but they could no more take it, or hold it, than they could take and hold Washington. Inside the Kremlin walls lie heaped thousands of bronze cannons, bright and beautiful as snakes, all decorated with eagles and N's and ambitious mottoes. Napoleon Bonaparte left them there when he fled, defeated and routed by the Russians, only to be still more soundly defeated by snow and storm and bitter cold. Those cannons are evidence indeed of the invincibility of Moscow.

Germany ought to know that a march on Moscow, however easy, would result in unifying the Russian army against the foe. Perhaps Germany does not know this, for she seems not to know anything about the hearts and minds of any people. The mechanics of nationality she knows and understands. The psychology of it she never understands. However, I do not believe that Germany's recent attack and partial conquest of the islands before Riga[7] are a prelude to a march on the capital or on Moscow. What Germany probably wants is the splendid loot to be found in Courland and Estonia. Riga, which is a city of 400,000 inhabitants, is, next to Petrograd, the most important port on the Baltic Sea. Out from Riga go immense exports of timber, flax and hemp, linseed and many cereals. The country east and south of Riga produces these things in great quantity, and Germany needs them in her business just now, and needs them badly enough to risk a few of her ships and men to get them.

Germany is not after conquest, this trip; she is after food and fuel and supplies. A little south of Riga lie the governments of Kovno,[8] Vilna[9] and Minsk,[10] and a little south and west lie Russian Poland, already partially in German hands. I traveled through part of that country last summer and watched through the train windows vast fields of rye and wheat, and thousands of acres of potatoes. I did not see many sugar-beet fields, but they lie somewhere in that region—hundreds of thousands of acres of them, already harvested or waiting to be harvested. And Germany is hungry for those harvests.

There may be other reasons why Germany is pounding so desperately at the defenses of Riga. Not very far away, to the north, washed by the same Baltic Sea, lies the grand duchy of Finland, the one province of the Russian Empire that has shown friendliness to Germany. Finland is also the one province that has already declared its unalterable determination not to belong further to the Russian Empire. Finland wishes to set up a separate government and to be an independent state. At least the mass of the people, expressing themselves through a Socialist majority in the local Diet, has declared for this policy.

It would be tremendously to the advantage of Germany to have the big Russian Empire split up into separate states, and the German government has worked assiduously to encourage the Finnish people in their secession policy. Finland is such a Mecca for German agents, and so many Finns are in the pay of these agents, that the Provisional Government last July practically shut the grand duchy off, marooned it, so to speak, from the rest of the empire. A traveler cannot go to Finland from Russia without special permission obtained from the war ministry. A resident of Petrograd could not go down to one of the numerous and charming Finnish seaside towns near the capital, even for a weekend visit, without such a permit. I have spent some time in Finland and know a great many people in Helsingfors, the capital. I tried to get a permit to stop in Helsingfors on my way out of Russia, but the war ministry refused to grant the permit.

When the traveler left Russia for England or the United States, for any country, for that matter, he had to take a certain train leaving Petrograd at 7:30 in the morning, and he left that train just once before he reached the frontier. That once is at Bely Ostrov,[11] for the customs inspection. After that the traveler was a prisoner in his train until he reached Tornea,[12] where he was finally inspected and convoyed across a narrow stretch of water to Sweden. That was the attitude of the Russian Provisional Government toward Finland.

The grand duchy is rightly considered one of the greatest menaces to the future integrity of the empire. It is rightly considered by Germany a hope for the future of Germany, and it may very well be that the German navy expects and hopes to follow up the conquest of the Baltic port of Riga with a conquest of the Baltic port of Helsingfors. Finland detests Russia to such an extent that she is apparently blind to the danger of a friendship with Germany. For 50 years she has hated and feared Russia, and she apparently cannot get it into her head that the thing she hated and feared has gone forever. I have observed this state of mind in Poles as well as Finns. They have hated Russia so long that they cannot stop all at once. The Finns have hated Russia so hard that they would not even look at the Russian soldiers quartered on them by the old government. I spent the winter of 1913 in Helsingfors, and it was one of the sights of the place to me to watch the Finns cut the Russians in the street every day. A regiment of Russians marched through the streets, bands playing, swords clanking, feet tramping, a gorgeous sight. But the soldiers might as well have been invisible phantoms for all the notice taken of them by the Finns. They walked quietly along, attending to their business, conversing or chatting with their neighbors, never looking at the Russians. In fact, it was a point of honor with the Finns never to look at a Russian. As for speaking to one, knowing him, inviting him to his house, a Finn who did such a thing would have been ostracized. Even the smallest children knew that.

This being the state of mind of the Finns, it is explainable to a degree why, in order to wring their independence from Russia now, they are willing to run a very great risk of being absorbed or badly exploited by the Germany of after the war. They became part of the Russian Empire willingly, having been on very bad terms for a number of years with their old overlord, Sweden. This was in 1801. Then the Tsar made a solemn compact with Finland, both for himself and his heirs, that the country should have almost complete autonomy. It was to maintain its own army, which would never be called upon to serve on Russian soil but should defend the Finnish coast and border in case Russia was involved in war.

Finland was to have her own coinage, postal systems, schools, courts, language and her own local diet. The Tsar retained the right of vetoing legislation, the right to collect foreign customs and other imperial rights. Almost every promise made in that treaty has been broken by the tsars of Russia, especially by Nicholas II, now in Siberia. This Nicholas tried to break the treaty altogether, abolish it, but the Finns were too intelligent, too clear-headed and too united to let him do it. Their resistance to his tyrannous treachery is a thrilling story in itself. Finland has never broken any part of her treaty with Russia, but now she wants to abolish the treaty. The contention is that the treaty was made with the tsars of Russia, and, now that there are no more tsars, the treaty has ceased to hold good. Finland is full of German agents, and they must have invented this brilliant piece of reasoning and taught it to the Finnish Socialists. At all events, they must have fostered it with might and main, and perhaps the German navy believes that a visit to Helsingfors would convert the whole country to it.

There is even a better reason why the German navy has been pounding away in the Gulf of Finland, and why in the spring it will pound again. Germany seeks to separate still further Russia and her allies. There are only three ways by which Russia can communicate with Europe and America. One of these ways is across Siberia and the Pacific Ocean, a long distance. Another way, through Arkhangelsk,[13] is a summer way only. The third and shortest way is through Finland and Sweden. If Germany can partially take Finland and seize the railroad that leads to Sweden, and there is only one main line of railroad, she can cut Russia off from her allies very effectively. Perhaps her next step would be to interfere, by means of submarines, with Russia's other outlet in the Pacific.

Notes

1 Peter the Great, Peter I (1672–1725) was the Tsar of Russia who reigned jointly with his half-brother Ivan V (1682–96) and alone thereafter (1696–1725) and who in 1721 was proclaimed Emperor. He was one of Russia's greatest statesmen, organizers and reformers, founded the Russian navy and formed a regular army based on compulsory military service for all nobles and on recruitments from the peasantry. Peter the Great transformed Russia from an isolated kingdom into a transcontinental superpower.

2 The U.S. Steel Corporation was founded in 1901. At the beginning of the twentieth century, a number of businessmen were involved in the formation of the U.S. Steel Corporation, including Andrew Carnegie, Elbert H. Gary, Charles M. Schwab and J.P. Morgan. Carnegie had founded the Carnegie Steel Company headquartered in Pittsburgh, PA, and Gary had founded the Federal Steel Company headquartered in Chicago. In 1900 Schwab became president of the Carnegie company, and he eventually approached Gary with the idea of a giant consolidation. With the aid of J.P. Morgan, they bought Carnegie's interests for more than $492 million and formed a new steel company. U.S. Steel was capitalized at $1.4 billion. Gary was made chairman of the board (he held that post until his death in 1927).

3 St. Isaac's Cathedral is an iron-domed cathedral in St. Petersburg that was designed in the Russian Empire style by Auguste de Montferrand. Covering 2.5 acres, it was completed in 1858 after four decades of construction. It is dedicated to Saint Isaac of Dalmatia, a patron saint of Peter the Great who had been born on the feast day of that saint. St. Isaac's Cathedral is the third largest domed cathedral in the world.

4 Ivan the Terrible (1530–1584) was the Grand Duke of Moscow (1533–84) and the first to be proclaimed Tsar of Russia (from 1547). His reign saw the completion of the construction of a centrally administered Russian state and the creation of an empire that included non-Slav states. Ivan engaged in prolonged and largely unsuccessful wars against Sweden and Poland, and, in seeking to impose military discipline and a centralized administration, he instituted a reign of terror against the hereditary nobility.

5 Saint Basil's Cathedral was built between 1555 and 1561 by Ivan the Terrible in Moscow. Legend has it that the cathedral's builders were blinded post-construction so that a structure of such beauty could never be built again.

6 The first tsar of the Romanov dynasty, Mikhail Fyodorovich Romanov, was believed to be born in the House of the Romanov boyars (the Chambers of the Romanov Boyars) in 1596. The Romanov family lived here in the sixteenth century. Today, it is a museum devoted to the Russian nobility's lifestyle of the sixteenth to seventeenth centuries.

7 Riga, a city that lies on the Gulf of Riga at the mouth of the Daugava River where it meets the Baltic Sea, was captured by Russians during the Great Northern War (1701–1721). At the beginning of the twentieth century, Riga was one of the largest export ports in the Russian Empire.

8 Kovno Governorate was an administrative-territorial unit (*guberniya*) of the Russian Empire with its capital in Kovno (today's Kaunas). It was formed in 1842 by Tsar Nicholas I from the western part of Vilna Governorate.

9 Vilna Governorate was an administrative-territorial unit (*guberniya*) of the Russian Empire with its capital in Vilna (today's Vilnius). The governorate bordered on Minsk Governorate in the south, Grodno Governorate in the southwest, Suwalki Governorate in the west, the Kovno and Courland Governorates in the north, and Vitebsk Governorate in the east.

10 Minsk Governorate was an administrative-territorial unit (*guberniya*) of the Russian Empire with its capital in Minsk. It was created from the land acquired in the partitions of Poland and existed from 1793 until 1921. Its territory covered the majority of modern-day Belarus.

11 Bely Ostrov is a small artificial island in the delta of the Neva.

12 Tornea is the Swedish name of Tornio, a city in northern Finland.

13 Arkhangelsk lies on both banks of the mouth of the Northern Dvina where it flows into the White Sea; the city was the chief seaport of medieval and early modern Russia until 1703, when it was replaced by the newly founded Saint Petersburg. In 1722, Peter the Great decreed that Arkhangelsk should no longer accept goods in excess of the town's domestic needs. The economy of Arkhangelsk revived in the late nineteenth century when a railway to Moscow was completed, and timber became a major export.

Chapter 24

RUSSIA'S GREATEST NEEDS

It would be a very terrible thing for democracy and the world's peace if the Allies, observing the anarchy into which Russia has fallen, should relax any of their efforts to help her back to a sound military, economic and social foundation. The first impulse is to beseech the U.S. government to refuse to loan money to such an unstable government, and even to decline to send Red Cross relief to a people who will not try to help themselves. But second thought reveals the unwisdom of deserting Russia in her crisis, however wilfully the crisis was brought on. We must loan money to Russia even though we lose the money. We must send her food and supplies, even though they be received without much gratitude. For the sake of democracy, to which revivified and regenerated Russia has a world to contribute, we must help her now. The task will not be as difficult as the surface facts indicate. Russia is rapidly approaching the climax of her woe.

Aside from her military situation, bankruptcy is coming if it is not already there. Bankruptcy for the national treasury, for few taxes are being paid. Bankruptcy for food, clothing, fuel for all the people except a few on the farms, and even they will suffer for many things. Hunger and cold are at the door. The Russian army may rally, may turn on the Germans and magnificently retrieve its lost reputation as a fighting force. But there is no way in which the army of producers, the farmers and the working people can rout the enemy they have admitted within the lines.

The farmer class of Russia this year did not produce full crops, and they refused to send to market a very large proportion of what they did produce. They hoarded their grain for their own use and some of it at least they have turned into vodka. In the towns and cities of Russia prohibition almost prohibits, but the peasant very quickly learned the art of illicit distilling, and I heard on authority I could scarcely question that stills have been established in half the villages of Russia. The statement is borne out to some extent by the fact that drunkenness among soldiers is increasing, especially in places remote from the larger cities. In Petrograd I saw little drunkenness, but the farther I traveled southward into the farming area the more I saw and heard of it. At the military position in Poland where the Bochkareva's Battalion of Death was stationed, I talked with a soldier who had lived in America. In the course of our conversation, he mentioned that a group in his regiment had got drunk and were in trouble.

"Where could they get liquor?" I asked.

"Oh, they get it," he replied. "It's new and it's quite horrible, but they drink it."

Serious as the grain shortage was, the transportation situation was still more serious. Food for which Petrograd and Moscow would pay almost any money rotted on the ground, spoiled in the half-loaded freight cars and wasted in congested way stations for lack of transportation facilities and for lack of labor. In the industrial world, things were as bad. The working people, blind to their own peril, had shortened hours of work, had gone slack on their jobs and had voted themselves wages far in excess of their productive activities. The consequences were rapidly accumulating. Factories were closing down, partly because they could not get coal and partly because of the extortions of labor. Soon there will be gaunt famine in the land. The working people will know what it is to go hungry with their pockets full of money.

When these troubles culminate—and in a few weeks at the most, the world will stand aghast at Russia's state—the orgy of the Bolsheviki, the riot of the dreamers will end. Human nature is the same in Russia as it is elsewhere, the same as it is in New York or in Emporia, Kansas. We all know how, when hard times pinch the country, the Republican Party elects its candidates. The people follow their theorizing and dreaming leaders in good times, but when the hard times come, they turn to the party of strong businessmen to set them on their feet again. The full dinner pail argument is going to appeal strongly to the Russian masses this coming winter, and if the constituent assembly is postponed until the autumn of 1918, I am confident that the people will vote in favor, not of a socialistic millennium that will not work, but for a sane, practical democracy that will.

What Russia needs above all other things is leaders. What the people of this country must do for Russia is to help her find and develop those leaders. They are there somewhere. Russia has shown that she can produce great men and great women, people whom any nation might be proud to follow. But under tsardom the only people permitted to lead were so corrupt, so reactionary and tyrannical that the Russians learned to fear and distrust all leadership. When they overthrew tsardom and banished the tyrants and the corruptionists, they thought they could get along without any leaders. The world knows now how fatal their mistake was, and very soon the blindest of the blind in Russia will know it.

Russia needs not only political leaders, she needs, even more urgently, leaders in the economic field. She needs at the present time a businessman of the caliber of Mark Hanna,[1] a man who, with a better ethical standard, possesses Mark Hanna's great genius for organization, his marvelous executive ability. Such a man rarely dazzles the public with oratorical powers. He wastes little energy in speech. But he knows exactly what to do. He says to one man, "come," and to another man, "go," and you may depend on it they are precisely the right men for the right jobs. He says to all about him, "Do this," and they do it "to the king's taste." Russia needs many such men.

Nobody need be a slave under leaders, responsible and removable, like that. We were, in the United States, until we got our eyes a little open. We sink back once in a while still. Witness some of our municipal governments. But freedom under strong leadership is entirely possible. In fact, it is the only real freedom there is in the world.

The Russians may have a difficult time achieving it, for they are not quite the hard-fibered, ambitious, struggling race the English, French and Americans are. They are fatalistic and dreamy. That is the reason they endured their autocrats so long. But in the end, they will achieve it.

Russia needs education, and here again America must show her the way. A public school system on the best lines we have been able to develop will make over the Russian people in one generation. Ninety percent of the present population is said to be illiterate. The old government tried within the past ten years to extend the common schools, but with little effect on illiteracy. The mass of the children was given two years of schooling, with the object of teaching them at least to read and write. Most of them barely learned and practically all forgot, because they were not encouraged to use their tiny bit of knowledge. Russia has no conception of the public library as we have developed it. There are libraries, magnificent ones, in the cities. But they are reference libraries for the learned, not reading and lending libraries for the masses. I am sure there is not such a thing in Russia as a children's library, much less a librarian especially trained and paid to teach children how to use and to love books. Russia needs schools to teach children knowledge, and she needs libraries very near, if not directly attached, to the schools. I talked to many people in Russia about the wonderful Gary schools, in which children work, study and play their way to fine, strong, thinking manhood and womanhood, and in every case the response was the same. "We must have schools like that all over Russia. Will you help us, when the time comes, to organize them?"

They cannot hope, of course, to go at once into all the intensive work of the Gary public school system, but they can adopt its general principles and its duplicate use of the school plant. In this way, they will be able to educate more children in each schoolhouse and thus hasten the day when all the children will be in school. William Wirt's[2] next great work may be organizing school systems in new Russia. Having no old system to replace, he will not meet with the stupid and criminal obstruction and opposition with which his labors in New York were met.

Russia needs wholesome popular amusements to entertain and instruct her adult population. If I were to write a detailed list of Russia's most pressing needs, I should place near the head of the list plumbers and moving pictures. The empire is back in the Dark Ages as far as building sanitation is concerned. That is no small thing, because it affects both the health and the morals of a people. It affects their manners also, as anyone who ever had to enter the lavatory of a Russian railroad carriage or station can testify.

They have some moving picture theaters in Russia, but they are poor in performance and frightfully high-priced. You pay as much to go to the movies in Russia as you pay to hear a high-class symphony concert. I never saw a 10 and 15 cent motion picture house, nor could I learn that they existed anywhere in the empire. Mrs. Pankhurst and I went to the movies one night, paying something like a dollar and a half for our seats. The play was a long, dreary drama, ending in suicide and general misery. The acting was poor and the actors fat and elderly. For current events pictures, they presented the Cossack funeral, reeled off at such a dizzy pace that it looked less like a funeral than an automobile race.

Moving pictures, carefully selected, offered for a small admission fee, would be a boon to Russia. They would teach the grown people a thousand and one things they have never had a chance to learn, and they would perhaps get the Russian mind out of its habit of ingrowing, self-torturing analysis that leads to nowhere. They would also give the *Tavarishi* something to do besides soap box spouting, and their listeners something more to think about than half-baked social theories. Because of the great illiteracy of the masses, Russia would have to introduce into her picture theaters an institution which Spain has already established. In Spain few people can read the titles and captions that run through the picture dramas, so each theater has a public reader, a man with a strong voice and clear enunciation, who reads aloud to the audience and also makes any explanations that are necessary.

I know exactly where moving pictures for the masses could be shown in Petrograd without waiting for private enterprise to open theaters. On the west bank of the Neva, not far from the sinister fortress of Peter and Paul, stands the best and most democratic monument to Russian enterprise in the capital. This is known as the Narodny Dom, or People's House, a combination clubhouse, restaurant, theater and general meeting place of the working classes, founded by Prince Alexander of Oldenburg[3] and liberally supported by the late Tsar.

They have some fine concerts there, in times of peace, and an excellent drama for the more intelligent of the workers. Admission prices are fairly low and the performances good. For the less intellectual, there are certain Coney Island[4] features, and these are so well-patronized that the concessionaires were well on the road to vast wealth. Long lines of people waited every evening for a turn on the chutes or the roller coaster. Their absolute hunger for a little amusement, a chance to laugh and be gay is pathetic to witness.

Another thing Russia needs is the soda fountain. A cold soft drink in summer and a hot chocolate in winter, easily accessible and cheap, would do more to take Ivan's mind off moonshining vodka than all the laws in the world. Last summer there were times when I would cheerfully have given a dollar for a frosty glass of soda, any kind, any flavor. And there were plenty of others in Petrograd of my mind.

The best place to have luncheon in Petrograd is at the officers' stores in the street which bears the appalling name of Bolshaya Konyushennaya. Here the food, government supplied, is good and it is sold for something approaching reasonable prices. The best meal I had every day was luncheon at the officers' stores. The place is crowded from 11 to 4 every weekday, military men and their families predominating. Once, on a hot July day, there appeared on the counter where hors d'oeuvres were sold a cold delicious drink. It was a sort of cherry phosphate, and there were glass pitchers and pitchers of it, literally gallons. It sold for about twenty cents a small glass, and within half an hour it was gone, every drop. The crowd swarmed to that counter waving its money in the air, swallowed the cherry phosphate in one gulp, so to speak, and clamored loudly for more. I remember that I pleaded almost with tears for a second glass and could not get it. There is a fortune waiting for the capitalist who will take cold, soft drinks to Russia, and he will have besides the fortune the additional satisfaction of bringing hope to the sodden victims of vodka.

An army that will obey orders; a government that will govern; leaders in business, in transportation, in agriculture and a people willing to obey those leaders; education, wholesome life. Russia needs all these, and in her coming mighty struggle to achieve them the whole world of democracy, and especially our United States, must lend willing and sympathetic help and guidance.

Notes

1 Hanna, Mark (1837–1904) was an American industrialist. The prosperous owner of a Cleveland coal and iron enterprise, he soon expanded his interests to include banking, transportation and publishing. Hanna successfully promoted the presidential candidacy of William McKinley in the election of 1896 and personified the growing influence of big business in American politics.

2 Wirt, William Albert (1874–1938) was a superintendent of schools in Gary, Indiana. Wirt developed the Gary Plan for the more efficient use of school facilities, a reform of the Progressive Movement that was widely adopted in over 200 cities by 1929.
3 Alexander of Oldenburg, Prince (1844–1932) was the second son of Duke Peter of Oldenburg and Princess Therese of Nassau-Weilburg. Though he had a German title and ancestry, Alexander and his siblings were born and raised in Saint Petersburg as the grandchildren of Grand Duchess Catherine Pavlovna of Russia. Alexander served as adjutant general to Alexander III of Russia and as commanding general of the Imperial Guard. At the outbreak of World War I, Nicholas II appointed Alexander, a medical doctor, as supreme chief of the medical service of the military and naval forces. Alexander and his wife Princess Eugenia Maximilianovna of Leuchtenberg were noted for their philanthropy; they established schools, hospitals, orphanages and other charitable organizations.
4 Coney Island is a neighborhood and entertainment area in the southwestern section of the New York City borough of Brooklyn. By the mid-nineteenth century, it had become a seaside resort, and by the late nineteenth century, amusement parks had also been built at the location. The attractions reached their historical peak during the first half of the twentieth century.

Chapter 25

WHAT NEXT?

Man must hope. He must believe that his fight is a winning fight, or he must give up in despair. That is why the Americans place credence in every dispatch from Russia which seems to indicate that the disorganized fighting forces are being whipped into form again. That is why any hint that Kerensky had not succeeded in restoring order in the empire was for some time received with incredulity by the reading public. But why refuse to face the facts? We must face them sometime.

In late September I read in one of the newspapers a headline that stated that the so-called democratic congress then in session in Petrograd had voted to sustain Kerensky's demand for a coalition ministry. The headlines were wrong. What the dispatch really stated was that the congress had voted not to form any coalition with the bourgeois element, or with members of the Constitutional Democratic party. That is, the congress would not support a ministry that had any non-socialist members in it. "All the power to the Soviets" was retired as too conservative a slogan. It was "all the power to the Bolsheviki" then, for that is precisely what the vote in that so-called Democratic Congress meant.

Since June 1917, no fewer than six congresses or conventions have been held in Russia with the object of finding a way out of the chaos with which the country is threatened. Every one of them was hailed beforehand as the one that was going to be a revelation of the intentions and desires of the people. The most important of these was the all-Russia congress of Soviets held last July, and before that the preliminary convention to prepare for the constituent assembly. The one was to decide once and for all whether or not the moderate or the extreme element in the Soviets was to rule, and the other was to quiet both elements by showing that the government intended to prepare a liberal and a democratic constitution for them to debate, amend and adopt when the time came. Lastly, there was the great Moscow congress of last August.[1] I don't remember what the stated object of that congress was, but it does not matter much. The real object was to find out which was the stronger man, Kerensky or Kornilov. Kerensky won by a narrow margin, a very narrow margin. And then they held another convention, and Kerensky lost.

What will happen next in that distracted country? Into what new morass are the people being led? Frankly, I do not know. I do not know anybody who does. The only analogous situation in modern history is that of Poland in the eighteenth century.[2] Poland had a government quite as bad as that of the Russian Soviets or the Council of Workmen's and Soldiers' Delegates. Instead of being an all-socialist affair, Poland's parliament was made up entirely of noblemen. These men were so proud, so "free" in the New Russia sense of the word that they wouldn't yield on any question even to a majority vote. A single dissenting voice in their parliament was enough to kill any measure. The people of Poland had no more to say about government than the middle class and the rich have in Russia of today. And when a European war on a limited scale broke out, and Frederick the Great[3] started the era of frightfulness which William the last thought he could bring to a triumphant conclusion, the three great eastern powers of Europe—Russia, Prussia and Austria—sliced up Poland and handed each of the three monarchs a piece. Maria Theresa,[4] who ruled Austria of that day, wanted it printed in the records that she wept when she took her piece, but she took it just the same, and Poland has wept ever since.

This could happen to Russia. She could be dismembered and handed around. But this is not likely to happen. The Allies would never be so foolish or so cruel as to permit it to happen. Russia could fall apart and become an aggregation of small separate states, but each one of those would still have its Soviets, and consequently a government without stability or permanence. Finland and Ukraine are two Russian states that are trying to bring about this end, and they may succeed, but a dissected Russia would furnish such good material for future wars that the Allies can hardly afford to consent to it.

Civil war is a fine possibility in Russia just now, except that there seems to be no one at hand to organize the two forces. The strongest probability is more guerrilla warfare, more street fighting, more motor trucks loaded with machine guns rushing up and down Petrograd, more battle, murder and sudden death, and then the reaction. Just what form the reaction will take nobody knows. But the mad Bolsheviki know that it is coming, and though they almost court it they also fear it. They call this inevitable reaction the counterrevolution, and they excuse all their vagaries, their obstinacy, their pigheaded resistance to a coalition with non-socialists on the ground that they are fighting the counterrevolution. I have heard Americans in Russia, college professors, businessmen, correspondents, even members of American commissions, say: "Don't blame these people too much for their radicalism. They are afraid they will lose all they gained by the revolution. They fear the return of autocracy."

WHAT NEXT?

I can say with all confidence that whatever may happen in Russia, there is not even the remotest chance of any counterrevolution, in the sense meant by the extremists, nor is there the slightest risk of a return of autocracy. The autocracy collapsed like a house of cards, and the real surprise there was in it for the Duma members who deposed Nicholas was that the thing was so easy. I can imagine Miliukov, Rodzianko, and the others getting together afterward and saying: "Why on earth didn't we do this in August 1914?"

Nobody wants the Tsar back unless it is the Romanov family, and doubtless each one of the Grand Dukes believes that if anyone came back, it ought to be himself. The only possibility of a return of monarchy in Russia would result from desperation on the part of the men who will finally restore order there. The situation may be so bad, when the time comes to do that, that they may decide on a limited constitutional monarchy as the best form of government for people who are not yet ready for self-government. A figurehead king, something visible to the people and symbolizing government, but a king with responsible ministers who really rule, is a possibility for Russia. The inevitable reaction, especially if it is long postponed, may take that form. I have heard many Russians say so. Some said it with sorrow, some with satisfaction, but there are plenty of educated and liberal-minded people in Russia who would welcome it. If it comes, I predict that the capital of Russia will be moved back to Moscow. The constitutional monarch, if they have one, may be that brother of the late Tsar who is known in Russia as Michael Alexandrovitch, who is one of the ablest and most enlightened of the Romanov family. He is the man who was chosen by the first provisional government to succeed the Tsar when the latter was deposed, and the governments which have followed have all treated him with rather especial consideration. Last June he asked permission to leave turbulent Petrograd and spend the summer in his villa on one of the Finnish lakes. This permission was granted, and Michael has lived in Finland in comparative peace and comfort ever since. The government has not treated any other Romanov as well.

Most of the Grand Dukes and Grand Duchesses are virtually prisoners on their estates. The Empress Dowager is confined to her estate in the Crimea, and the government would not even allow her to leave it to bid her exiled son goodbye. But Michael Alexandrovitch must have convinced the government that he is trustworthy, and he seems to be regarded as a man who could be brought out of his shadowy background and set up for the people to call a king, if the worst comes to the worst and they have to have a king. This is the most severe form the reaction could permanently take in Russia, as far as I can judge. Of course, a military dictatorship may precede this, but the dictatorship would be a temporary thing, a war measure to crush the Bolsheviki and bring order out of chaos. Nobody in Russia, as far as I know and believe, wants a counterrevolution in the sense suggested by the Bolsheviki. But the counterrevolution, as a bogey to be held over the heads of the timid dreamers and of those half-hearted ones who shrink from bloodshed, is so useful that the Bolshevik leaders worked it hard all summer and in the latest developments they were still at it.

The experience of the French people after their revolution is often cited by the timorous in Russia. It is true that the Bourbons came back, but the people of France did not call them back. They were put back by the allied monarchs of Europe, aghast at the spread of republicanism in the Eastern Hemisphere. Following the revolution and the two score years of Napoleonic wars, these rulers got together, signed a secret agreement that the peace of Europe, depended on France remaining a monarchy, and in 1814 they put Louis XVIII[5] on the throne. By virtue of giving the French a liberal constitution he kept the throne until his death, ten years later. The allied monarchs saw to it that his brother, Charles X,[6] succeeded him, but the allies could not prevent the French from turning him out of the country within six years. Nor could they stay the revolution of 1848 which banished Louis Philippe,[7] the last Bourbon.

Times have changed since the French Revolution. Kings have lost most of their power and almost all of their popularity. They cannot get together and, under the direction of a Metternich,[8] agree that the peace of Europe demands that Russia remain an autocracy. They could not do this even if the old combination, Russia, Prussia, Austria, England and France, had not been violently disrupted. No country in Europe is interested in restoring the Romanov dynasty, unless it be the country of the Hohenzollerns,[9] and that country is not going to have much to say about the world's business for the next few years.

There may be no counterrevolution in Russia, but there will ultimately be a return to sanity and order. There will be a constitutional convention, not too soon, it is to be hoped, and in that convention the voice of the leaders of the moderate parties will be heard. Trotsky may be a delegate, but so will Prof. Paul Miliukov, the leader of the Constitutional Democrats, or *Kadets*, as they are colloquially known. All through the riot and turmoil of the summer, Prof. Miliukov and his colleagues worked steadily to keep the party alive, to keep it constantly in the foreground as the liberal-conservative force that might at least share in shaping the new constitution.

There are plenty of wise, sane statesmen, plenty of good citizens in Russia. They are not very conspicuous just now, and for good reason. A fine old French abbe who was asked what he did during the Reign of Terror,[10] replied simply, "I lived." Avoiding assassination is a career in itself just now in Russia. Many of the wealthy classes and the estate owners spent the summer in Finland.

WHAT NEXT?

Some went to England or the United States. The peasants in many parts of the empire, falling in joyfully with the Kerensky plan of dividing up the land, began the process by sacking and burning the homes of the estate owners, destroying their fields, orchards and vineyards, and cutting and burning their forests. These acts, in conjunction with riots and excesses in the towns, have encouraged the intellectual classes to leave the country and to take no part in politics.

Despite everything that has happened, despite these excesses, there is no question that the Russian people in revolt have contributed greatly to the world's democracy. They will make still greater contributions, I believe. They have a long road to travel before they establish their new civilization. The Russians are not as developed as the English, the French or the Americans. In some respects, they are no further developed than the English of the reign of Henry the Eighth.[11] They ride in streetcars, but the streetcars were made in Germany. They use the telephone and go upstairs in a lift, but the telephone and the lift came from Sweden. They have only recently learned to use modern tools with skill or to farm scientifically. But they are learning very fast. They are learning to cooperate in their farming faster than almost any other people in Europe, which to my mind is the most hopeful sign of all.

For I am just as much of a socialist as when I went to Russia in May 1917, and just as little of an anarchist. I believe that the next economic development will be socialism, that is cooperation, common ownership of the principal means of production, and the administration of all departments of government for the collective good of all the people. I believe that the world is for the many, not the few. But Russia has demonstrated that there is no advantage to be gained by taking all power out of the hands of one class and placing it in the hands of another. Too much power rests now in the hands of a small class. But that class never abused its power more ruthlessly than the Russian *Tavarishi* did in the 1917 Revolution.

The lesson of Russia to America is patient, intelligent, clear-sighted preparation for the next economic development. Beginning with the youngest children, we must contrive for all children a system of education that will create in the coming generation a thinking working class, one that will accept responsibility as well as demand power, and into whose hands we can safely confide authority and destiny.

Notes

1 The Moscow State Conference took place on August 12–15 [25–28], 1917.
2 In the eighteenth century, Poland, officially called the Polish–Lithuanian Commonwealth, was a democracy of nobles who elected their King and who

undertook their deliberations both in provincial assemblies and in the central *Sejm*, or Parliament.

3 Frederick the Great, Frederick II (1712–1786), was the King of Prussia (1740–86), a brilliant military campaigner who, in a series of diplomatic stratagems and wars against Austria and other powers, greatly enlarged Prussia's territories and made Prussia the foremost military power in Europe. He was the last Hohenzollern monarch titled King in Prussia, declaring himself King of Prussia after annexing Royal Prussia from the Polish-Lithuanian Commonwealth in 1772. An enlightened absolute monarch, he favored the French language and art.

4 Maria Theresa (German: Maria Theresia) (1717–1780) was Archduchess of Austria and Queen of Hungary and Bohemia (1740–80). She was the eldest daughter of Emperor Charles VI, who promulgated the Pragmatic Sanction to allow her to succeed to the Habsburg domains. She helped initiate financial and educational reforms, promoted commerce and the development of agriculture, and reorganized the army, all of which strengthened Austria's resources. A key figure in the power politics of eighteenth-century Europe, Maria Theresa brought unity to the Habsburg monarchy and was considered one of its most capable rulers. Conflict with Prussia led to the War of the Austrian Succession, the Seven Years' War and to the War of the Bavarian Succession. After her husband's death (1765), her son became Emperor as Joseph II.

5 Louis XVIII (1755–1824) was the King of France by title from 1795 and in fact from 1814 to 1824, except for the interruption of the Hundred Days, during which Napoleon attempted to recapture his empire. After Napoleon's defeats in 1813, Louis issued a manifesto in which he promised to recognize some of the results of the Revolution in a restored Bourbon regime. When the Allied armies entered Paris in March 1814, the brilliant diplomatist Talleyrand was able to negotiate the restoration. After Waterloo, Louis XVIII's reign saw France's first experiment in parliamentary government since the Revolution. The legislature, though, had a strong right-wing, royalist majority.

6 Charles X (1757–1836) was the King of France from 1824 to 1830. After the Bourbon Restoration in 1814, Charles became the leader of the ultra-royalists, a radical monarchist faction within the French court that affirmed absolute monarchy by divine right and opposed the constitutional monarchy concessions toward liberals and the guarantees of civil liberties granted by the Charter of 1814. Charles succeeded his brother Louis XVIII in 1824.

7 Louis Philippe I (1773–1850) was the King of the French from 1830 to 1848 and the last French monarch to bear the title "King." Having based his rule on the support of the upper bourgeoisie, he ultimately fell from power because he could not win the allegiance of the new industrial classes. Louis Philippe abdicated during the French Revolution of 1848, which led to the foundation of the French Second Republic.

8 Prince von Metternich, Klemence (1773–1859) was an Austrian statesman and diplomat. In 1809, Francis I of Austria appointed him minister of foreign affairs, a position he would retain until 1848. He is remembered for his role in restoring Austria as a leading European power. As the organizer of the Congress of Vienna (1814–15), he was largely responsible for the policy of the balance of power in Europe intended to ensure the stability of European governments. After 1815, he remained firmly opposed to liberal ideas and revolutionary movements. He was forced to resign by the revolution of 1848.

9 The Hohenzollerns were the ruling house of Brandenburg-Prussia (1415–1918) and of imperial Germany (1871–1918).
10 Reign of Terror was a period of the French Revolution from June 1793 to July 27, 1794, during which the Committee of Public Safety exercised virtual dictatorial control over the French government. The "Great Terror" that followed, in which about 1,400 persons were executed, contributed to the fall of Robespierre on July 27 (9 Thermidor).
11 Henry VIII (1491–1547) was the King of England from April 1509 until his death.

INDEX

Note: Page number in **bold** denotes figures, while 'n' denotes note numbers

Admiralty Quay (Admiralty Embankment) 33, 34n4
Alexander of Oldenburg, Prince 163, 164n3
Alexander Palace xxii, 70, 90
Alexander Theater (Alexandrinsky Theater) 57, 64n1
Alexandra Feodorovna, the Empress of Russia (Tsarina) ix, xix, xxii–xxiv, xxxin56, xxxiiin72, 5, 67–68, 70–71, 73n1–3, 75–81, 83–94, 95n4, 97, 100–1, 152
Alexei Nikolaevich, the last Russian Tsarevich 73n2
All-Russian Extraordinary Commission, The 64n9
American Federation of Labor 22n4, 33, 34n6
American Relief Administration (ARA) 25
Andrei Vladimirovich, Grand Duke 21n2
Anthony, Susan B. xiv, xx, xxixn34
Arkhangelsk xxxiiin71, 155, 157n13
Asquith, Herbert Henry 130, 134n7

Beatty, Elizabeth Mary "Bessie" xxi, xxixn42, 17, 114
Red Heart of Russia, The xxi, xxxn46
Bell Syndicate xxi
Bely Ostrov 154, 156n11
Bochkareva, Maria Leont'evna vii, ix, xxi, xxiv, xxixn44, xxx, xxxn44, 4, 35–37, 41, 43, 45, 49–52, 55, 132
Bochkareva's Battalion of Death xxiv, 37–42, 51, 53
Bolshaya Konyushennaya, street 163
Bolshevik(i) (*Tavarish*) ix, xiv, xxi–xxv, xxviiin13, xxxn44, xxxin53, xxxiin62,
xxxiin64-66, xxxiii, xxxiiin72, 2–4, 5n2–4, 7, 9, 12n8, 13n13, 13n15, 15–23, 28, 28n1, 31–32, 41–42, 52, 61–65n9, 65n10, 73n1, 82n3, 88n1, 92, 96n5, 98, 105, 107, 110, 111, 123–24, 126, 129, 131–33, 146–48, 150n4, 160, 162, 165–78, 170n1
Bonaparte, Josephine 87, 88n5
Borgia, Lucrezia 75, 81–82n1
borzoi 11, 13n14
Boston Transcript xvi
bourju 98
Breshko-Breshkovskaya, Ekaterina Konstantinovna **v**, xvi, xxiv, xxviiin13, 61
British Tommy 10, 13
Brusilov, Aleksei Alekseyevich 22
Bryant, Louise xxi, xxv, xxixn43, xxi
Six Red Month in Russia xxi, xxxn46
Bullard, Artur xviii
Bund (General Jewish Labor Bund in Lithuania, Poland and Russia) 62, 65n11

Carlyle, Thomas 58, 64n2
Cat and Mouse (Temporary Discharge for Ill-Health) Act 130, 134n5
Catherine II, the Empress of Russia 40n2, 73n11, 151
Cazalet, William Lewis 98–99, 103n2, 127, 127n2
Charles X, the King of France 168, 170n7
Cheshire, Daniel 123–24, 126–27
Chicago 26, 62–63, 156n2
Chkheidze, Nikoloz 105, 110n2
Communist Labor Party of America xxxn45
Coney Island 163, 164n4

Constitutional Democrats (*Kadets*) xxi, xxiii, xxixn39, 28, 71, 168
Corday, Charlotte xxii, xxxin51, 60
Cossacks xxiv, 16, 17, 20–21, 23, 24, 26, 28, 34–35, 57, 133, 140
Courier-Journal, The xxxivn87
Kovno 153, 156n8
Cross of Saint George (Medal of St. George) 40n2

Danton, Georges Jacques xxii, 141, 142n3
Demidov Palace 6n16
Dewey, John 73n12
Diet of Finland 150n2
Dmitri Pavlovich, the Grand Duke of Russia 68, 71, 73n9
Dolgorukov, Vasily Alexandrovich, Prince 94, 96n5
Don, river 26, 28n2
Dosch-Fleurot, Arno 42, 44n2
droshky 2, 6n10, 19, 22n6, 42, 107
Duncan, James 16, 22n4
Dvinsk xxiv, 2, 6n7, 90
Dzerzhinsky, Felix Edmundovich 64n9

Eddy, Mary Baker 88n2
Elizabeth Feodorovna, the Grand Duchess Sergei xxxiiin72, 6n15, 97–**100**, 102, 103n1
Engineer's (Mikhailovsky) Castle 56n5
English Fabian Society xvii
Everybody's Magazine xv–xvi

feminism xviii, xxvi
  feminist xiii, xv, xvii, xix, xxiv, xxixn43, 103
  Heterodoxy feminist circle xvii–xviii
  National Woman's Party xix, xxviin2
Figner, Vera Nikolaevna xxiv, xxxiiin71, 59, 60, 64n3
Francis, David Rowland 29, 34n1, 134n10
Frederick the Great, Frederick II, the King of Prussia 166, 170n3
French Revolution of the 18th century xx, xxii, xxxin51, 1, 7, 33, 34n5, 58, 88n4, 92, 95n2, 141, 142n2, 168, 171n8
  Girondists xx, xxii
  Sans-Culottes xx, xxii, 33, 34n5
fortress of Peter and Paul 21, 22n11, 67, 76, 82n3, 91, 162

Gary system (Gary school) 72, 73n12, 102, 161, 164n2

General Federation of Women's Club xv
Gompers, Samuel 34n6
Good Housekeeping magazine xvii
Gordeeva, Valentina Sergeevna 99, 103n3
Graham, Stephen 101, 104n5
Grand Morskaya, street 5, 6n16, 19, 107, 111–12, 133
Grey, Edward 130, 134n8

Hampton's Magazine xviii
Hanna, Mark 161, 163n1
Hard, William xvi
Harper, Florence xxxn47
  Runway Russia xxxn47
Harper's Weekly xvi, xxviiin12
Helsingfors 92, 95, 148, 150n5, 154–55
Henry VIII, the King of England 169, 171n12
Hohenzollerns 168, 171n10
Hossein, Robert xxxin60
Hotel d'Europe 6n9
Hotel Military (formerly the Astoria) 4, 6n12

International Wagons-Lits 114, 116n3
Irina Alexandrovna, the Grand Duchess xxiii, xxxin57, xxxin60, 68, **69**
Iskra 12n8
Ivan the Terrible, the Tsar of Russia 152, 156n4, 156n5
izvostchik 19, 22n6

Jacobstadt 2, 6n8
Jezebel 75–76, 82n2
Journal de Petrograd 19
July Revolution (July uprising, July Days, July crisis) of 1917 xxi, 5n4, 15–16, 19, 23, 28n1, 31, 102, 132, 146
June offensive 22n5

Kaiser: *see Wilhelm II, the German Emperor, Kaiser*
Kazan Cathedral 41, 44n1, 51
Kenney, Jessica "Jessie" 129, 134n3
Kerenskaya (born Baranovskaya), Olga Lvovna 60, 64n6, 133, 142
Kerensky, Alexander Fyodorovich viii, ix, xxii–xxvi, xxxin53, xxix, xxxin61, xxxin62, xxxin65, xxxin66, xxxin69, xxxiiin73, 9, 11, 15, 17–18, 22, 24–25, 27, 28, 28n1, 30, **31**, 48, 55, 60, 64n6, 90–94, 98, 102, 105, 129, 131–33, 137–42, 147–49, 150n4, 165, 169

INDEX 175

Khrustaliov-Nosar, Georgy Stepanovich 8, 12n4
Kiev 148–49
Kirsanov 145, 150n3
Kornilov, Lavr Georgiyevich xxiii–xxiv, xxxin62, 22n5, 25–28n1, 140, 165
Kovno 153, 156n8–9
Kronstadt 10, 16, 18–21, 92, 145–47
Kropotkin, Maria Dmitrievna, Princess 55, 56n3
Kropotkin, Pyotr Alekseyevich, Prince 55, 56n4, 60, 64n7
Kschessinskaya (Kschessinska), Mathilde-Marie Feliksovna 15, 21n2

lazaret 32, 34n3
Lebedev(a), Aleksandra Petrovna (born as Princess Aleksandra "Sasha" Kropotkin) 60, 64n7
Lenin (Ulyanov), Vladimir Ilyich 2, 5n3–4, 9, 16, 19, 21, 22n10–11, 23, 28, 42, 88n1, 105, 107, 110n1
Leninists 16, 18, 20, 42
Leslie's Illustrated Weekly Newspaper xxxn47
Lewis, Harry Sinclair xviii
Liteyny Avenue 5, 107
Lloyd George, David 22n8, 129–31, 134n2
Lomnovskiy, Pyotr Nikolaevich 50n2
Loskov, Aleksand Vasilievich 55
Louis Philippe I, the King of the French 168, 170n8
Louis XVI, the King of France xxii, 88n4, 92, 94, 95n2
Louis XVIII, the King of France 170nn6–7, 168
Luzhenovsky, Gavriil Nikolaevich xxxn50, 64n8
Lvov, Georgy Yevgenyevich, Prince xxxiin70, 7, 12n2, 25, 137–38

MacDonald, Ramsay 130, 131, 134n9
McKinley xv, 163n1
Marat, Jean-Paul xxxin51, 141
Maria Dmitrievna, Princess 55, 56n3
Maria Feodorovna, the Dowager Empress 64n5, 88n1
Maria Theresa, Archduchess of Austria and Queen of Hungary and Bohemia 166, 170n5
Marie Antoinette xxii, 87, 88n4
Marie Palace (Mariinsky Palace) 4, 6n14, 18, 22n7

Martha and Mary (Marfo-Mariinsky) Convent xxxiiin72, **100**, 103n1
Masses, The xxxn45
Maxim Gorky (Alexei Maksimovich Peshkov) 9
Mensheviki 9, 12n8, 31
Metropolitan, The xxxn45
Metternich, Klemence, Prince von 168, 171n9
Michael Alexandrovich, the Grand Duke of Russia 84, 88n1, 167
Miles, Basil 113
Miliukov, Pavel Nikolayevich xxiii, xxxiin68, 7, 24, 28, 137–38, 149, 167–68
Miller, James Russell 86, 88n3
Minsk 15, 21n1, 153, 156n9–10
Mirabeau, Honoré Gabriel Riqueti, Count xxii, 141, 142n2
Moika, river (*Dorr: Canal*) 68, **69**, 71, 111, 114
Moscow ix, xxiii, xxviiin14, xxxin61, 3–4, 11, 12n8, 13n13, 28, 35, 55, 59, 60, 64n3, 72, 73n10, 97–100, 109, 110, 113–15, 116n1, 118, 121, 127, 127n1, 133, 151–53, 156nn4–5, 157n13, 160, 165, 167, 169n1
muckraker xiii, xv, xvii, 22n3, 65n12
muckraking journalism xiii, xv, xvii

Nachalnik 42–44, 48–50
Napoleon Bonaparte 25, 88n5, 111, 116n1, 135n11, 153, 170n6
Narishkina, Elizabeth Alexeevna 94, 95n4
National Association for the Advancement of Colored People 22n3
Nekrasov, Nikolai Vissarionovich 116n2, 117
Neva, riva 16, 21, 22n11, 33, 34n4, 70, 114, 133, 146, 151, 156n11, 162
Nevsky Prospect ix, xxiixn42, 5, 6n9, 16, **18**, 57, 63, 107, 111
New York xiv, xvi, xix, xx, 3, 43, 62, 64n7, 99, 105, 160, 162, 164n4
New York Evening Mail xviii, xxii, xxv, xxviiin27, xxxin58, xxxin61, xxxiin65–67, xxxiin69, xxxiin70, xxxiiin73, xxxiiin76, xxxiiin78, xxxiiinn80–81
New York Evening Post xv–xvi
New York Times xxviiin29, xxixnn36–37, xxxn47

New York Tribune xix
New York World 42
Nicholas II, the Emperor of Russia xxii, xxxin56–57, 8, 12n5, 21n2, 64n5, 73nn1–2, 73n9, 82n3, 88n1, 90–95, 96n5, 97, 121n2, 155, 164n3, 167
Nikolai station in Petrograd 19, 52, 115
Novaya Zhizn 9
Novoe Vremya 51, 56n1

Odessa 148–49
Olga Constantinovna, Princess 60, 64n4
Orlova, Alexandra 43, 52

Panina, Sofia Vladimirovna, Countess 134, 135n12
Pankhurst, Christabel Harriette 129, 130, 134n4
Pankhurst, Emmeline viii–ix, xvi–xvii, xxviiin15, xxviiin20, xxxiiin76, 20, 22, **37**, 67, 129–33, 134n1, 134nn3–4, 162
Pankhurst, Sylvia 134n4
Paul Alexandrovich, the Grand Duke of Russia 73n9, 76, 82n3
Paul I, the Emperor of Russia 56n5–6
Pereverzev, Pavel Nikolaevich 150n4
Peshkova, Ekaterina 64n3
Peter the Great, Peter I 151–52, 155n1, 156n3, 157n13
Petrograd viii, xix, xxi–v, xxix, xxxi, xxxiin62, xxxiiin66, 2–5, 6nn11–12, 7–8, 10, 11, 12nn8–9, 15–16, 19–21, 22n7, 23–24, 26–33, 35, 37–38, 41, 43, 49, 50, 52–53, 55, 56n7, 57–65, 68, 70, 77, 81, 89, 92, 102, 105–8, 110–15110n2, 118–19, 123–24, 131, 133, 138, 142, 146–47, 149, 151–54, 159, 160, 162–63, 165–67
Pictorial Review xix
Pittsburgh Daily Post xxxivn87
Political Red Cross 59, 64n3
Poole, Ernest xvii
Pravda 9
Protopopov, Alexander Dmitrievich 67, 73n6
Provisional Government xxii–v, xxixn39, xxixn42, xxxn44, xxxin53, xxxiin66, xxxiin68, 4–5, 6nn13–14, 8, 11, 12n2, 12n9, 16, 20, 22n5, 22n7, 22n10, 25–26, 28, 28n1, 30, 61, 63, 71, 76, 90, 92, 94–95, 103, 116n5, 126, 129, 132, 137, 140, 145–46, 148, 149, 153–54, 167

Purishkevich, Vladimir Mitrofanovich xxxin56

Rasputin, Grigori vii, ix, xxiii, xxxin56–58, xxxin60, 5, 67–71, 73n2, 75, 77–79, **78**, 80–81, 83–84, 87–89, 94
Red Cross 30, 32, 38, 41, 43, 54–55, 85, 159
Reed, John Silas xxi, xxixn43, xxxn45, 63
Ten Days That Shook the World xxxn45
Reign of Terror 7, 141, 142nn3–4, 156n4, 168, 171n11
Riga 53, 153–54, 156n7
Robespierre, Maximilien xxii, 141, 142n4, 171n11
Rodzianko, Mikhail Vladimirovich 7, 12n1, 24, 167
Romanov(s) (Romanov family, Romanov dynasty) vii, xxxin56, 12n5, 56n5, 58, 64n4, 67, 71–72, 73n10, 80, 82, 87–90, 93, 98, 102, 105, 141, 152, 156n6, 167–68
Root mission xxiii, xxxiin66, 10, 22n3–4, 113
Roosevelt, Theodore xv, 40n1, 142, 143n5
Russell, Charles Edward 16, 22n3
Russian State Duma xx–xxi, xxixn39, xxxin56, 7–9, 13n13, 17, 20, 28, 36, 76, 105, 110n2, 113, 167, 169n1
Russian Revolution v, ix, xxiii–xxvii, xxviiin13, xxix, xxxiii, 7, 34n1, 63, 145
of 1905–7 xx–xxi, 64n3, 110n1
All-Russian Congress of Soviets (Councils) of Workers and Soldiers 13n15, 64n9
All-Russian Central Executive Committee of the Soviets of Workers' 13n15
June offensive ("the Kerensky offensive") 22n5
Kornilov affair (Kornilov putsch) 28n1
Moscow State Conference of August 12 [25]–15 [28], 1917 13n13
of October 1917 xxi, xxvii, xxxiin62, xxxiiin66, 5n2, 56n7
Order No. 1 9–10, 12n9
and Soldiers' Deputies (VTsIK) 13n15
of February 1917 xviii, xxi–xxii, xxxiin68, 2, 6n13, 12n8, 106, 111, 123, 137
Russo-Japanese War, 1904–5 36, 39n1, 143n5

Saint Basil's Cathedral 152, 156n5
St. Isaac's Cathedral 23, 152, 156n3
St. Louis Post-Dispatch xxv, xxxin61, xxxiin70
San Francisco Bulletin xxi, xxixn42, 17, 114
San Francisco Chronicle xx5, xxin61
sanitaries 54, 56n2
Sergei Alexandrovich, the Grand Duke of Russia xxiv, xxxiiin72, 6n15, 73n9, **100**
Shepherd, William Gunn 42, 44n3
Skobelev, Matvey Ivanovich 121n1
Skrydlov, Nikolai Illarionovich, Admiral 37–38, 40n3
Skrydlova, Maria Nikolaevna 37–38, 40n3, 41–42, 49–52, 112
Social Democratic League of America 22n3
Socialist Party of America 22n3
  Greenwich Village (Highbrow) branch xvii–xviii
Socialist Revolutionary Party (SRs) of Russia xxviiin13, xxixn40, 64n7, 138
Society of Russian Women to Help the Country, The 55
Soviets (Councils of Soldiers' and Workmen's Delegates) xxiii–xxv, 7, 11–12, 13n3, 13n5, 13n15, 17, 28, 28n1, 33, 61, 64n9, 92, 105–6, 111, 132, 141, 165–66, 169n1
  Petrograd Council of Workmen's Deputies 8
Spiridonova, Maria Alexandrovna xxii, xxiv, xxxn50, xxxin53, xxxiiin71–72, 27, 64n9, 65n9
Stanton, Elizabeth Cady xiv
Stavka (Staff Headquarters) 47, 50n1
Steffens, Joseph Lincoln 63, 65n12
Stevens, John Frank 115, 116n5, 117
Sturmer, Boris Vladimirovich 67
suffrage xiii, xv–xvii, xviiin15, xxi, xxviin1, 129–30, 133, 134n1, 134n3
  Congressional Union for Suffrage xviii
  National Suffrage Association xiv
suffragist (suffragette) xiii, xvi–xvii, 20, 129–30, 134n3, 134nn5–6
Suffragist, The xvii–xviii
suffrage movement xiii, xviii, xxviiin15, 134n1
Sukhomlinov, Vladimir Aleksandrovich 30, 34n2
Sumarokov-Elston, Felix Felixovich 71, 73n10
Sveaborg 148, 150n5

Tauride Palace 20, 22n7, 132
Tavarishi, Tavarish xxiii, 3, 9, 17, 21, 23, 32, 62–63, 92, 105, 123–24, 147, 162, 169; *see also* Bolsheviki
Taylor, Frederick 73n12
Tchaikovsky, Nikolai Vasilyevich 149, 150n6
Tereshchenko, Mikhail Ivanovich
Thomas Cook & Son 116n4
Tobolsk 92, 94–95, 95n3, 96n5
Tomsk xxxn44, 55, 145, 147
Tornea (Tornia) 10, 13n11, 62, 154, 156n12
Trans-Siberian railroad 63, 115
Treaty of Portsmouth 40n1
Trotsky, Leon (Bronstein, Lev Davidovich) 5n4, 105–7, 110n1, 168
Tsaritsyn 145, 150n1
Tuileries xxii, 92, 95n2

Ufa 65n9
Ukraine 22n5, 145, 148–49, 166
United Press 42
United States Steel Corporation (Dorr: Company) 151, 156n2
Ural Mountains 26, 28n3, 95n3

Vilna (Vilnius) 2, 6n6, 153, 156nn8–9
Vladivostok 63, 115
Vyborg, district of Petrograd 15, 119, 121n2, 124
Vyrubova, Anna Alexandrovna xix, xxii, xxiv, 67, 73n3, 75–77, 79–81, 83–86, 89–91, 94

Walling, William English xvii
Washington Evening Star xxv, xxxiin65, xxxiin67, xxxiin70, xxxiiin73, xxxiiin76
William II, the German Emperor (Kaiser) xviii, 2, 6n5, 21, 42, 62, 170n4
Wilson, Woodrow xxiii, xxxn44, xxxiin66, 22nn3–4, 34n1, 116n5
Winship, North 138, 142n1
Winter Palace xxixn42, 22n9, 56n7, 61, 132, 142
Wirt, William 73n12, 162, 164n2
Witte, Sergei Yulyevich 8, 12n6
Women's Battalion of Death: *see* Bochkareva's Women's Battalion of Death

Women's Social and Political Union 129, 134n1, 134n4

World War I xviii, xx, xxixn39, xxixn44–5, xxxiiin74, 13n15, 35, 40n3, 44nn2–3, 64n4, 73n1, 73n5, 106, 121n2, 134n2, 134n6, 164n3, 170n4

Young, Arthur xxii

Young Men's Christian Association xviii

Yusupov, Felix Felixovich xxiii, xxxin56-7, xxxin60, 67–72, 73n10, 75, 81, 83–84

Yusupov Palace xxxin57, 68, 71, 73n7, 83